070.1
G82t

75924

DATE DUE		
Aug 1 '72 Mar 3 '82		
Aug 3 '72 Apr 30 '82		
Nov 20 '75		
Apr 7 '75		
Apr 7 '75		
Oct 15 '75		
Feb 18 '76		
Mar 31 '76		
Aug 10 '76		
Mar 7 7 9		
Feb 25 '81		
Aug 11 '81		

Television News

Anatomy and Process

Television News

Anatomy and Process

Maury Green

Wadsworth Publishing Company, Inc.
Belmont, California

To Evelyn,
who made it all worthwhile

Preface

The purpose of this work is to explore three aspects of television news: its techniques, its journalistic concepts, and its effects on society. The argument is that the techniques are more complex than those of other media, that the relationship of technique to concept is extremely intimate and widely misunderstood, and that the effects of television news on society are so profound that they should be the concern of all men, let alone the television journalist.

Because of the intricate interrelationship of technique, concept, and effect, the author has chosen to develop his exploration along all three lines as nearly simultaneously as possible. This accounts for the structure of the book, in which, for example, relevant particulars of concept are discussed at appropriate points as the argument proceeds from fundamentals to more complex considerations, from basic elements to writing, reporting, production, and management.

Like the film motion picture, to which it is incestuously related, the electronic motion picture makes its points most effectively not by the familiar method of stating facts, but by generating emotional reactions within a factual context. This is not a matter of choice on the part of the purveyors of television news, it is inherent in the medium. This emotional factor is both the power and the weakness of television news; the wisdom with which it is used is of fateful importance to society.

The television journalist is more deeply and directly involved in the anatomy and process of his medium than are journalists of other media; therefore this work is necessarily in large part a discussion of technique, of "how to." Future works on the subject undoubtedly will concentrate more on concept and less on technique. But until the moment arrives when the feedback between technique and concept is as well comprehended in television as it is in print, works of this nature must speak of both.

Because of the economics of television, small stations generally tend to use simpler, less costly techniques than larger stations. Most of the common techniques, simple and complex, are included herein, so that the reader can extract whatever he finds of value in his own work.

However, this is not a book for the technician. It is primarily for the journalist—writer, reporter, or producer—and secondarily for the critic or general student of television news. The discussion of technicalities, extensive though it may appear to some, is barely the minimum needed by the competent journalist; it is deliberately inadequate for the craft specialists, such as video operators or film cameramen.

While this work is largely the product of personal experience, observation, and conviction, in human affairs no work is the product of a single person. The author wishes to express his gratitude for the advice of Michael Kizziah of KNBC (formerly of KNXT); Al Mann, news director of KMOX-TV; the late Edwin Miller, production manager of KNXT; Professors Walter Wilcox and John M. Smith of the Department of Journalism, University of California, Los Angeles; and Robert D. Wood, president of the CBS Television Network division of the Columbia Broadcasting System, Inc. For extensive and invaluable critical suggestions, the author is deeply indebted to Professor Edward Borgers, chairman of the Department of Telecommunications, University of Southern California; Professor John Roberts, School of Communication, Temple University; and Professor Ben Yablonky, Department of Journalism, University of Michigan.

Maury Green
Encino, California

Contents

Part One

An Introduction
to Television
News

Chapter 1

Past
and
Present

In the beginning, a little history . . .

When television first faded in on the American scene, circa 1948, station managers regarded news as a bothersome but necessary interruption between wrestling matches and Milton Berle. Unlike entertainment programming, which made money, news was a nuisance which served the sole useful purpose of keeping the Federal Communications Commission off the station's back.

This attitude was understandable. The FCC is empowered by law to require that an unspecified portion of a station's broadcast time be devoted to programs serving the "public interest, convenience, and necessity." News is so defined.

But the average station manager knew little about news. He had no reason to know much about it. He was usually a former radio time salesman graduated to management and conditioned to think in terms of production costs, sponsor whims, Nielsen ratings, adjacencies, and advertising rate cards. News to him was alien and annoying, made up largely of unpleasant information about such matters as war and rebellion, civil rights, and social problems—the kind of information which makes sponsors, who also know little about news, downright unhappy.

But with the ingenuity of his kind, the station manager soon devised a news formula that had at least one prime advantage: it was cheap. A staff announcer, or perhaps an otherwise unemployable old actor, ripped the news off the Associated Press radio wire and read it to the video camera.

Essentially "rip and read" remained the news formula at most television stations for a decade or more, and in those early days many a television newscast was written with a stapler.

The Rise of Personality

Those days came to an end when the public began to favor one newscaster over another, with a resultant effect on program ratings. The newscasters so favored were not always the best informed or the most responsible, but they were almost always those who most effectively managed to project a personality through the tube and who read the news with distinctive style. There was a definite dramatic flair about the most successful newscasters, a flair usually evidenced in either or both of two ways: (1) the projection of a "manufactured" personality, such as patriot, old family friend, or trench-coated foreign correspondent; or (2) the flavoring or slanting of the news with personal opinions—liberal, conservative, or whatever—which appealed to large blocs of audience.

This trend toward emphasis on personality was predictable to those who viewed television news as both information and entertainment, but the station managers who took this view in the earliest days of television were rare. To most of them, news was one thing, entertainment another. The truth is that they cannot be completely separated. This truth is still unpalatable to many television newsmen and to many critics of television news, but their tastes do not determine the facts. The public's tastes do.

Thus began the "cult of personality," on which we shall have more to say later. By the late 1950s the cult of personality was firmly established as the basis of one type of news show, a common type in which such revenue as the news program produced went largely to pay the talent. (The term "talent," by the way, is not indicative of ability; it merely differentiates those who appear on the air from those who do not. The latter may *have* talent, but the former *are* "talent" regardless of ability.) Even the networks were not entirely immune to the trend, although from the beginning they were clearly if slowly moving toward a more responsible type of news presentation. One prominent network news personality, known to his colleagues as a "reader" (of news scripts) rather more than as a genuine newsman, finally lost his job because he insisted on making speeches about television news (in return for gratuities which increased his income considerably), embarrassing his employers with his obvious ignorance of the subject. Subsequently, he was more appropriately employed as a successful commercial announcer.

Although most local news shows in the personality era were largely "rip and read" operations, the more affluent stations, having discovered that they could profit or at least break even by selling personality, began to hire a few writers to rephrase wire copy in better broadcast language, and they began to shoot some film, mostly silent, of local events. Sound film was still rare, and the reporter accompanying a film crew in the field was even rarer. Station managers, having recognized that personality was as valuable in news as in entertainment, were willing to let it go at that. The typical television news show in the late 1950s was still little more than a radio show with an accompanying motion picture of the personality reading the news.

The Short Format

Another inheritance from radio was the short news format, 5 minutes or, less frequently, 15 minutes. It was more than a decade before any sizable number of station managers began to realize that 15 minutes, however adequate it may have been for radio news, simply was not enough time for television news. Even the networks stuck with the 15-minute format for their main news shows until well into the 1960s.

Even the 15-minute format created a programming problem; it did not fit well into the half-hour blocks of which the television program structure is built. For most entertainment or discussion shows, the half-hour seems to be a natural minimum length. It is natural, perhaps, because ours is what Marshall McLuhan calls a linear, fragmented society and time (as we see it) is a line, and its fragments of half-hour dimensions are easy to conceive, instantly recognizable in newspaper program logs, and as convenient to merchandise as identical bars of soap. Whether the material fits the time slot seems to be of little importance.

Various solutions were found for the problem of fitting 15 minutes of news into a half-hour time block. Some stations, especially in the Midwest, filled the other quarter-hour with musical programs. Network-owned or -affiliated stations often piggybacked the 15-minute network news with an equal length of locally produced news.

The Segmented Show

Whatever the length of the show, it was almost always segmented. A 15-minute show might consist of three separate sections, each invariably 5 minutes in length: for example, 5 minutes of general news, 5 minutes of sports, and 5 minutes of weather. Sometimes it was ten minutes of general news and 5 minutes of commentary. The weatherman was the only new phenomenon, in comparison to radio; the new visual dimension of television had increased his value to the news (it is extremely difficult to draw an isobar on a blackboard in radio). In today's terms it seems ridiculous to equate general news with, say, sports news by allotting each the same amount of time, but it was common practice in the 1950s.

By happy coincidence, this rigid, segmented format was easy to sell. The television quarter-hour is too rich a diet for any but the most affluent advertiser. But the segmented show was in reality a collection of little shows, each with its own star personality and its own separate identity. Advertisers love identity. And in the specialist segments each little show had the advantage of a personality who customarily developed and wrote his own material, and was often a better newsman than the star, or anchorman, who delivered the general news. Many an advertiser who could not afford the quarter-hour could and did ante up the cash to sponsor a 5-minute weather or sports segment, and got his money's worth in return.

This, then, was the established pattern of television news as the medium confidently entered the 1960s: the personality-newsman; the abortively brief, segmented news show; the two-bit advertiser calling the tune because he paid the piper—rip and read and forget it. But fortunately, change was on the way.

The News Explosion

The change, which began in the early 1960s and is continuing at this writing, was characterized by the lengthening of the news show to 30 minutes or longer, by a consequent increase in responsible origination of major news, and by adoption of what has come to be known (rather inaccurately) as the "magazine format." The result was an astounding explosion of television news programming, enormous increases in the size and scope of television news operations at every level from the smallest local station to the networks, and the rise of television to the position of the nation's dominant news medium, surpassing newspapers, news magazines, and radio in acceptance, credibility, and influence.

This explosion, probably unprecedented in the history of news, was documented for the first time in the Land Report, a study prepared for the President's Task Force on Communications Policy and commissioned by the National Association of Broadcasters.[1] The thrust of the study is in opposition to the "wired city" concept of closed-circuit television program distribution, which the NAB could be expected to

---

[1] *Television and the Wired City,* by Herman W. Land Associates, Inc. (Washington, D.C.: National Association of Broadcasters, 1968).

oppose; but in marshaling the arguments against that concept, the study leans most heavily on news—its influence and effectiveness, its costs, and the relationship of costs to the flow of information in American society. The study summarizes the findings of a survey of 329 commercial television stations in every part of the United States.

The descriptive word is "growth." In a comparatively short period of time television news has experienced a dramatic change in quantity, quality and character. Today news is *the* major element in local programming, and the local television station has become the chief source of information for the country at large. . . .

In numerous instances, stations report their news airtime has doubled in the last three to five years. . . . Station after station across the country reports it has doubled, even tripled, its news gathering force in the last five years.[2]

The scope of the expansion, in terms of actual news broadcasts, is also detailed:

Of the 297 stations that reported on their news operations, 228 stated that they were producing at least one half-hour newscast a day; 127 stations reported that they were producing at least two half-hours daily; and 44 stations claimed that they were doing three. There is a noticeable increase, too, in the number of stations broadcasting longer local newscasts—45 minutes, 60 minutes, and more. Even in the smaller, one-station markets, the trend toward the 30-minute newscast is marked; 17 of 20 reporting noted 30-minute local news programs. The total number of half-hours devoted to news today in the one-station markets (networks plus local) ranged from 13 to 32. In the six-station markets the news volume ranged from 89 to 168 half-hours a week. The high point is reached in Los Angeles —264 half-hours of news per week.[3]

The report further documents the rise of television to its present position as the nation's major source of news, as indicated by studies made by Roper Research Associates.[4] By 1967, these studies indicate, 70 per cent of all Negroes and 64 per cent of all whites (roughly two thirds of all Americans) obtained most of their news from television. The comparable figures in 1960 were 40 per cent of Negroes and 53 per cent of whites.

A New Dimension in Coverage

Increasingly stations are expanding their outlook, reaching out with their own facilities and staffs in their attempts to detail the impact of national

---

[2] *Ibid.*, p. 175–180.

[3] *Ibid.*, p. 8.

[4] *Ibid.*, p. 26.

and international events on local community life. In a world in which a Middle Eastern flare-up, a financial crisis of an ally in Europe, a "hot war" in the Far East, or riots here in this country, are all too quickly reflected in our daily lives, the old parochial concept of "local news" has undergone and is undergoing change.[5]

In other words, television is finally beginning to fulfill one of the main functions of any news medium, that of interpreting the *meaning* of complex events. It is still only a beginning—the paragraph just quoted still cannot be applied accurately to many stations—but it *is* a beginning. And part of the rising public demand for television news is undoubtedly in response to this beginning effort; it is probably accurate to say that news audience ratings today give some indication of which stations are making such an effort.

What that effort may mean to station management is also hinted at by the Land Report: "The effort in manpower put into informational programming is indicated by that of one of the nation's foremost stations which estimates it last year devoted 115 'man years' to news, public affairs and community affairs programs."[6]

This new dimension in coverage is also indicated by the growing number of specialist newsmen in television—political analysts, investigative reporters, business reporters, beat reporters, entertainment specialists, farm experts—and by the growing number of stations which maintain permanent out-of-town bureaus at significant sources of local news, such as state capitals. These practices, long common among better newspapers, have only recently been adopted by television stations, and not yet by any means to the extent that they should be. But the medium is growing up, and the public is responding to this new evidence of maturity by giving television news its confidence and its attention.

The Magazine Format

Another of the principal causes of the television news explosion, perhaps the most fundamental cause, was the abandonment of the segmented news program format in favor of the magazine format. The change was fundamental because it freed the news show from the restrictive rigidity of the older format; without this new freedom the longer show, the greater coverage, the more meaningful coverage in depth, would not be possible. Television simply burst the breeches of the segmented format.

---

[5] *Ibid.*, pp. 183–184.

[6] *Ibid.*, p. 182.

This development was inevitable, but someone had to start the new trend. For this the credit must go to the two men primarily responsible for inaugurating the news show which, more than any other in the nation, has stimulated imitation by its remarkable success: *The Big News*, broadcast by KNXT, the CBS-owned station in Los Angeles. Two or three other somewhat similar programs were on the air ahead of it, but it was the success of this particular program, in the most competitive television news market in the nation, which evoked the sincerest form of flattery throughout the nation. Its success may be measured by the fact that in 1968 its audience was the fourth largest for any television news show in the United States, being exceeded in size only by the audiences of the three main early evening network shows of ABC, CBS, and NBC. The show was the concept of Robert D. Wood, then (in 1961) KNXT's general manager, now president of the CBS Television Network division, and the concept was implemented by Sam Zelman, then KNXT's news director, now manager of the West Coast bureau of CBS News in Los Angeles.

The original show in 1961 was 45 minutes in length, followed immediately by the *CBS Evening News*, which was then 15 minutes in length. When the network show was expanded to 30 minutes in 1963, the local Los Angeles production was simultaneously expanded to a full hour.

But the length was only a corollary of the format, in which the elements of the show are variable both in length and in their relative positions in the show. If the top story of the day, for example, is a sports story, sports tops the show; the viewer does not have to wait until a preset time to get a preset amount of sports (or any other) news. If a major local story justifies 25 solid minutes of coverage, it gets it.

This idea was not original; newspapers have always been made up that way. An analogy more appropriate to television would be the medieval town crier, who certainly did not shout out his weather report last when the weather was the big news, simply because the weather was customarily his final segment, or who certainly did not arbitrarily limit the time he gave to a certain type of news regardless of its importance. Yet these limitations were characteristic of television news prior to the adoption of the magazine format, which today is almost universal. The failure of the medium to adopt this format earlier is explainable only by the fact that it is dominated by salesmen, not by newsmen.

The format also included the use of several reporters on the air, and this aspect also has been almost universally copied by news organizations large enough to do so. The original *Big News* included an anchorman, an investigative reporter, a feature reporter, a sports reporter, and a weatherman. In later years others were added: several field reporters, three out-of-town bureau reporters, a political editor, and an entertainment reporter. But the principle remained the same. The various news stories, reported by specialists and by reporters on the scene of the event, carried greater authority because they were so reported. And the flexibility of the format, combined with the changes of pace occasioned by the mere variety of faces and voices presented, almost automatically gave the news broadcast the structure of a show. This last factor was of great significance in making the longer broadcast not only acceptable but inviting to the public, and its importance will be discussed in detail in later chapters.

The magazine format has another result, one which was not entirely anticipated at the time it first became popular: it inevitably leads the station to sell only participating spots in a news show, rather than complete or partial sponsorship. Sponsorship includes sponsor identity with show both on the air and in advertising in other media, a lower time rate in return for a firm commitment for several weeks or months of sponsorship, plus 20 seconds or so of billboards to open and close the sponsored section of the show ("This portion of tonight's news is brought to you by Gold Dust Federal Savings"). But where the magazine format is successfully applied, advertisers line up in such depth that the station finds it advantageous to sell only spots, which are more remunerative when they can be sold out consistently.

Elimination of sponsorship helps to separate the station "image" from the advertiser's "image" in the public mind. Inferences of advertiser influence on editorial content are harder to draw. No one advertiser is identified with most successful television news shows today, just as no one advertiser is identified with *The New York Times*. Thus the news becomes more believable, and at the same time it draws more revenue. To the station manager this is like getting paid to go to church.

In summary, adoption of the magazine format had results of unexpected "megascope." Or, better, megaprofits. Money is one of the main advantages of the magazine format; it is the real reason for the television news explosion.

Costs and Revenues

Information on news department costs and revenues is closely guarded, for obvious reasons. However, it requires very little calculation to demonstrate that the production of television news is very expensive. Salaries are comparatively high, comparatively large numbers of people are required, and the proportion of total program time devoted to news (and therefore to news revenue) is comparatively low.

Further, equipment costs are high, especially for a small station. One film camera crew represents a capital investment of some $10,000 in vehicle, cameras, sound recorders and amplifiers, lights, radio communications equipment, and all the necessary accessories. A single video camera may cost $70,000, and the supporting system to make it usable may cost as much as $1,000,000.

Nor can this equipment be used indefinitely. Newspapers may be printed on presses half a century old (which is one reason many newspapers find themselves in financial difficulties), but a ten-year-old video camera is obsolete. The advance of technology in electronics is so rapid that much equipment becomes obsolescent if not obsolete before

Table 1-1
Costs of Television News
Operations

(110 reporting stations)

Cost Range (Yearly)	Number of Stations
$20,000 or less	5
$20,000 to $49,999	8
$50,000 to $99,999	21
$100,000 to $199,999	32
$200,000 to $499,999	27
$500,000 to $899,999	14
$900,000 to $999,999	—
$1,000,000 or more	3

Source: *Television and the Wired City*, by Herman W. Land Associates, Inc. (Washington, D.C.: National Association of Broadcasters, 1968), p. 189.

it can be amortized to best advantage. The advent of color television, for example, is requiring the rapid replacement of untold millions of dollars worth of black and white video equipment.

Costs of materials are also high. Color film, an outstanding example, costs approximately 15 cents per foot for raw stock and processing. (One foot of film equals less than two seconds of air time.) Station WKY-TV in Oklahoma City runs about 750,000 feet of film a year,[7] for which the cost must be reckoned at $112,500. Major metropolitan stations shoot as much as 50,000 feet of film a week, at an annual expense approximating $400,000.

The Land Report summarizes information on news operation costs provided by 110 stations (Table 1-1). A more accurate idea of specific

---

[7] *National Press Photographer* (July 1968), p. 6.

costs may be obtained from Table 1-2, which lists in round numbers some of the significant items from the budget of an Eastern station in a market area of some 1,000,000 population.

The annual news budget of the station referred to in Table 1-2 is $475,000. The news department consists of 23 people, and it produces 7 hours of news programming weekly. The $475,000 figure is smaller than

Table 1-2
Selected News Budget Items
of One Station

(Eastern U.S., area pop. 1,000,000)

Item	Budgeted Expense (annual)
Personnel:	
News director	$ 23,000
Anchorman	46,000
Weatherman	40,000
Reporters (6)	110,000
Producer	13,000
Writer-editor-producers (4)	45,000
Clerical, etc. (3)	16,000
News film crews (3)	103,000
Other:	
Film (raw stock and processing)	110,000
Syndication news film	16,000
Press wire services	36,000
Line charges (telephone, cable, teletype)	4,000
Special projects	8,000
Transportion, travel, and entertainment	12,000

Source: Data obtained privately by the author.

the total of the costs listed in Table 1-2 (which are not all-inclusive) primarily because talent salaries, a total of $196,000, are charged against the program department rather than the news department. Disregarding that accounting procedure (the type of procedure which makes budget figures deceptive), and adding miscellaneous costs plus a percentage of the costs of technical and studio personnel which must be attributed to news, it seems obvious that this station's news operation actually costs well over $600,000 a year. Or, to approach a final figure another way, by simply adding talent costs to the stated budget one arrives at a probable yearly cost of $671,000.

Obviously no management is going to spend such large sums of money without some expectation of profit; that simply would not be good business. The manager of a Southwestern television station, asked by the author whether his 19-man news department is profitable, replied, "We don't do anything that doesn't make money." (However, he politely declined to reveal his cost and revenue figures.) His attitude is not only typical, it is proper in a (hopefully) profit-making business.

It is one thing for critics, who have no responsibility except to criticize, to demand that stations present news and public service programming even at a loss. It is quite another thing for the manager of a station to report to its owners that his management is losing their money. No amount of argument about the free use of the public's air waves, no platitudinizing about public service, is going to alter the hard facts of a communications business operating in a capitalistic society.

Fortunately for television news, the revenues to support its costs are available. Contrary to the prevailing public impression, many television news shows make money—and not just a little of it.

The Land Report, taking reporting stations at their word, indicates that 41 per cent of stations make a profit on their news operations, an equal percentage lose money on news, and the remainder (18 per cent) break-even.[8] However, in apparent contradiction the report also attributes to station managements the conviction that expanded news service is "good for business."[9] And it concludes that "stations that do the best news job and spend the most money on news are most likely to show a profit. In a single city, for example, one station spends over $100,000 a year on news and calls it a loss operation; a second spends over $150,000 and breaks even; and a third spends over $400,000 on news in the same market and makes a profit."[10]

Some speculation of the type in which any station manager can engage concerning the possible revenues of the nation's currently most successful local news show, KNXT's *The Big News,* may be illuminating as to the possibilities for any station, large or small, willing to make an all-out effort in news. By simple multiplication of the number of 1-minute commercial spots in the show (take 10 for a daily average) by the average cost of a spot (which varies seasonally, but for which $2,000 is a conservative figure), it is easy to determine that the 5-day strip show's approximate gross revenue is at least $5,000,000 annually.

Against this must be set the cost of the news operation; there are

---

[8] *Television and the Wired City,* by Herman W. Land Associates, Inc. (Washington, D.C.: National Association of Broadcasters, 1968), p. 191.

[9] *Ibid.,* p. 179.

[10] *Ibid.,* p. 189.

several ways of arriving at an educated guess on this without looking at the books. For example, the KNXT operation is roughly four times as large (90 people) as that of the Eastern station whose costs were listed in Table 1-2; multiplying $671,000 by four, then, we arrive at a cost figure of $2,684,000. Or, take the $3,000,000 news budget publicly announced by a comparable and competing Los Angeles station, KNBC. Either way, the show's net income before taxes would appear to be at least $2,000,000, or 40 per cent on the gross, even without writing off a portion of the costs against the station's other news programming.

Interestingly enough, that percentage corresponds closely to the combined net incomes of the 15 O&O (owned and operated) stations of the three networks in 1966, as announced by the FCC. The 15 stations netted $108,000,000 before taxes, or 41.2 per cent of their combined gross earnings. In contrast, the networks themselves, with far greater revenues but proportionately even higher expenses, in that same year netted only $79,000,000, or 8.7 per cent on their gross revenues.

If a single news show can account for almost 2 per cent of the combined net incomes of the O&O stations, it seems highly probable that the local news operations of all 15 stations accounted for an extremely large percentage of their profits. In other words, television news has become big business.

The critics of television might well ponder these figures, even allowing for their highly questionable accuracy. News programming, whatever its faults, is rather generally conceded to be television's finest product. Considering the tremendous cost of news production, the public is fortunate that the news can be profitable. If it did not make money, and a great deal of it, there would be much less news on the air. And the public would be the poorer.

Summary

Since its advent (circa 1950) commercial television news has progressed from "rip and read" and the segmented show to the misnamed "magazine format" with a group of newsmen and specialists presided over by an anchorman, and with personality always an important element.

The longer magazine format, by helping to satisfy the public's desire for information within the attractive context of television, was primarily responsible for the "news explosion" of the 1960s. The result was a steady growth in the public confidence in television, and a concomitant and enormous increase in station revenues from television news.

Suggested Assignments

1. Investigate the comparative audience ratings of local television news shows in your community, and give your opinion as to why they differ.

2. Compare local television news shows in terms of (a) length of show, (b) type of format, (c) programming adjacencies with respect to network news shows aired by the same stations, and (d) number and types of reporters seen on the air.

3. Comment on the apparent news responsibility demonstrated by a local television station in terms of (a) coverage given stories of local importance, (b) coverage given stories of regional importance, (c) coverage given stories of national or international importance, (d) reporting in depth, (e) analysis or commentary, and (f) slanting of news.

4. Interview the station manager or news director of a local television station and report on such information as he supplies concerning costs and revenues of his news operation.

5. Compare the coverage given a major local story by a local television station and a local newspaper. Discuss the reasons for the differences.

6. State your personal opinion of the social relationship and interaction between commercial television news in your community and its local government. In other words, does television news in your community have any effect, beneficial or deleterious, on your local government?

Chapter 2

Opportunities and Requirements

Most jobs in television news demand a diversity of skills not required in any other medium. Because of this the job categories overlap endlessly, some of them stretching across the entire range of skills.

Types of Jobs

To avoid the confusion caused by this overlapping of functions, we can begin by separating the journalistic skills of television news into four somewhat arbitrary categories: (1) writers, (2) talent, (3) producers, and (4) executives.

Writers The news writer in television is, in the simplest terms, the man who writes all or part of the script of the news show. This includes the wording of news stories, but of equal importance are scripted cues for the use of film, video tape recordings, and graphics and for the shots to be taken by the video cameras.

In addition to news writers, television stations employ two other types of writers, who are usually graduates from the ranks of experienced news writers:

Documentary writers. In writing terms the television documentary is similar to a news show except that it usually confines its concern to a single story, and that more time and care are taken in its production.

Editorial writers. Television editorials are also similar to news stories in writing terms, except that they espouse a point of view or urge a course of action. The opportunities in this field are severely limited; there are probably fewer than 300 television editorial writers in the United States.

Talent There are three general categories of talent, or persons who appear on the air, either from studio or on film:

Field reporters. These are news reporters who go into the field, as the saying goes, to cover news at its source. Most network field reporters are called "correspondents." Whatever their title, field reporters are the television equivalent of the newspaper's general assignment reporters. The television field reporter is accompanied by a film camera crew or a mobile video unit, either of which makes a motion picture recording of the event being covered. The reporter's duties also usually include narration explaining the event, and recorded interviews with participants in the event.

Specialists. More and more television news is using reporters who specialize in coverage of particular topics or areas of news, such as weather, politics, farm news, or urban affairs. For the most part these men function in much the same manner as field reporters except for the specialization of their subject matter. Some, notably the weather reporter, may work almost entirely in the broadcast studio.

Anchormen. Most news shows are threaded together by one or, occasionally, more air men known as anchormen. The anchorman is the principal figure seen in studio, where he reads the script prepared in the newsroom. Field reporters and specialists may also appear in studio, but they disappear after completing their individual reports, whereas the anchorman remains and reappears throughout the show.

Producers The producer is the newsman who decides what news goes into the show and what is omitted, and the order in which the various news stories are presented. His concern is with the over-all style and content of the show, and his function is comparable to that of the makeup editor of a newspaper.

News department executives The top executive of a television news department is usually titled the *news director*. He has the over-all responsibility for news production and the hiring and firing of personnel; in consultation with higher management he helps to determine news programming schedules and budgetary policies. His function is comparable to that of the managing editor of a newspaper.

Subordinate to the news director are various other executives, of which the two most important in most shops are the producers of the various shows and the *assignment editor*, who decides which stories to cover and assigns reporters and crews to cover them.

The producer's functions were listed in a separate category above. Although he is an executive, we have listed him separately because his duties are more closely related to those of the writer. In fact, the most inexperienced writer is very likely to find himself functioning in part as a producer on his very first job.

Overlapping of Functions

The double function of the producer illustrates the difficulty of attempting to categorize jobs in television news; in most shops the producer is better described as a writer-producer. Only in very large organizations does the producer cease to write and simply produce.

The writer does far more than merely write. One of his most important functions is to edit film and VTR (video tape recording), or to supervise the editing. Whether or not he functions as the producer of a show, he functions as the producer of each story he writes.

The reporter is of necessity a writer, whether he commits his copy to script before he reads it to the camera, or ad libs his "writing" vocally. In smaller news shops he may have to be a film cameraman as well, and perhaps record sound as he runs the camera. In almost all shops the reporter functions as a film director; he directs the film crew as to the style and content of the film coverage. And even though his primary work is in the field, he is usually expected to be a competent air performer in studio; he may even be the anchorman. On top of all this, in some shops he may also produce the show.

The news director in a small shop may function as assignment editor, reporter, writer, producer, and anchorman. In larger shops the subordinate executive functions may be divided among platoons of executives commanding battalions of specialized writers and reporters.

An excellent example of the typical overlapping of functions is provided by the eleven-man news operation of station WKY-TV in Oklahoma City, honored in 1968 as Newsfilm Station of the Year by the National Press Photographer's Association.

Every man on the staff, including News Director Ernie Schultz and the two air men, shoots film. Everyone also edits and scripts his own film and film shot by other staff members. On weekends the newsmen on duty even operate the station's color film processor. "Although some specialization of function develops under the pressure of deadlines, the idea of everybody being able to do anything is a cardinal principle at WKY."[1]

The larger the staff, the more specialization one finds. But even in the largest station and network operations, most writers are expected to be competent producers, and reporters are expected to be film directors as well as reporter-writer-producers. And regardless of the size of the news operation, the television newsman who cannot supervise the editing of film is so rare as to be almost nonexistent. A study of the list in Appendix A (page 317) will confirm the need for a multiplicity of skills.

Pay Scales

In television as in so many other media, the importance of good writing is seldom recognized by management, and the writer therefore is paid less than other newsmen in proportion to the value of his contribution. However, the television news writer's pay compares favorably with the pay of writers in print media and radio. Further, the tendency to combine writing with production, which stands higher on the pay scale, offers the television news writer many more opportunities to increase his income. Since writing often provides the quickest entree to television, these factors make television news writing especially attractive for the journalism graduate or for the experienced newsman who wishes to move into television from another medium.

Producers are paid more than mere writers, not only because more skills and greater experience are required, but also because a producer is obviously an executive of a sort, however minor, and management respects and understands the executive function. For the same reasons assignment editors and news directors rank fairly high on the pay scale.

But in television news the top pay goes to talent. In many cases the top news talent is paid twice as much as the news director who is his boss. One reason is the combination of skills required. Another is the peculiar and apparently permanent shortage of truly effective talent; many otherwise good newsmen fail miserably at projecting their competence through the television tube to the audience. Still another reason is the personality factor which causes the audience to identify a news show by its talent, not by its writers or producers, and not to a comparable degree by the station which broadcasts the show. This

---

[1] "Film: At WKY-TV It's the Name of the Business," *National Press Photographer* (July 1968), p. 6.

factor, unique to broadcasting, gives talent a bargaining leverage which is beyond the grasp of most other newsmen.

Television's position vis-à-vis other news media in competing for journalism graduates is documented by the annual studies of starting salaries compiled by The Newspaper Fund, a research and information organization established by Dow Jones & Company, Inc. Table 2-1, compiled by the Fund, covers reports from 4,609 out of a total of 5,320 graduates of 126 schools and departments of journalism during 1968.

Table 2-1

Average 1968 Starting Salaries

	BAs	MAs or PhDs
Advertising	$129.89	$168.47
Public relations	127.55	179.48
Daily newspaper advertising	122.17	120.00
Radio news	121.80	156.67
Magazines	118.97	138.20
Wire services	114.43	151.60
Daily newsroom	114.19	140.82
Television news	*112.68*	*137.50*
Weekly newspaper advertising	112.28	—
Weekly newsroom	109.76	143.25

Source: *Where They Went to Work 1964–1968*, The Newspaper Fund (Princeton, N.J., n.d.), pp. C2–C3.

Of the graduates reported on, 114, or 2.5 per cent, entered television news. This was an increase of 52 per cent over the number entering television news in 1967.

The Fund's report unfortunately fails to indicate which job categories were filled by those entering television news. However, it is a fairly safe assumption that most were employed primarily as writers.

The actual list of job openings (Appendix A) is more helpful as an indicator of both prevailing pay scales and skills requirements in television news. And it should be remembered that nearly all television news jobs involve some writing, and that many writers must also be producers.

In the Appendix A list, a salary stated as "plus fees" or "plus talent" indicates a base pay supplemented by fees for air work; fees vary from one locality to another, and they are calculated on an extremely complicated basis involving the number and type of air appearances made each week. In many cases fees may equal or surpass the base pay. A large flat salary for air work is usually a minimum guarantee against fees, and the employee can seldom expect to make more than his guarantee.

Most jobs, except for unionized jobs in larger cities, call for a 6-day week; in some cases overtime is paid for the sixth day. Talent is a notable exception; talent may work any number of days or hours in a week without extra pay, because talent pay is seldom calculated on the basis of time worked. At many stations talent also does not participate in company benefit and retirement plans, as do most other employees in the news department.

Major Market Stations and Networks

As might be expected, pay scales range higher in major markets (large cities) and at the networks than at small stations. However, much of this additional income may be consumed by higher living costs; thus the difference in real terms is not as great as the figures may indicate.

Writers Typical of the labor union contracts for major market writers are the current contracts between NBC and NABET (National Association of Broadcast Employees and Technicians) covering both local O&O and network writers in Chicago, Los Angeles, and San Francisco. The contracts call for a sliding scale of minimum pay based on experience and ranging from $181 per week for writers with no experience to $235.96 per week for those with more than 18 months of television news or comparable experience. In September 1969, these minimums rose to $188 and $245.40, respectively.

This base pay is supplemented for most writers by certain fees. A writer functioning in an executive capacity (for example, as a producer) gets additional "desk pay" of $8.50 per day. Writers for commercial network shows get additional pay depending on the length of the show, from $6 (for each 5-minute show) up to $35 (for each show of 30 or more minutes in length). These show fees may be reduced somewhat, however, if the writer is regularly assigned to a strip show; for example, the writer of a 5-day strip show receives a fee equal to three times the daily fee, not five times that fee.

Thus the experienced writer of a 30-minute commercially sponsored network strip show would at present receive his base pay of $235.96, desk pay of $42.50, and commercial show fees of $105, for a total weekly pay of $383.46.

NABET has a similar contract with ABC for local and network news writers in the same three cities; the variations in the terms are relatively minor. And the WGA (Writers Guild of America) contracts for network and O&O news writers in such cities as New York, Philadelphia, Chicago, and Los Angeles are also on approximately the same pay level, with innumerable minor variations.

The type of experience required to attain a news writing job for a network or a major market station is clearly indicated by the WGA agreement covering CBS news writers in Los Angeles. The contract defines a "senior staff writer" as one who has one or more years of news writing experience under the following circumstances:

(1) Employment as a staff news writer by any nationwide radio or television network, or

(2) Employment as a reporter or rewrite man on the staff of a metropolitan daily newspaper with a circulation of at least 100,000 copies, or

(3) Employment as a news writer on the staff of AP or UPI in a marketing area with a population of 500,000 or more, or

(4) Employment as a news writer on the staff of a 50,000 watt radio station in a marketing area with a population of 500,000 or more, or

(5) Employment as a news writer on the staff of any VHF television station in a marketing area of 500,000 or more.

However, less experienced news writers are often hired by major stations and even networks on a probationary basis. The same WGA-CBS contract makes provision for this in the form of a category known as "junior staff writers" with less than one year of radio or television news writing experience or the equivalent. Junior writers must be promoted to full senior writer status within six months or else be laid off. Under this contract junior writers currently receive base pay of $135.75 per week, as compared to $235 per week for senior writers working on local shows.

Similar opportunities for the less experienced writer exist almost everywhere, no matter how large or prestigious the news operation. All the writer has to do is prove his merit; the doors are never completely closed.

Talent The bargaining agent for news talent in all networks and major markets is AFTRA (American Federation of Television and Radio Artists), the union which also represents all actors, announcers, singers, and dancers who perform for television either live or on VTR. (Those who perform on film, *except* news film, are represented by the Screen Actors Guild, even if the film is destined primarily for television distribution.)

AFTRA's contracts with the ABC, CBS, and NBC networks all call for a weekly minimum guarantee of $350 for news talent. On top of this the newsman receives a fee for each air appearance, although half of the fee is "recapturable," which means that a portion of the fee may be credited against his base pay. The manner in which performance fees are computed is incredibly complicated; suffice it to say that the newsman who appears on the air with some regularity can expect to make $400 or $500 a week, and occasionally much more.

AFTRA agreements covering O&O newsmen guarantee a minimum of $300 a week, plus fees, which in some cases are recapturable. Local fees are usually smaller than network fees. Talent employed by independent stations in major markets tend to receive a minimum of at least $200, plus fees.

That more than a few local newsmen in major markets tend to make far more than contract scale is indicated by the provision for a "money break" in the AFTRA contract for CBS O&O newsmen in Los Angeles. The money break is set at $26,000; local newsmen who are guaranteed that much per year suffer the penalty of 100 per cent recapturability of fees. It is a penalty to be borne lightly.

Actually, AFTRA's fee system makes little sense when applied to the news business, and should be radically revised if not abandoned. The system was devised for the benefit of entertainers, who may work here today and there tomorrow, and who need protection against the unscrupulous employer; few entertainers would like to see any major change in the system. But it has been transferred to television news without regard for the greatly differing conditions of employment. The newsman usually works regularly for the same employer for long periods of time, and his employer seldom tries to cheat or defraud him.

But the worst aspect of the fee system in news is that it restricts the management from making full use of the employee, and in the process not infrequently leads to subtle distortion of the news. This distortion is seldom significant, but any distortion of news is cause for concern.

One form of distortion is caused by the newsman himself. If he gets an additional fee for every air appearance, he tends to inject himself into the story, visually or vocally, without regard for the news values involved, just to earn extra money. A second form of distortion originates with the news executive, usually the assignment editor, who in assigning a reporter to a story may be required to consider which newsman will cost the company the least in fees; as a result, the least qualified man may get the assignment.

A far more sensible system would be to hire talent on the same basis that most other employees are hired: so much money for so many days and hours of work, overtime beyond that. There would be difficulties; for example, it would be difficult to work out a schedule for an air man who anchors shows at noon, 6 P.M., and 11 P.M. But the difficulties are not insuperable, if both union and management will approach the problem open-mindedly.

Journalistic Requirements

Training and experience   The first and most obvious requirement for the television newsman is the same as for any other type of journalist: a knowledge of news. While news for television differs strikingly in certain details from news for other media, the fundamental principles are the same and the fundamental need is the same: professionalism.

Until recently almost the only school for the training of professional television newsmen was the school of experience, and it is still unqualifiedly the best. To gain experience the newcomer in television usually must first find a job at one of the smaller stations; at least, his chances are better here than in the large stations. UHF (ultra high frequency) stations, with their smaller audiences (and therefore smaller revenues and lower pay scales), offer opportunities for the newsman with little experience. Radio, too, is full of opportunities; there are many more radio stations than television stations, and much radio experience is directly applicable to television.

Newspapers and news magazines have provided stepping stones into television for many writers and reporters, but this route seems likely to carry somewhat less traffic in the future. During the first two decades of television the print media provided perhaps the largest pool of experienced newsmen upon which television could draw, and draw it did; the author suspects that more television newsmen came out of print than out of radio, although he can find no proof to support this thesis. The newspaper man may know nothing of the technical aspects of television news, but he has the basic equipment on which to build that knowledge; and it is easier to teach a man technical tricks than to teach him to understand the evaluation and gathering of news.

Today, however, the aspiring television newsman is more likely to look directly to television for his first job. This new direction reflects in part the rapidly increasing scope and competence of the academic training available for television news. Journalism schools and departments, until only a few years ago primarily print-oriented, with an occasional bow to radio writing, are recognizing the increasing need for television news training and are providing it. More and more telecommunications schools are springing up, and existing schools are expanding their curricula. Today the would-be television newsman can undergo his basic training here, rather than in the college of hard knocks. While newspaper or radio experience is always valuable, it is the side door entry to television; the television major may open the front door.

Technical knowledge The television news major is especially valuable, in that it provides the technical knowledge which is required of the television newsman to a degree astronomically exceeding the comparable requirements in any other medium. The fully competent television newsman combines the abilities of writing, reporting, video production, film editing, and film direction. All of these are not merely crafts; they are arts, and they require of the newsman that he be an artist in the fullest meaning of the word.

To some newsmen television's technical details are boring or overwhelming. Obviously, television news is not for such men. But for those who enjoy overcoming the technical problems and making technique a form of artistry, television is the most challenging and the most rewarding of all the news media.

Performance To the list of abilities above, the television reporter (but not the other newsmen in television) must add the ability to perform before the camera. His is the face the audience sees, his is the voice it hears; and if his personal presentation is not at least acceptable, at best authoritative and convincing, his message will never get through.

Performance consists of two parts: speech and appearance. The reporter whose grammar is atrocious, who speaks in accents undecipherable to the average American, or who stutters, stammers, or mumbles is not likely to find a reporting job in television. Nor is the reporter with a wart on his nose, a bald head, strikingly unusual facial expressions, or clothing which is noticeably unconventional. There are probably a few exceptions to all of these rules, but they are so rare as to prove the rule. The one rule to which there are *never* any enduring exceptions is that the reporter must not betray nervousness or panic on camera; in fact, he must not even *be* nervous, because nervousness cannot be concealed from the camera.

These conditions may seem to be a defense of conformity, and in a superficial sense they are. But there is one very good and simple reason for all of them: each of the conditions named attracts attention to itself and thereby distracts the viewer from the reporter's message, which is the news.

The reporter is therefore advised to mend his fractured language, have the wart removed, buy a toupee, dress conventionally, and—if possible—keep his cool. That, or seek a job outside the talent area.

Education The television newsman should be a knowledgeable man, aware of social, political, technological, and theological trends and their implications, acquainted with as many leaders in these fields as possible, and always on the lookout for hints of change in the society on which and to which he reports.

He is therefore an educated man, which means a man who seeks wisdom as well as facts. He may obtain formal education in a college or university, or he may be self-educated; the important thing is for him to recognize that education is an endless process, and that the wisdom he pursues is ultimately unattainable but must nevertheless be sought.

In practical terms this means that his technical knowledge of television production is only a tool, a means to an end. The professional is more than a technician; his greater concern is the end to which he puts his means. His fundamental purpose is to help provide a continuing flow not just of information, but of the *kind* of information society needs to order its affairs, to improve itself, and to recognize and solve the new problems which every improvement creates. His aim is the betterment of his profession and, through that, of mankind.

From this point of view it becomes immediately evident that the television newsman must study a range of subjects extending far beyond journalism. He must be reasonably well versed in anthropology, art, economics, history, languages, law, philosophy, and the social and physical sciences. If for lack of time he be master of none, he must surely be jack of all; the alternative is incompetence. Recognition of this is more and more apparent in departments and schools of journalism and telecommunications, many of which are adopting an interdisciplinary structure within which the student journalist is exposed to the broad spectrum of knowledge which his profession will demand of him. Further, the emphasis in virtually all such schools is on the conceptual values of journalism and the meaning of the term "news," rather than on such technical training as may be necessary. The values of responsibility and adequacy of coverage, the philosophical judgment which the student acquires here will help to guide him throughout his career no matter how many changes occur (and many will) in the technical methods by which news is gathered and disseminated.

Beyond formal schooling, the television journalist should continue his process of self-education, by extensive reading, by suitable formal study (for example, university extension courses), by travel, and by maintaining personal contacts above and beyond the necessities of his daily work with leaders and potential leaders in every field of human endeavor.

This is a demanding requirement. It calls for a commitment of time and effort which not all journalists are willing to make. To consider only one item, there is never enough time for reading; the conscientious journalist is nagged by the knowledge that every year he falls another eleven months behind in the reading he should do. And since his work is extremely demanding of both time and physical effort, and since sabbaticals are almost unheard of in television news, he must somehow try to squeeze in some of the precious reading time he needs by foregoing other pleasures. The penalty for failure to make this effort will be visible in his work, for nothing is more relentlessly unkind to the narrow mind than the television camera.

Ethics   There is a moral imperative which drives some men beyond their capacities toward the fulfillment of dreams, and the best television newsmen are made of such stuff. The responsibility which accident of time and circumstance has placed in their hands is awesome, and its exercise demands care of a magnitude new to journalism. In a society drowning in information, it is the television newsman's chosen duty to select the information the majority of the American public is to know about. Amid a confusion of images, false and true, he must try to find the true. As Western society pays the rising price of technology in the coin of alienation, the television journalist more than any other is responsible for discerning the causes and pointing to the alterations in that society which may promise its survival.

It is a time of revolution, born, like all revolutions, of frustration. The Age of Reason, in which ever expanding knowledge was to guarantee eternal progress toward happiness for all, seems to be collapsing amid the wreckage of its own promises. As disenchantment becomes endemic, the system that bred it must change or die. For the television journalist's task in such an age, knowledge—the driving force that has failed—is plainly not enough. He must have faith. He must be moved by a moral imperative.

The moral imperative of Western civilization is embedded in the Judaeo-Christian ethic, with its commandments to love. This is the faith which gives the newsman a rule by which to measure himself and his work. And if this seems a far connection from the customary preachments of journalistic ethics, the newsman might ask himself why he is a journalist if not out of love for his fellow man. Why tell anyone anything unless he *needs* to know it? And why *care* about his need? The bedrock answer, which provides clues to all the other answers, is love of man.

The television journalist has not only the responsibility to his fellow man, he has uniquely the opportunity to carry out that responsibility. He is equipped with one of the most powerful artifacts of the Age of Reason: television itself. It is a person-to-person medium, and never more so than when the individual newsman steps electronically into another individual's home and speaks to him of important matters, as one person to another. Television is a mass medium, true, but its message is received not by people in the mass but by individuals, each alone and unique. Mass man is an abstract, statistical conception; he does not exist. Individual man does exist, and it is to him that the newsman speaks, with all the power of personal communication.

The newsman's responsibility is to speak to this man with care and concern for his future. He needs no other code of ethics. Let him read the codes, if he wishes. They are in all the books, and they are all useful, and they are all inadequate.

Not one of them mentions love.

Summary

The four fundamental job classifications in television news are *writers, talent, producers,* and *executives.* In most shops their functions overlap.

Pay scales for most television jobs are comparable with those in other media, with the anomaly that talent is often higher paid than the executives who command its services.

Journalistic requirements include training and experience, technical knowledge, continuing education, and ethical motivation, plus ability to perform in the case of reporters.

Suggested Assignments

1. Make arrangements to visit a local television station and observe the operations in the newsroom, film editing rooms, telecine, VTR room, control room, and studio. (Most television stations are happy to cooperate in showing their facilities to television news classes, especially if arrangements are made well in advance.) Write a report on the overlapping of functions observed.

2. Interview one or more newsmen at a television station with particular reference to the types of skills (writing, producing, film editing, film direction, air work) which their jobs require, and report on same.

3. Write a report on the opinions of one or more television newsmen interviewed as to the background needed to be competent in television news.

4. Analyze a television news show in terms of each of the following: (a) educational background needed for adequate coverage of one or more specific stories, (b) apparent technical polish of the production, (c) performance characteristics of the air men and field reporters, and (d) apparent ethical standards maintained by the news staff as evident in the selection and style of presentation of the various news stories.

5. Write a brief statement of your own aims in television news, and the motivations underlying those aims.

Chapter 3

News
Sources
in Television

Television uses the same sources of news that are used by other media, plus two sources in particular, the microwave feed and the syndication film, used by no other medium. However, the manner in which television uses the information it obtains is sometimes quite different from the manner in which other media use it.

Press Wire Services

The primary source of both national and international news in television is the press wire service teletype (Associated Press, United Press International, Reuters, etc.). Even a network news organization, with dozens of correspondents in many nations, cannot hope to keep track of events occurring all over the world without relying principally on the wire services.

These include many specialized wires, such as those carrying only regional, business, sports, or weather information, but with the exception of regional and sports wires these are not widely found at the smaller stations. Many television stations subscribe to the radio wire services, which carry the same basic information as the full report or "A" wires except that it is transmitted in condensed form prepared for broadcasting of 5-minute and 15-minute radio news shows. Smaller stations may simply "rip and read" the radio wire summaries, but for most stations this is a backup service used only in emergencies; they prefer to rewrite their own script copy from the A-wires, which are seldom written in a style suitable for broadcast use. In a few of the largest cities local wire services provide news of local events only, and these are of great value to stations in those cities.

Still photographs transmitted by facsimile wire services are widely used in television, especially for visual coverage of late-breaking stories on which film or VTR is not available.

However, the use which television makes of wire service information is somewhat different than the use to which it is put by newspapers. A newspaper may take an AP wire story and print it without change. For television use the same story usually must be rewritten, for two reasons: (1) to condense it by distillation of its essential elements so that it will not take up so much air time, and (2) to recast it in a form and wording more suitable for broadcast delivery. If film or VTR coverage of the same story is available, the wire service information will be used only to supplement the information provided by the visual coverage, this supplementary information being scripted in the form of either standup or voice-over copy (that is, copy to be read on camera or over the film or VTR).

Like the other media, television also uses wire services as a source of information on future events which it may wish to cover in its own fashion, which most often means film or video coverage.

Microwave Feeds

The microwave feed is television's own unique version of the wire service. It is an electronic transmission of news stories originally recorded on film or VTR, edited, assembled into a single package usually of 15 or 30 minutes duration, and fed by closed-circuit micro-wave to subscribers who record it on video tape and select from it any stories they wish to use on their own local news broadcasts. The networks are the major distributors of these microwave feeds, which are transmitted once daily at a preset time, usually early enough for use in early evening news shows.

Network O&Os and affiliates frequently make a somewhat similar use of the network news shows which they receive, but only after the network show is aired locally. For later local shows parts of the VTR of the network show may be "cannibalized" for use in the local production.

Syndication Film Clips

Similar to the microwave feed, although seldom as timely, is the news film syndication service. This is a daily shipment, usually via Air

Express, sometimes by Air Freight, of filmed news stories on matters of broad enough interest to warrant showing on many television stations. Because of the time delay involved in producing many prints of a single story and shipping them, the film syndication service at the present is giving way, although slowly, to the more up-to-date microwave feed. However, it is usually less expensive, and the films often provide excellent background footage for current stories even though they may be a day or more old. In cases where no visual report on an otherwise outdated story has been seen before, the film report may have current value simply because the audience has only heard about, but not seen, the event.

Stringers

Film coverage of many spot news events, such as fires, highway collisions and emergency police actions, is often difficult to obtain if staff cameramen were not on duty at the time the event occurred or were unable to reach the scene fast enough to record it. However, such film is sometimes shot by free-lance cameramen lucky enough to be on the scene; this film may be purchased for television use.

These free-lances, or "stringers," are often newspaper photographers who carry a film camera in the hope of picking up extra money. The customary arrangement is for the station to buy the film at a standard price ($25 for the average story in larger markets), process it at its own expense, and give the stringer an amount of unexposed film equal to the amount purchased.

In localities where staff cameramen are unionized, labor union contracts customarily forbid the purchase of stringer film for any but spot news stories. In other words, stringer film of scheduled events cannot be purchased, on the theory that the station which wants film coverage of such an event should assign its own staff cameramen to the story.

Other Television Stations

When film coverage of distant events is desired, the film can sometimes be obtained from a television station in the locality where the event occurred, provided that station has covered the event. If special coverage is desired, this often can be arranged in advance. This coverage may be in the form of a film print shipped by Air Express; or if time is short and budget allows, the visual coverage may be transmitted by microwave and recorded on VTR.

Competitors

No television station can expect to originate all of the news in its own community, no matter how great an effort it makes to do so. Other stations, radio news operations, and newspapers frequently "break" important stories which warrant coverage by all media. For this reason other broadcast news should be monitored regularly, and all editions of the local newspapers should be purchased and scrutinized carefully for such news. In most communities the newspapers do most of the work of originating local news and are thus the most likely source of major stories.

In some shops there is a tendency to ignore such stories unless they are too important to ignore. The theory seems to be, "It's *their* story, so let *them* follow it up." The author finds little to admire in this theory of competitive inaction. If the competitor has found something new and worthwhile to report, the story should be judged purely on that basis—that is, on its news value.

Staff Reporters

Most stations maintain a staff of reporters who gather news. In quite a few cases the staff includes one or more reporters stationed in out-of-town bureaus. These reporters all function as news sources.

Personal contacts are the reporter's major source of news. Newspapers have long recognized this by maintaining "beat reporters" who are permanently assigned to certain beats or news source areas (city hall, police department, schools, etc.) and whose primary duty is to develop and maintain a broad range of personal contacts in those areas. Their function is not only to cover stories but to *discover* them and notify the newsroom of events pending or in progress. Some beat reporters never write a story, and the author recalls one who was illiterate but nevertheless an excellent reporter; he telephoned all his information to rewrite men. Beat reporters spend much of their time dropping in on possible news sources for casual conversation with the sole objective of maintaining a close personal relationship; when something newsworthy develops, the reporter who is a personal friend of the source contact is often the reporter who gets the story first.

Television has not yet developed the beat reporter system to anything like the extent that newspapers have. A frequently used substitute, however, is the tipster whose personal contacts give him access to news of certain types. Often the television tipster is a newspaper beat reporter who is not averse to receiving a nominal weekly retainer from the television station, in return for which he tips the station's assignment editor to the same stories about which he informs his own news desk. Such an arrangement is in most cases a secret between the television station and the tipster, because newspapers object to the practice as a conflict of interest. However, all is considered fair in love and news competition.

The television specialist has a particular advantage in the maintenance of contacts in his specialty area. This advantage is conferred by the station's public recognition of his specialist status, evidenced by promotion and advertising. His contacts are invariably impressed by the stature accorded him by his employers, although that impression is quickly dissipated if he proves incompetent.

Any television reporter has some advantage over his newspaper or radio counterparts because of the personal prestige ("glamor," if you wish) which results simply from regular appearance on a television news show. Television reporters quickly become minor celebrities, the degree of public recognition being approximately proportionate to the degree of "exposure" or time spent on the air. The reporter who appears regularly on a daily news show receives more exposure, at least in his own community, than the most famous stars of network entertainment shows. This circumstance has distinct handicaps for the newsman, particularly in that he cannot go about his work unnoticed and unrecognized, but it opens doors and disposes personal contacts to talk, and out of such entree many news stories develop.

Public Relations Representatives

Public relations representatives of business firms, governmental offices and agencies, political parties and candidates, foundations, civic and community organizations, and numerous other groups provide a large amount of news which appears on television in one form or another.

Their most obvious activity is the issuance of "news releases" containing information about the activities of their clients. They also arrange and announce news conferences which television may cover.

Of particular interest to television is the PR distribution of free film clips or video tapes ("handouts"), many of which find their way into news shows. Some of these are of great value because they provide visual reports on activities which television cannot possibly cover, or which it could cover only at great difficulty and expense. Examples of such visual reports are the films shot by American astronauts in space and distributed by NASA, the National Aeronautical and Space Administration, and films of aquanauts shot underseas during the Sealab experiments and distributed by the United States Navy.

In general, however, the PR men do not "score" as well with television as with newspapers, for two reasons: (1) Because of its time limitations television cannot cover as many stories as the newspaper, and many PR releases are therefore rejected as too trivial or too limited in interest, and (2) many PR releases are so promotional in nature that to incorporate them into a news show would constitute a "plug" (free advertising) for the PR client. Especially since the "payola" scandals of the late 1950s, television is far more sensitive about plugs than are many newspapers.

Periodicals

Certain periodicals, not directly competitive with television, constitute an extremely rich source of news for the newsman who is willing to cull their contents. For the most part these are specialized publications of limited circulation: the journal of the American Medical Association, the *Bulletin of Atomic Scientists,* many so-called "little" magazines, a host of publications put out by legal societies, trade unions, and professional groups, and publications catering to the special interests of various businesses and industries. News of many important developments or pending events appears first in such publications and becomes known to the general public only when a reporter for one of the mass media takes the trouble to dig it out of the source publication and give it wider distribution.

Colleges, Universities, and Foundations

The academic community, in which by broad definition we include numerous privately endowed foundations engaged in research and study, constitutes an increasingly important source of news for television. Under the growing system of government and foundation research grants amounting to billions of dollars, the professors and savants have emerged from their ivory towers to involve themselves deeply in the practical and pressing problems of international peace, transportation, air and water pollution, urban decay, race relations, politics, and every other thing under the sun that makes news. Their studies, discoveries, and opinions daily produce stories of national and even international import.

The newsman who develops his contacts in the academic community will quickly discern a bonus. Its name is integrity. Nothing has greater value to the man or woman who has devoted his career to academic pursuits, for intellectual dishonesty is the incurable leprosy of the professor. This is not merely a matter of concern for reputation. With rare exceptions those who are attracted to academic life see truth as the highest form of beauty and its pursuit as man's noblest occupation; most of them could make more money in business, but they do what they do because they prefer it. They may fall short of truth by error or overshoot it by zeal, but their opinions, while fallible, can usually be relied upon as honest. The same generality cannot be made about any other group except perhaps the cloth and, hopefully, the fourth estate.

The General Public

A surprising number of news stories develop out of letters and telephone calls from television viewers. Most such stories involve localized community or personal problems which have relevance beyond the persons immediately concerned. Residents of a neighborhood, for example, may be disturbed about a proposed zoning change, but if the zoning change appears to involve bribery or a violation of master planning concepts, then the area of interest extends beyond the immediately affected neighborhood to the entire community.

To attract information from the general public on such matters—matters which otherwise might never become news—the station's entire news programming must be of the type to instill public confidence in the station's responsibility to and concern for its constituents. Such confidence is won only by continued adherence to a news policy which demonstrates in word and picture and deed, day after day, that the station truly intends to operate as much in the public interest as for its own convenience and necessity.

All news is a matter of public interest, and the public is quick to discern deception, distortion, bias, and irresponsibility in the news. The newsman who treats the public with the respect to which it is entitled, not only legally but morally, will find that the public repays him a hundredfold with its confidence.

Summary

Television's sources of news are the same as those of other media—press wire services, stringers, staff reporters, other stations and other media, public relations representatives, the academic world, and the general public—plus syndication film and microwave feeds.

Television's handling of news differs from that of other media in several respects: wire copy is usually recast in broadcast form, public relations representatives do not "score" as well as with other media, and the average station's development of news at the source is still inadequate.

Suggested Assignments

1. From observation during a visit to a television station (see Suggested Assignments, Chapter 2), name the types of press wire service, facsimile, microwave, and film syndication services to which the station subscribes, and give a specific example of the use made of each.

2. If the station maintains out-of-town bureaus, note and report on the extent to which reports from the bureaus are used in the news.

3. Try to identify any public relations film "handouts" used in a news show, and explain why you think they originated with public relations agencies. Check your guesses by asking the show's producer.

4. Monitor a news show and try to identify the original sources of the various stories, whether film or standup. If any story seemed inadequate, explain what more you would have done in reporting it.

5. List as many potential news stories in your community as you can which to your knowledge have not been covered and which in your opinion warrant coverage. Explain why you think these stories should be reported, and how you would go about it.

Chapter 4

News
Values
in Television

While news is fundamentally the same in any medium, the news which appears on television is distinguishable by certain striking characteristics not found in other media. Obviously, then, it is based on a different set of values, which are derived from the peculiar conditions applicable only to television. The television newsman needs to know television's news values, how they differ from the values which set the patterns of news in the other media, and why these differences exist.

The Newspaper Analogy

To arrive at such an understanding, it may be useful to compare television news with the news found in the more familiar newspaper.

Time limitations The length of a news broadcast severely restricts the amount of news which can be incorporated into the typical daily television news show. Time is to television what space is to the newspaper, and television has much less time than the newspaper has space. Only so much can be said in a given amount of time; measured by wordage alone, a 30-minute television news show is the equivalent of less than the front page of a newspaper. Further, the newspaper's space is expandable, but television's time is not. The paper can be made larger simply by adding pages; television program schedules permit the addition of more time to the news show only in exceptional circumstances.

This time limitation forces television news producers to be highly selective in the stories they include in their shows. Television news is basically "page one" news; there is no time to include the stories which might appear on page 38 of the newspaper. Thus only the most important news of the day is likely to find its way into the show.

Because of the lack of time, television news is likely to be covered with extreme brevity as compared with the newspaper's coverage. The writing is concise, striking directly at the heart of the matter. Lengthy, rambling reports are seldom seen; occasional reports "in depth" do appear, but their depth is usually found, on examination, to be quite shallow in comparison with that of a newspaper report in depth.

Time of broadcast   The hour at which the news show is aired may significantly alter the news values upon which the show is based. While the newspaper has its copy and makeup deadlines and is delivered to the home or newsstand at a certain time of day, the reader is free to peruse it when he chooses. But the television viewer can watch the show only when it is on the air. (This condition will become less restricting as home video tape recording equipment becomes less expensive and is more widely used than at present.)

The time of broadcast therefore restricts the potential audience to those persons who *can* watch the show, and this in turn raises the question of who these persons are and what their principal interests are. The midday audience, for example, is composed largely of housewives; their interest in fashion news can be presumed to be high, but their interest in sports news can be presumed to be almost nonexistent. The early evening audience is a general family audience with a wide diversity of interests. The late evening audience consists mostly of adults who would be bored by a feature story appealing primarily to children.

Even the same person has different interests at different times of the day. The commuter gulping his breakfast before starting to work in the morning has no time or patience for in-depth reports which might interest him greatly at dinner time; he wants the top of the news in a hurry. At ten or eleven o'clock in the evening this same viewer is tired, relaxed, receptive to a more sophisticated and entertaining type of news than he was earlier in the evening before the children had been put to bed.

All this is not to imply that major news stories are not of interest at any time of the day or night. But whereas the newspaper is a potpourri of items appealing to every possible taste and interest, the content and style of the television news show must to some extent be tailored to the tastes and interests of its potential audience.

Signal area Here is another obvious consideration in the news values of television. And here again the newspaper has an advantage; it can be delivered anywhere. *The New York Times* is sold in every major city in the United States and in many foreign countries. But a television show cannot be received beyond its signal area, the geographic region covered by its video transmission. The video broadcast signal follows a straight line, eventually moving out into space as the earth curves away beneath it. Nor is the signal area a geographic circle; many obstructions, such as tall buildings or mountains, may block the signal.

This factor primarily affects the use of stories of localized interest in communities outside the signal area—stories which many newspapers might cover. But if the story has no particular interest outside that community, there is little point in broadcasting it.

Similarly, if the signal area is extremely broad, as is the case with network news shows which are broadcast by many stations, news that is of interest only in one locality—even within the signal area—is inappropriate for the show. Here the content of the network news show resembles the content of a national news magazine; the appeal must be to the broadest audience. To a lesser degree the same is true for stations in metropolitan areas; matters of purely neighborhood interest are not important enough to include in the show.

Visual elements These are obviously more important in television than in any other news medium, and the show tends to favor news which can be reported with pictures—moving pictures, especially—over news on which no picture is available.

Personality Here again is a significant and complicating factor in determining television news values, simply because most of the news must be transmitted through the person of a reporter. The personality of the reporter inevitably affects the story to a much greater degree than in radio, let alone newspapers.

These last two factors—visual elements and personality—are in fact so important that separate discussions will be devoted to them.

Importance of the Visual

Only television among the news media has the motion picture, and the best of its news values are based on this fact.

This is most strikingly evident in the television news special, in which regular programming is interrupted for the presentation of a major news event. Outstanding examples of this type of coverage in recent years were the network specials on the national political conventions; numerous activities of the American space program; the assassinations of President John F. Kennedy, Dr. Martin Luther King, Jr., and Senator Robert F. Kennedy; the funeral of Sir Winston Churchill; and innumerable sports events such as major golf tournaments, the Olympic games, and baseball's World Series. Local specials far too numerous to mention have been contributed by stations conscious of their responsibility to provide extensive live coverage of major events in their own communities.

Through such television specials the world was able to see these important events as they happened, even to witness the actual shooting of Lee Harvey Oswald. Not only did the public see what happened, it saw it in more detail and more comprehensively than persons on the scene, because of television's ability to leap instantaneously from one locale to another.

Even more important, in all probability, is the sense of participation in great human events which the television special makes possible for the public. Many persons, even those who had no fondness for President Kennedy or his policies, wept in the quiet of their living rooms as they watched their nation mourn, and few failed to be impressed with television's visible witness to the mortality of man and the continuity of his institutions. No other medium could begin to convey the reality of the tragedy as television did.

But the special is, as its name indicates, a rare type of news coverage. Far more common is the routine motion picture coverage seen on regularly scheduled news shows. And if the magnitude of the events depicted is usually less, the effect of witnessing them and vicariously participating in them is the same. The effect is an *emotional* reaction, whether to the death of a President or the tragedy of a missing child. *It is this ability to generate an emotional reaction which is the principal distinction between television news and all other news.* It accounts for the greater impact of television news, also for much of the controversy which it generates. It is a "moving" picture in more than one sense.

What this means is as difficult to assay as the career determinants of a teen-ager. Many critics, responding instinctively to television's emotional impact, decry it; this is futility. The real problem is how to deal with it. It is neither good nor bad in itself, but only as good or bad as we make it. And the business of the television newsman is to make it good.

What he must understand is that much of the information conveyed by the motion picture is conveyed indirectly, by stirring the emotions, rather than by the conventional journalistic method of stating facts in an appeal to reason. This is not a new technique. It is a method of communication long understood by practitioners of certain arts, among them priests, business executives, witch doctors, clairvoyants, politicians, and con men of all eras. The method cannot be judged by its practitioners; such a judgment constitutes guilt or approval by association, a principle only too common but abhorrent to justice. The motives and knowledge of the practitioner must be examined. And in the case of television news, the newsman must examine his own motives and his knowledge of his art.

If the television newsman's instinct draws him to the visual story, he must also recognize the dangers implicit in its emotional impact. The picture seldom tells all of the story; it must be supplemented by words. Sometimes what the picture shows is not what really happened, and the truth of the matter must be explained. The threatening words of the black militant may strike fear and consequent anger in the heart of the white viewer, but if the threat is translated accurately by the newsman the viewer's fear and anger may give way to reasoned concern and a sense of purpose. To return to the death of President Kennedy, it has been widely remarked that television's calculated counterpoint to its own visual coverage, in the form of the deliberately calm voices and reasoned explanations of network newsmen reporting the facts and quieting the rumors of those tragic days, helped to allay the public's alarm. By showing the public what was happening and simultaneously explaining the meanings which the motion picture alone could not convey, television more than any other news medium contributed to the emotional catharsis essential to the continuity of the governmental system and the avoidance of anarchy. This was a remarkable achievement, a magnificently professional use of a medium which transmits its information primarily by the imperfectly understood method of generating emotion. A medium which operates in that manner cannot be all bad, any more than it can be all good.

The television newsman who does not understand this and conduct himself in the light of that understanding is like a child playing carelessly with the trigger mechanism of a hydrogen bomb. In his use of the motion picture the newsman must try to generate the emotional response which corresponds to the reasoned opinion arrived at by examination of the facts. If he fails to understand this he cannot be forgiven for his ignorance, for he is not a child; he pretends to a profession.

The Cult of Personality

Much has been said, most of it critical, about the "cult of personality" in television news. By this the critics usually mean the predominance of the newscaster's personality and opinions over the style and content of the news.

Considered in the abstract, the injection of personality or, worse, opinion into the news is undesirable. We all would like to believe that the news we get from television is "objective" as to both content and style of delivery. Certainly no one can reasonably argue that it is preferable to get the news from newscasters who inject their opinions into the stories they report, or who alter the meaning of those stories by vocal inflection or facial expression.

But this *is* an abstract point of view, an opinion formed in a vacuum. And television news is not reported in a vacuum under ideal, abstract conditions. Television news is not anonymous; it is not distributed in the nameless, faceless way of printed news. Each story wears not a byline but the man himself. Television news is reported by men and women who have faces and voices and philosophies which they cannot or will not alter. Those faces are seen on the air, those voices are heard, and those philosophies to some extent determine the facial and vocal expression. Until science can create a computer with a David Brinkley's wry grin or a Walter Cronkite's wince of distaste for the tasteless, television will continue to be gut personal. It cannot be otherwise.

To view it another way, given the technical means of broadcasting, talent is the only indispensable element in television news. Without talent there can be no show; with talent there may be. The indispensability of talent exerts a constant pull on television news, steering it toward the "star system" so prevalent in the entertainment world. The star system dates back to the earliest days of the medium. Unlike the old movie newsreels, which presented only the news they had been able to film with an unseen narrator voicing comments over the film, television from its beginning attempted to cover *all* of the important news, whether or not film of every event was available. For those stories lacking visual coverage, it was necessary to present the newsman on camera, talking directly to the audience. The simple fact of such visual exposure tends to make a star, or at least a celebrity, of the newsman.

In addition, the star system is one with which the entertainment-oriented managers of the television business are both familiar and comfortable. Stars "sell," whether in entertainment or news; many viewers tune in as much to see and hear their favorite newscasters as to get the news itself. And, again as in entertainment, there are not too many newsmen with the partly intangible attributes which add up to star quality. Further, once a newsman who does project star quality has been established for some time with a particular show or station, his audience becomes in part a "habit" audience and this increases his value to the station; management assumes, often correctly, that if he transfers to a competitive news operation he will take a sizable portion of his audience with him, and this assumption gives him powerful bargaining leverage not only with regard to salary but also with regard to control of the style and content of the shows on which he appears.

Among the newsmen who currently fit into this star category are Walter Cronkite, Chet Huntley, David Brinkley, Frank Reynolds, Howard K. Smith, and Eric Sevareid, on the network level. Every local television community has its own local star or stars who shine just as brightly in their own more confined firmaments.

As long as the newsman who finds himself in such a powerful position uses his power responsibly, with concern for the public interest, the problems presented by the star system are, if not negligible, certainly more subtle than most of the system's critics have discerned. Unfortunately not all of television's news stars are as concerned with the public's interests as with their own. A small but significant minority of such stars may still be observed, usually at independent stations in larger cities, shaping the news to fit their own opinions or the opinions they conceive to be the most marketable; it is not coincidental that these opinions happen to match the predispositions and prejudices of their selected audiences. There is always a market for prejudice, and it is a profitable market; newsmen of this type attract viewers who want confirmation, not information.

One such news star, featured by an independent station in one of the nation's largest metropolitan areas, thrives on the adulation of an ultraconservative audience which gives him a consistent rating high enough to provide him with a publicly reported salary of $300,000 a year and to provide his station with an estimated net income from his news shows of at least $500,000 a year. The *ultimate* justification of the star system is purely economic.

Even when the star system is used responsibly, as by the networks in recent years, the effect on the news is not always beneficial. One of the most discerning comments on the subject was made by social critic Desmond Smith:

. . . the star-dominated format is still TV's basic news pattern. It has served the public better than most critics realize, but it is overdue for revision of its aims and methods. The three main criticisms are: The format is tired, worn out, old-fashioned; twenty years ago a case could be made for the star system on the ground that there really weren't any news departments; today the journalistic superstar survives only as an anachronism. Second, there has been little encouragement of investigative reporting and insufficient regard for independent judgment. Third, the system has worked better as a news pipeline than as a news-gathering organization.[1]

---

[1] Desmond Smith, "The Seven O'Clock Supermen," *The Nation* (March 18, 1968), pp. 375–377.

In short, dependence on the star has led to neglect of the most fundamental function of a news operation, the *origination* of news. With a few shining exceptions, most of them in the documentary field, television does not *make* news by aggressive and imaginative journalistic enterprise; instead it *reports* news originated by others. In the light of television's importance among the news media, as attested by many polls and governmental commission reports, this failure is a basic breach of responsibility.

However, while it is easy to deplore the star system, it is not so easy to conceive of an acceptable alternative. One suggestion is to return to the old movie newsreel concept: always cover the face of the newsman with visuals of the event. But for many events no visuals of any kind are available; this is especially true for late-breaking stories, with which the newsreels were not concerned but which television with its greater immediacy rightly feels it must report.

The adoption of the magazine format in the early 1960s was a step away from the star system; it diluted the image of the anchorman (the superstar) with the images of several other reporters. True, these other reporters quickly became stars in their own right, but the anchorman was no longer the whole show.

A further step in this direction might be considered. Why have an anchorman at all? Why not let a group of responsible experts report the news, each covering his own field of expertise? This system, long followed by newspapers, would at least obviate the pretense of omniscience on the part of a single newsman, while at the same time the authority of the various reports would be enhanced by their presentation by specialists who might reasonably be presumed to have some knowledge of their subjects. The specialists would still acquire luster from their exposure, but none would be of the first magnitude; their relationship to the show would be more comparable to that of the featured writers and columnists of a newspaper.

For management such a system would have the advantage of increasing its bargaining power with its reporter-employees with regard to salary; the loss of a single specialist among several would not be as likely to threaten a show's rating as the loss of an anchorman. For the news department the advantage would be the development of genuine expertise by newsmen free to devote their time and energies to their specialties, as opposed to the prevailing system under which most reporters are assumed to know all about everything and consequently know too little about anything.

However, the fiercely competitive economics of television news make it unlikely that the star system will be abandoned as long as it remains profitable. For the present, certainly, the cult of personality remains one of the major values of television news.

The News Broadcast as a Show

Many persons working in or concerned with television news deplore the use of the word "show" to describe television news broadcasts. Dr. Frank Stanton, the president of CBS, went so far as to ask the employees of CBS to avoid the use of the word in that connection. Dr. Stanton's point was well taken in the light of his responsibilities, one of which was to see to it that CBS projected an image of dignity and responsibility. "Show business" carries some connotation of the cheap, the tawdry, the phony, and to call a news broadcast a show might tarnish it by relating it to show business."

It seems doubtful, however, that CBS need worry that its corporate image will be stained if its news broadcasts are called by some other name; their quality speaks for itself. Besides, the evidence of politics in recent years would seem to indicate that show business has taken on a new respectability.

But more significantly, news broadcasts *are* shows, and attempts to change the name will not change the game. What is distributed by television is as much a show as it is news. With its emphasis on the visual, television tries to *show* the news as it happened.

In a much more subtle sense the news broadcast is a show because it must be structured in accordance with the same psychological principles which determine the structure of a stage play, a motion picture play, or, perhaps more precisely, a variety entertainment show. The *Random House Dictionary of the English Language* gives the premier definition of "entertain" as "to hold the attention of agreeably." That is exactly the aim of a television news show, not as to content but as to style. It must be a calculated blend of news and personality, presented in a pattern designed to hold the attention and interest of the audience.

To achieve this in the kind of time-space continuum which television simulates requires of the newsman a set of values which differ considerably from those of the print media and to a lesser degree from those of radio. The television newsman is required to think of the total broadcast not as a collection of news stories but as a *show*, the primary purpose of which is to convey the news. Television news shows which leave the viewer vaguely dissatisfied are nearly always the product of newsmen who either fail to apprehend this characteristic of their medium or who, consciously or subconsciously, reject any connection with "show business." But whether they know it or like it or not, they *are* in show business.

The construction of a news broadcast in the form of a show involves the methods of individual reportage, the style of the writing, the arrangement of the various stories and air men within the show, and the transitions by which the stories are interconnected. Each of these facets of television news will be considered in its appropriate place in the chapters which follow.

The Criterion of Significance

The trouble with a system of news values based on visual, personality, or entertainment criteria is that it ignores the significant. A visually dull event, such as a public hearing on proposed changes in welfare laws, may have far greater portent for society than a noisy and colorful student demonstration against the housing policies of a university administration. Yet there is a tendency, when the choice must be made, to use the visually stimulating story of the demonstration and drop the more important story on welfare. When this tendency is permitted to dictate the content of the news show, the viewer is denied his right to be informed of events that matter most to him. Instead, he is entertained and kept in ignorance.

The author recalls vividly a CBS television interview several years ago in which Edward R. Murrow asked Dr. J. Robert Oppenheimer whether the development of nuclear weapons had reached a point where mankind could destroy itself by accident. For something like 45 seconds the brilliant nuclear scientist pondered the question, and for the full time the camera held on Dr. Oppenheimer. Murrow did not interrupt; there was only silence. Finally the physicist replied, "Not quite." In a medium addicted to sound and fury even 5 seconds of motionlessness and silence is an eternity, and 9 times that is unthinkable. Yet that 45 seconds was one of television's finest moments. The suspense of watching one of the world's great scientists think through the intricate ponderables of the proposition was almost unbearable, and his answer, when it finally came, left the viewer with the certainty that his world had been given no more than a momentary reprieve. This was a motion picture only in the technical sense; what elevated it to greatness was understanding of context: the wisdom of the director in holding the static shot of Dr. Oppenheimer, and Murrow's wisdom in holding his tongue. The answer implied the destiny of the species of which the show's audience was representative.

This incident illustrates the most fundamental principle not only of television news but of all news: significance. The first question is how important the event is, and to whom. The more people it concerns, the greater its news value. The more it is likely to change their lives, their society, and their destiny, the greater its news value.

Journalism schools customarily implant the so-called "five Ws" in the minds of their students. Who, What, When, Where, and Why must be asked about any news event, but of these the most important is Why. Not just the conventional Why of the event itself, but even more importantly the introspective Why the reporter asks of himself: Why is this news? Why is he covering it? Why is it worth bothering with? The prime criterion is significance, and all other values by which news may be judged are subordinate.

With such a standard the newsman can quickly measure the relative values of any news stories. The mayor's admission of corruption in his administration is bigger news than the turnpike accident in which eight people died because the scandal affects the entire city and its body politic whereas the accident affects only the few people directly and indirectly involved. It might be argued that the turnpike accident is more important because of the fact that some 50,000 Americans die in automobile accidents every year, but this particular accident is merely illustrative of that well-known problem, whereas the mayor's admission is the revelation of a problem of immediate concern to the city and it discloses a need for action. The opening of a new community cultural center is more important than a fashion show; fashions are shown everywhere, but the new cultural center promises to raise the community's level of understanding.

Naturally there are many instances where it is difficult to determine the relative news values of events, even by applying the measure of significance, because the underlying causes are extremely complex and the potential effects indeterminate. Was the capture in London of the alleged killer of Dr. Martin Luther King, Jr., more significant than the almost simultaneous appointment by the President of a commission to study the causes of violence in the United States, including the kind of violence which killed Dr. King? Both stories held portents for the nation's future attitude toward violence, but in neither case could the portents be read clearly at the time. Further, it was a time in which news shows had to include details of the preparations for the funeral of Senator Robert F. Kennedy, whose assassination was the immediate cause of the President's action, and details of plans to obtain an indictment of Kennedy's alleged assassin. To determine the order of precedence of these stories required a complicated assessment of competing values.

It can be pointed out, however, that the capture of James Earl Ray signaled the beginning of a legal process that inevitably had to arrive at some specific conclusion, whereas the appointment of the commission would merely lead to publication of a report of a type that had been largely ignored in the past (for example, the Warren Commission Report and the Report of the National Advisory Commission on Civil Disorders); on this basis, the story of Ray would take precedence. It is a better basis for judgment than the basis of audience interest, by which the newsman would arrive at the same conclusion. (Specific information about specific individuals, such as Ray, is always of more interest—but not necessarily of more significance—than abstract information such as the commission story.)

The prominence given television reports of Ray's capture demonstrated that newsmen were not judging the story on its visual values, which were almost nonexistent. For the earliest reports of Ray's capture only file photos of Ray, distributed earlier by law enforcement officials, were available. Later, when film and video reports from London became available, they had little visual value except to show the locale because of the severe British restrictions (much more severe than most in the United States) on pretrial information. Any decision about how to use this story *had* to be based on an evaluation of its significance, not on its visual values.

The Robert F. Kennedy funeral itself posed difficult problems of significance and visual values for the networks. For many hours, while the funeral train moved slowly from New York to Washington, only intermittent visual coverage was available as the train passed an occasional video camera. CBS filled part of this nonvisual time with discussions over a running film shot of the roadbed over which the train was moving, and with graphics showing its position; both were obviously preplanned devices to add visual interest to a story which the network could not cover adequately in the television manner. There were occasional radio reports from correspondents aboard the train, but most of the time was filled with live or taped interviews with persons who had known Kennedy, philosophical discussions by the network newsmen, replays of video tapes of portions of the services at St. Patrick's Cathedral in New York, and bulletins on other news.

The question of the value of this coverage has been raised. Certainly the coverage contributed little to the public knowledge, although perhaps it contributed to the national catharsis. Television critic Hal Humphrey questioned the coverage by wondering whether the medium was not overcommunicating, then added: "Television may be overcommunicating in instances like this, but not communicative enough on a day-to-day basis, because if it were, perhaps such tragedies would not happen to us so frequently."[2]

This comment expresses the very heart of the meaning of significance as it must be interpreted by the television newsman. It is his business to discern the underlying trends in his community and to report events which bring those trends to public attention and help to clarify their meaning. Lacking such reporting, the community may find itself suddenly facing a crisis of which it has no real comprehension and with which it cannot cope.

---

[2] *The Los Angeles Times* (June 10, 1968), part 4, p. 34. Copyright, 1968, by the Los Angeles Times. Reprinted by permission.

The first of the big city riots of the 1960s, in Watts, surprised all of Los Angeles and, indeed, the nation. Two years and scores of similar riots later the same thing was happening in Detroit, Newark, and many other cities. Obviously little had been learned in the meantime. The significant factor here is that so many communities, large and small, have been surprised by rioting. This surprise in itself indicates a failure of the news media to apprise the community of its own internal weaknesses and disruptive tendencies. It is all too easy to accept and publicize the self-serving statements of local officials who blame "outside agitators." It is not so easy to examine the community's own contributory actions and thereby force the community to search its soul, but this is the only path to a solution. The newsmen had been covering the plaudits of the Chamber of Commerce and ignoring the growing frustration in the ghetto. They did not cover what was most significant.

That newsmen did not comprehend these riots even after they occurred was proved by their repeated use of the term "race riots" to describe civil disorders which had their roots not in racial antagonism but in social and economic frustration. It was three years after Watts before this understanding began to permeate the news with any consistency.

Critics of television may argue that the newsman cannot be expected to read the crystal ball and predict the future. But certainly he should know what is going on in his own community, especially when the viability of the community is at stake. And knowing, he should report. A community fully informed of the problems of the ghetto is a community not likely to be surprised by violence originating in the ghetto, a community hopefully even moving toward solutions for the causes of the despair that breeds violence.

Tomorrow's problems will not be the same, but the newsman's approach to the prevention of the breakdown of the community is always the same: report the significant. The newsman who fails to do this must take his share of the responsibility for whatever tragedy follows.

Summary

Factors peculiar to television which affect its news values are broadcast time limitations, the hour of broadcast, signal area, visual elements, and personality; the last two, in particular, inject value considerations which differ markedly from those of other media.

The motion picture's ability to generate an emotional reaction in the audience constitutes the principal distinction between television news and all other news.

Television's inclination to profit by use of the "cult of personality" is both natural and necessary, but imposes a need for restraint to prevent news distortion. One result of excessive dependence on personality has been failure to originate news to a degree corresponding to the medium's importance as measured by size of audience.

Audience psychology requires that the news broadcast be structured in the form of an entertainment show.

All other values are subordinate to the criterion of significance, which can be measured roughly by the number of persons affected by the news and the depth of that effect.

Suggested Assignments

1. Compare a local television news show and a local newspaper of comparable date (remembering, for example, that an evening show covers approximately the same news as the next morning's paper) in terms of the following: (a) number of stories covered, (b) relative time or space given to major stories, (c) depth of reporting, (d) limitations apparently imposed on the show by signal area, time of broadcast, and length of the show, and (e) emphasis on visual values.

2. Analyze one television news film story for its use of emotion to convey information, in particular with respect to whether the information thus conveyed was accurate and responsibly reported.

3. Analyze the use of personality in the over-all presentation of a particular news show, in particular with respect to the responsibility demonstrated.

4. State your opinion of a local television news operation's effectiveness as an originator of news, and substantiate with examples.

5. Discuss a local television news show, not as news but as a show. If it is entertaining and holds the viewer's interest, how does it do so; if not, why not?

6. Analyze a local television news show for its adherence to the principle of significance in the evaluation and presentation of news.

Chapter 5

Developing the Story

The typical television news story begins, like all news stories, at the source, but from that point its progression to broadcast on the air follows a different production route than the same story as covered by any other medium. A brief description of this route and some of its important waystops may help to explain how the story gets on the air.

At the News Source

At the point of origin of the story television is most likely to be represented by a reporter and a film camera crew (Figure 5–1). Much of the event is recorded on film; for the rest the reporter makes notes, but his primary purpose on the scene is to capture the relevant portions and the flavor of the event on film. To do this he functions not only as a reporter, but also as a film director; he tells the camera crew what effects he wants and what portions of the event to record. He anticipates the problems to be encountered in editing the film, and makes sure that all of the shots the editor will need are recorded. In short, he is responsible for the content and style of the coverage.

In the Newsroom

Once the film is processed, the writer of the story takes over. His first task is to view the film in a projection room, which is customarily

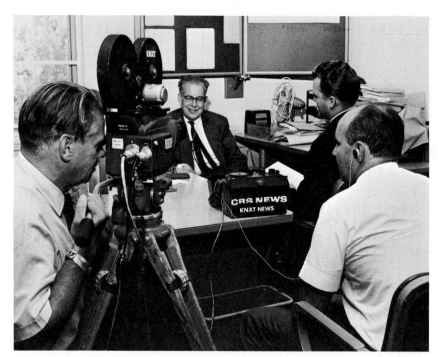

Figure 5-1   KNXT news crew (cameraman Jack Leppert, soundman Paul Nelson, reporter John Hart) conducts typical news film interview. Cameraman is responsible for camera position, shot composition, lighting, lens aperture, zoom and focus. Transistorized amplifier-mixer (on desk, center) receives audio signals from lavalier microphones worn by reporter and interviewee, feeds signal mix to recording head inside 16-millimeter Auricon camera modified to accept 400-foot magazine of single-system film. Soundman controls gain (volume) of signals from both microphones, listens to instant playback on earphones. Reporter is responsible for conduct of interview, also functions as director except when interview is in progress, when cameraman becomes director. Photo courtesy KNXT.

located in or near the television newsroom (Figure 5–2). His purpose is to evaluate the film for editing purposes, both as to content and as to technical quality. Content includes how much of the story the film tells, and how well. Technical quality includes such considerations as proper focus and exposure, sound quality, determination of whether damage has occurred in processing, and deciding whether the film was shot in such a manner that it is possible to edit it effectively.

Information not contained on the film the writer obtains from any of the conventional sources, such as wire copy, notes made by the reporter, or telephone calls to the news source. Having evaluated both the film and the story itself, the writer confers with the producer, advising him as to the value of the story and how much time it will need on the air. The producer, who must evaluate this story in relation

Figure 5-2 KNXT newsroom near air time, showing assignment desk (foreground), production desk (right background), writers' desks (left). Teletype and editing rooms are nearby. Similarity to newspaper city room is deceptive, because functions performed here are only superficially similar. Maury Green Photo.

to all of the other news at his disposal, may allot it more or less time (usually less) than the writer recommends.

The producer's time assignment sets an approximate limit which the writer uses as a guide in editing the film (Figure 5–3), or in supervising the editing if the physical cutting is done by an editor. The most common news film editing equipment consists of rewinds, an action viewer, a film splicer, and a combination sound-reader and counter which measures the length of the film in seconds of time. The Movieola commonly used for editing of theatrical and commercial films finds little use in the news room, even for the editing of double-system film; it is too slow and cumbersome. Instead, multiple-track films are synchronized with a multiple-gang counter.

The relationship of the writer to the editor is rather similar to that of the reporter to his camera crew. The writer determines style and content, the editor advises on technical problems and physically makes the cuts and splices. If both are competent, each will know a great deal about the other's task, and the resulting teamwork makes for a better final cut. Once the final cut is made, either writer or editor writes a *film rundown* which indicates, to the second, the total length of the

Figure 5-3 Film editing bench showing (top to bottom) rewind, hot splicer, four-gang combined sound reader and film counter, editing viewer (which projects small picture on screen out of picture at left), rewind. This bench can accommodate up to four-track synchronized 16-millimeter production, far beyond normal television news requirements. The Movieola, almost universally used in production of feature films and documentaries, commercials, and industrial films, is seldom seen in the daily news editing room. Maury Green Photo.

film and each point in it where any change in picture or sound must be made in the control room (to which we will come in a moment).

Finally, the writer goes to his typewriter to script the story. The actual writing begins *after* the cutting of the film. Not only is the film the heart of the story (unlike the newspaper photograph, which is

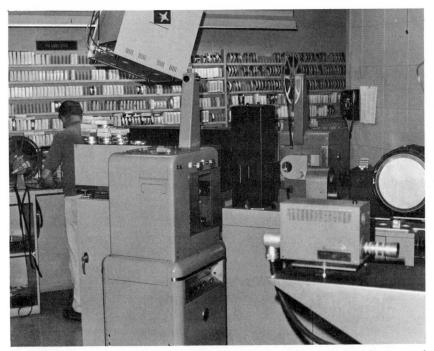

Figure 5-4 Telecine in KOOL-TV. Note 16-millimeter film projectors (foreground and right rear) and drum-shaped slide projector (extreme right), which feed pictures to video camera through mirror system (rectangular black box, center). Camera can accept only one picture source at a time. Photo courtesy KOOL-TV.

usually merely supplementary), but the story cannot be scripted without the film rundown, which in turn cannot be written until the final cut is completed. The script must contain precise instructions, or *cues*, for the control room if the film is to be aired properly.

However, the film seldom tells all of the story, and what it does tell usually requires amplification and explanation in words. Related developments, not covered by the film, may also require incorporation into the story. All this is of course the writer's job. Whatever is necessary he writes in narrative form, to be voiced by the air man in studio. The script is written on copy "books," the various copies being destined for different users; in some shops each copy is of a different color, the color indicating its ultimate user.

Meanwhile the producer is blocking out the entire news show, a function comparable to that of the newspaper's makeup editor. He assigns the story a place in the show, and when he receives the story script he slips it into its proper spot in the complete show script. He also notifies the film editor of the story's position in the *film lineup*, which indicates the correct sequence in which all of the film stories are to be assembled, often on a single reel.

Figure 5-5a   Master control, also used for show control, at KOOL-TV. Monitors display pictures on air, on closed circuit (line), from network, for preview, and from the various film-slide chains and video cameras. Note audio mixing panel (lower right) and technical director's video controls (lower center). Control setups invariably differ, each being designed for its station's particular needs. Photo courtesy KOOL-TV.

Technical Areas

From the newsroom the story now moves into the technical areas where engineers and technicians take over most of the work of getting it on the air.

Telecine   The completed film reel is delivered to telecine (Figure 5–4), where it is placed on a *film chain,* a combination of film projector and video camera which converts the projected visual image of the film into an electronic motion picture, or *video signal.* Simultaneously it converts the magnetic impressions of the film sound track into an *audio signal.*

Control room   The completed show script meanwhile has been stripped (sorted into sets of copies) in the newsroom. Two or more of the copy sets are delivered to the control room (Figure 5–5), which as its name implies is the command center in which the show is assembled elec-

Figure 5-5b Monitor board and TD controls in Studio C control room, KMOX-TV, St. Louis, Missouri. The large monitor (center, showing Walter Cronkite) displays the air picture; the other monitors display the pictures originating with other studio cameras, line feeds, film-slide chains and the like. The line feed of the air picture, fed by network from New York, is displayed on the monitor upper left of the air picture. Peter Ferman photo, courtesy KMOX-TV, St. Louis, Missouri.

tronically and from which its assembled video and audio signals are fed to the broadcast transmitter.

Three key persons work in the control room (although there may be quite a few more, depending on the size and complexity of the operation). These are the *director,* the *technical director* or TD, and the *audio mixer.*

The director, who is not to be confused with the news director, runs the show while it is on the air. He is in command of the technical processes by which it is assembled. Before him are closed circuit television monitors showing not only what is being broadcast, but also portions of the show yet to be broadcast; these monitors enable him to see what each video camera is looking at and whether the next film or slide is properly cued. In the case of VTR, however, the preview monitor shows nothing but "snow" and "breakup" until the video tape achieves speed.

One copy of the script goes to the director, and he uses the scripted cues to order the rolling of each film or VTR, the takes on stills, slides, and other visuals. The director has intercommunications with everyone he may need to talk to, such as the video cameramen in studio, the director of a remote unit if one is in use, and the technicians in telecine.

The television news director, however, has little to do with directing talent in the way that his motion picture counterpart directs actors. He discusses performance with the talent only insofar as performance impinges on his own needs or duties. He is not necessarily a newsman, and even if he were he would have little if any time to tell the talent how to perform; his own chores are demanding enough.

The TD, on spoken orders from the director, actually manipulates the buttons and switches of the electronic picture controls. He rolls the film or VTR by remote control, he cuts to the studio shots, and he creates optical effects such as dissolves and fades.

The audio mixer does the same thing for sound, connecting or disconnecting microphones, audio tapes, ETs (electronic transcriptions) and film track sound. For this he requires a copy of the script, which contains his audio cues. If two sounds are to be heard simultaneously—say, an air man's studio narration over natural film sound of a parade—he "mixes" them in the proper proportions. The audio mixer or an assistant may also handle audio tapes and ETs in the control room, but the physical handling of these sound sources may be done elsewhere.

Video tape recording The particular hypothetical story which we have been following through the production process does not require the use of VTR, but many stories do. For this, special VTR machines (Figure 5–6) are required; in some stations they are located in telecine, in others they are situated elsewhere. VTR machines can record or play back, they can be used for dubbing (one machine recording the signal from another), and they are used for editing VTR. Any VTR signal to be incorporated into the news show must of course be fed to the control room.

Master control All video and audio signals ultimately go through master control on their way to the transmitter. Smaller stations may have only one control room, which functions both to control the production of a single show and to control the station's entire output. In larger stations the two are usually separate control rooms, similar in equipment but serving different functions.

Master control receives the output of all the various control rooms, takes from and feeds to network, sends signals to the transmitter for broadcasting, and can do all of these things and more simultaneously.

Figure 5-6 Portion of video tape facilities of KOOL-TV, showing two of the station's five RCA color video tape machines. All five machines are high band (high fidelity). The 2-inch wide tape used by these machines is the standard for professional broadcast use. Photo courtesy KOOL-TV.

The newsman may never enter master control, but the end product of all his work passes through here.

Studio

The studio (Figure 5–7) is the location where the live performance portions of the news show originate. It is usually large and hopefully soundproofed. It contains the video cameras, lights, microphones, sets, props and other equipment necessary for live performance. At most stations the newsman has nothing to do with any of this equipment and may in fact be forbidden to touch it; it is operated by technicians, electricians, stagehands, and other specialists.

In the studio copies of the news script go to the air man and the stage manager. The latter commands the studio activities and gives cues to the air man; he is the air man's only connection with the control room.

Figure 5-7a KNXT Studio B dressed for news show. Silhouetted figures in foreground are stage crew members and air men waiting their turn. Podiums for various newsmen are visible (center to left). The author (center) is on the air. Rear projection screen at right. Photo courtesy KNXT.

On the Air

Now the show is ready for broadcast, and air time is almost upon us. Let us assume that the story we have been following from its source is the first story to be told, the "top of the show." Let us also assume that the show uses a 15-second standard opening film, which identifies the show by title and perhaps names its newsmen. From here on we shall describe events in terms of the time at which they occur, measured in minutes and seconds before and after *air time*, the precise second at which the show is due on the air:

Minus 1:00—Director: "One minute to air. Places, please." Stage manager: "One minute!"

Minus :10—Director: "Ready 16–2." (The number here identifies the film chain—16mm projector on chain 2—carrying the opening film.)

Figure 5-7b Primary election (1968) studio, KMOX-TV. In the foreground are some of the many workers required for election coverage, when stations frequently call upon all employees and many specially hired workers in addition for tabulation of returns. In shots seen on the air these people do not perform; they simply do their work. The three video cameras are at extreme left and right and (not visible) in the position of the camera which took this shot. Note the separate desks for the anchorman (center) and for reports on congressional races and returns of local interest in Missouri. Area for live interviews is at extreme right; eager candidates spend election nights making the rounds of the more important television stations, hoping to be interviewed. Significant in this stage setting is the fact that each of the three cameras can cover all of the broadcast positions. Photo courtesy KMOX-TV.

Minus :05—Director: "Stand by, announce booth." Stage manager: "Stand by for opening film. Quiet in studio!"

Minus :03—Director: "Roll it!" The TD pushes a button, and in telecine the opening film instantly begins running through 16–2, gaining speed as it rolls off its Academy leader.

:00—Director: "Take it! Cue announcer!" The TD pushes another button, and the opening film appears on the home viewer's receiver at the instant its Academy leader comes to an end and the first frame of the film proper begins. The audio mixer simultaneously opens the microphone in the announce booth, and a staff announcer reads the standard opening over the film.

:10—Director: "Ready 16–1. Stand by, Camera One." Stage manager: "Stand by in studio."

:15—Director: "Take One! Cue him!" The TD switches the picture from 16–2 to Camera One in studio; the red tally light on Camera One turns on. The audio mixer switches from the AB microphone to the air man's microphone. The stage manager, just off camera, flings an arm toward the air man. The air man looks at Camera One, says, "Good evening," and begins reading the standup copy leading into the film of the story shot hours earlier.

:30—Director: "Roll it!" The film on 16–1 begins rolling off its Academy leader.

:33—Director: "Take it!" The air man finishes the lead-in copy, the TD switches from Camera One to 16–1, the audio mixer switches to the film sound from 16–1, and the viewer finally begins to see the film of our story.

And with all this, we are only 33 seconds into the show.

The Need for Technical Knowledge

From the above the television newsman's need for technical knowledge should be evident. Furthermore, the story we have followed from film shooting to broadcast, while fairly typical, does not contain many of the visual and audio elements which other stories may require. The television newsman must understand all of these elements, at least well enough to know when they can be useful to him, when their use is impossible, and when it is outrageous to ask for them. Therefore a detailed discussion of many technical elements of television news is essential; we shall not, however, carry such discussion any further than the needs of *journalistic* (as opposed to technical) expertise require.

If we seem to belabor this point, it is only because so many print-oriented journalists consider any study of television's technicalities superfluous. The fact is that the television newsman who is not a master of the technical complexities of his craft commands a ship of fools; he is helpless in the hands of inept technicians. Yet his is the responsibility for the concept of the story, the impression received by the audience. And that impression, like the conversation of Lewis Carroll's Walrus, is made of many things: writing, voice, personality, video techniques, sound techniques, film techniques. The newsman who would bring artistry to television must first apprentice himself to the technical demands of his medium; only after the competent craftsman comes the artist.

Sources of Picture and Sound

The television news show is composed entirely of two basic elements, picture and sound.

Video camera   The picture always originates with a video camera, which is a camera that generates an electronic or video signal which can be used by the proper receiving apparatus to reproduce a motion picture electronically.

Microphone   The sound always originates with a microphone which generates an electronic or audio signal with which the sound can be reproduced.

There are several types of video cameras and an almost infinite variety of microphones; the significant characteristic in every case is the generation of the electronic signal.

In a practical sense it is useful to distinguish five picture sources and an equal number of sound sources, keeping in mind that whatever its origin in practical terms the picture and sound must be converted into an electronic signal:

Picture Source	Sound Source
Video camera	Microphone
Video tape recording	Video tape recording
Film	Film
Still photograph	Audio tape recording
Graphic	Phonograph record

Video tape recording   The VTR is essentially similar to the audio tape recording with which almost everyone is familiar, except that the tape is usually wider and the information stored on it electronically includes a motion picture as well as sound. The recording is available for instant replay (as soon as the tape is rewound), it can be replayed any reasonable number of times, it can be dubbed onto another VTR if additional copies are desired, and the quality of both picture and sound is excellent.

The VTR has the disadvantage of being difficult to edit rapidly and precisely unless the editor has the use of some of the newer electronic editing equipment, the cost of which is astronomical. VTR can be edited either electronically (a dubbing process) or by cutting and splicing the tape; the latter method is laborious and time-consuming. In either case a disturbing picture "rollover" is likely to occur at the splice or the dubbing joint, and for this reason there is a tendency to edit VTR "in the black" when possible so that the rollover will not be noticeable. This means that whole scenes must be taken, rather than portions of shots edited together as in film.

Another disadvantage of VTR, especially for news purposes, is that its original input must come from a video camera. This means the cumbersome video camera and all of its required supporting paraphernalia must be transported to the scene of action to get the picture. Often it takes many hours to set up the connections for such a remote unit and get it into action, and the costs of a microwave connection to the station are high. For this reason most of the motion pictures of news events seen on television are originally shot on film.

However, the rapid improvement being made in video and VTR equipment promises an ultimate reduction in both cost and size to a point where it may well succeed film within a few years.

Film   Until that time comes, film will remain the staple of television news. It is usually the film cameraman, not the video cameraman, who is on the scene to record the event. His equipment is comparatively light and easily portable, and he can be recording the event within minutes or even seconds of his arrival on the scene. Sensitive color films permit shooting even at night without lights, and a reel of film can be processed in less than half an hour.

The importance of film in television news is perhaps exceeded only by the shocking ignorance of film technique in news shops. The men of the medium, fresh from other journalistic fields, are continually and laboriously rediscovering the discoveries of D. W. Griffith and Sergei Eisenstein. To shortcut the need for retracing the steps of the pioneers, we have included in this work separate discussions of the basic elements of film, its logic, film reporting, and film editing. It should also be mentioned that the newsman who has a thorough knowledge of film technique can quickly and easily translate that knowledge into a competent understanding of video technique; in most conceptual respects film and video are similar if not identical.

Audio tape recordings   Audio tapes are sometimes synchronized with film at the time of shooting, but there is no practical way to use the tape in sync with picture. The sound is first dubbed onto a sound film track and then replayed in sync.

A more common use of audio tape is as a *wild track*, in which no attempt is made to synchronize sound and picture. There can, for example, be no *lip sync* with a wild track; the sound of a voice cannot be synchronized with the movements of the speaker's lips. Typical uses of the wild track include the sounds of riots, automobile races, or forest fires played over film.

Audio tapes are also used for music, and for telephone "beeper" reports for which no picture is available; such a beeper tape might be played over a still photo of the newsman telephoning the report, or over a video shot of the anchorman in studio listening to the report. The tapes may be played on conventional reel-type machines or in special cartridges.

Phonograph records Phonograph records of any size or speed may be used for any type of nonsynchronous sound. This also applies to *electrical transcriptions*, or ETs, which are records made by a different process and intended solely for broadcast use.

In common parlance all disk recordings, however made, are referred to as ETs, and the term is also commonly if loosely applied to audio tape recordings.

Still photographs Still photographs are used in several ways in television:

When a video camera photographs the still picture, it is called a *still*.

The photograph may be reproduced in the form of a 2 × 2 or 35-millimeter slide and projected by a film chain camera; this is called a *slide*.

The photograph may be projected onto a screen in studio and the projected image shot by a video camera. Depending on whether the projector is in front of the screen or behind it, the process is called *front projection* (FP) or *rear projection* (RP).

Still another method of using a still picture, especially if it is desired to focus on various portions of the picture in rapid succession, is to shoot film of those portions and edit the film to obtain the desired effect.

Graphics Graphics is a term encompassing maps, charts, diagrams, and other art work useful in illustrating a story. Once completed by the artist, these may be used in any of the ways still pictures are used.

Simple techniques are often used to impart movement to a graphic display. One example is the *pull*, in which the display is constructed of two or more layers of material, one of which is movable; when the movable part is pulled by a stagehand, the bars on a graph appear to rise or a statistical chart line to "grow." Sometimes magnets moved behind, say, a map are used to cause objects on the surface of the map to move as if self-propelled.

Combination Effects

By combining various sources of picture and sound, and by using various electronic effects in the control room, innumerable possibilities are achieved.

One of the simplest is the effect achieved by moving the video cameras, or by using a zoom lens which gives the appearance of camera movement. (A detailed discussion of camera shots and movements, applicable to video as well as to film cameras, will be found in Chapter 8, Film Basics.)

Optical effects In television the same optical effects which are created on film in the laboratory are achieved electronically by the control room. These include *dissolves, fades,* and *wipes* in particular.

Where the picture slowly emerges from a black screen over a period of one to three seconds, it is a fade-in. In the fade-out the picture slowly goes to black.

In the dissolve one picture fades in while the other fades out; for a brief period both pictures are on the screen at the same time. The dissolve requires two video signals.

In the wipe one picture seems to wipe another off the screen in much the manner of a windshield wiper. This also requires two video signals. The wipe comes in many shapes, such as circular, square, sawtooth, or venetian blind.

The *split screen*, in which two pictures occupy different parts of the screen simultaneously, is nothing more than an arrested wipe. While occasionally effective it must be used with care and restraint. (In general, the more unusual a device, the more restraint needed.)

The *superimposition*, or *super*, consists of two pictures each occupying the full screen at the same time. It, too, requires two picture sources, and considerable restraint. However, one form of the super is quite common in news; it is the *superslide*, where the name of a person is supered over a film or VTR shot of that person, for identification. Any readable information can be conveyed visually by superslide—for example, closing stock market averages over a slide showing Wall Street.

A similar effect can be achieved by a different method called *matting*, in which one picture is electronically matted or cut into another. There are two methods of creating matte shots, the older and less successful one employing a black background for the shot to be matted in (the visual information in the examples above). When this shot is matted over the picture shot, the black background fails to register and only the words are cut into the picture shot.

The newer method, *chroma key*, employs a blue background and can be used only in color television (although the resulting matte shot can be transmitted in black and white). With this method the blue background is cut out of the shot "in key." This is sometimes called "shooting the blue." Theoretically any color can be used as the key color, but for reasons beyond the author's understanding blue works best. For example, if the air man in studio stands in front of a blue background, it vanishes and he seems to stand in limbo. If the second picture source is a film, the blue cuts a hole in the film picture that is exactly the size and shape of the air man; as he moves, the hole moves with him, so that he seems to be standing or moving in front of the motion picture.

In this example the air man can be eliminated from the picture by dissolving him out, by wiping him out, or by zooming in past him until he is out of frame. All three methods leave the film filling the screen; in the third method, however, the resulting shot will create a confusing illusion unlike anything in reality. As we zoom in, the air man gets bigger and bigger until he passes outside the frame of the shot, but our perspective on the film remains unchanged; thus he seems almost to fly off the screen. This unsettling effect can be eliminated by zooming in with both cameras at the same rate, but very few film chain cameras are equipped with zoom lenses; also, the resulting shot of the film will show only a portion of the picture in the original film frame. If we are working with two studio cameras shooting, say, the air man and a still, the problem is not so difficult but the coordination required between the two cameras and the need to select a portion of the still for the final shot make the whole thing much more trouble than it is worth.

"Shooting the blue" also requires care in the use of props and articles of clothing of the exact shade of blue used for the key. If the air man wears a blue tie of that shade, it will vanish, leaving a tie-shaped hole in his chest. If he has that particular shade of blue eyes, he will look like Little Orphan Annie.

The effects board in some control rooms can also be used to make the video picture spin, turn upside down, waver, and perform various other stunts which are seldom if ever used in news.

Frozen frame The frozen frame technique involves the projection of a single film frame. The film reel must of course be stopped, or "frozen." The effect is the same as the projection of a slide or the shooting of a still.

Perhaps the most common use of the frozen frame is to freeze the first frame of a silent film story, hold it on the air for a few seconds while the air man narrates over the picture, then start the film as the narration continues. Suddenly the still picture becomes a moving picture. The film must be silent, at least for the first few seconds of the film sequence, because until the film reaches proper speed any audio taken off its sound track will "wow," or be distorted in pitch.

Occasionally effective use is made of the frozen frame in combination with chroma key. The air man is matted into the frozen frame, the film starts, and finally the air man is dissolved out. As with all unusual effects, this should be used only occasionally when the story elements warrant. The overuse of unusual effects gives the news show a "gim-micky" style which detracts from its authority.

Summary

The most typical television news story is a film story, originating in the field with a reporter and camera crew. In the newsroom the writer supervises the editing of the film if he does not edit it himself; he also scripts the story, including film cues. The producer allots each story a time and place in the news show. The film editor assembles the show reel on the basis of the film lineup made by the producer, and the film is placed on a film chain in telecine.

The use of the film is controlled by the director in the control room, following the scripted cues. Audio is controlled by the audio mixer, video by the technical director, both operating on orders from the director. Talent functions in the studio, following the script and cues from the stage manager. The assembled show is fed through master control to the broadcast transmitter.

Technically the show consists of a motion picture originating with video cameras and sound originating with microphones; in the practical sense there are five sources of picture and five sources of sound. In addition to the video camera and microphone, there are VTR, film, still photographs, graphics, audio tape recordings, and phonograph records. Any or all of these sources may be mixed in a great variety of ways to create sound mixes and optical effects. Among the most important optical effects are the dissolve, fade, wipe, split screen, super, and matte shot.

Suggested Assignments

1. Arrange to accompany a television news reporter on a film story, and follow the story through to air. (Such arrangements are best made by the instructor, and for class members individually, not as a group; it is completely impractical for more than one or two persons to accompany a reporter and film crew.) Report and discuss the following: (a) how much of the story was filmed, (b) how much and what portions of the film were used in the final cut, (c) how much of the story was reported by narration, either on film or in studio, (d) how much of the story originated with sources other than the film and the reporter, and (e) how well the story was covered.

2. From observations made during a visit to a television station (see Suggested Assignments, Chapter 2) report the number of persons, their titles or designations, and their apparent functions, which were observed

in (a) telecine, (b) video tape recording, (c) control room, and (d) studio.

3. From observing a news show being broadcast in the control room, or by studying a complete show script, report the various sources of picture and sound used and the manner in which they were used.

4. Explain how optical effects are created in television news.

5. List four different ways in which a still photograph might be used.

6. Explain the function of the television news director and how it differs from the function of a theatrical motion picture director.

7. Discuss the advantages and disadvantages of television's technical aspects in relation to the function of television as a medium of information.

Part Two

Television News Writing

Chapter 6

The Writer's Style

Clarity is the prime essential of television news writing. The writer has only one chance to get his meaning through to the viewer. If he fails that chance it cannot be recaptured; the show, like Omar Khayyam's moving finger, has moved on. And the viewer, like anyone left behind, is frustrated and angry.

Elements of Clarity

Brevity Brevity is the soul of clarity. The point was made definitively three centuries ago by the French philosopher Blaise Pascal in his apology to a friend to whom he had written a long letter. He had not had time, he explained, to write a short one.

To be brief, the writer must organize the story in his mind before he puts it on paper. Usually the news story has a single main point, whatever the complexity of its details. It cannot be written briefly until the writer is able to grasp this main point firmly. With that point in mind, he is able to sort out the pertinent details and arrange them in the best order to illustrate the point, at the same time discarding all irrelevant details. This is no more than the news writer in any medium should do, but the time limitations imposed on the television news story make a grasp of its essentials in the interest of brevity more important than in other media.

The best writing is almost always rewriting, and if time allows the writer will usually find that he can improve on his first draft by rewriting it. The very act of putting the first draft on paper often exposes weaknesses in the writer's original conception: the structure can be improved, some essentials have been omitted, some nonessentials have been included. Rewriting usually shortens the story and tightens it so that its meaning stands out sharply and clearly.

Philosophy A philosophical approach to the organization of the news story helps to make its meaning clear to the writer. If he cannot make it clear to himself, he cannot hope to make it clear to the viewer.

And here we are back to Pascal again. He would have made a brilliant television writer. He strove for brevity, he brought to his work a sense of order, and he was a philosopher. Without a philosophical approach, a *Weltanschauung*, events have no meaning, and what the viewer seeks is meaning. As the world grows more complex and the interdependence of quarrelsome man more critical, the meaning of events becomes ever more important. The television viewer is instinctively if not necessarily consciously aware of this; it is, after all, his world at stake.

What the writer must strive for, then, is his own view of the world, his own intuition of the tides of men's affairs. Without a basic philosophy he cannot judge how to organize even the simplest story.

Metaphor The meaning of complicated events is often most quickly conveyed by metaphor, and for this reason television news writing makes much use of metaphor. But the metaphor cannot be obscure or esoteric; it must be crystal clear:

The police chief came out of the city council meeting with a smile on his face, but less than he wanted in his pocket.

This lead, taken from a broadcast script by Paul Udell of KNXT, is an excellent example of television's use of simple metaphor. It summarizes the whole story in a sentence and makes clear the meaning of the details that followed: the chief had asked for more money for the police department; he got part of what he wanted.

Eric Sevareid, perhaps the finest of all television news writers, once remarked of Harlem that it was like a place walled in glass, whose inhabitants could look out from their crowded misery and see the splendor and richness of Manhattan, but could not pass through the glass walls. The metaphor illuminates the whole problem of the urban ghetto with a single brilliant flash of inspiration.

It was the lack of this kind of writing in newspapers that led British press lord Cecil King to criticize newspaper writing as "quite appalling, long, loose, rambling and repetitive" because of a "fetish for objectivity." Newspapers, said King, "divest news of its own inherent drama. They cast away the succulent flesh and offer the reader dry bones, coated with an insipid sauce of superfluous verbiage. They reject the flashing, illuminating phrase, which can make an unknown foreign statesman come vividly alive, or a dash of wit which may relieve the tedium unavoidably contained in much important news."[1]

Newspapers may get away with the kind of writing King described, but it may also have contributed to the decline in their number. Television cannot afford it for competitive reasons, as King indicated: "In America, television journalism, radio journalism, magazine journalism are all livelier and more professional than the newspapers."[2]

Conversational quality   In addition to metaphor, one source of this liveliness is the casual, conversational, even slangy quality of writing demanded by television. It is spoken language, not literary language, and only the best writers write the way they speak.

The writer can easily demonstrate this to himself by reading a newspaper story into a tape recorder and listening to the playback. The odds are that he will find the story difficult if not impossible to read aloud effectively, dull and confusing when played back. But if he turns to any of the better syndicated columnists and repeats the experiment, he will discover why some reporters work for low pay on general assignment and others write columns and get rich. The writing of the columnists is livelier, more meaningful, often as conversational in style as television writing.

Counterpoint   If the word description differs in the slightest from the television picture, the viewer tends to believe the picture and distrust the word. The exception is where the picture alone is misleading and therefore requires qualification. British journalist Henry Fairlie took note of this: "Most television reporting just describes the pictures, and by so doing, reinforces them. But the object of words in television news should be to distract from the picture, to say, 'It was not quite so. This was not the whole story.' "[3]

Fairlie contends that television news "jerks from incident to incident. For the real world of patient and familiar arrangements, it substitutes an unreal world of constant activity . . . It is almost impossible, these days, to consider any problem or any event except as a crisis; and by this very way of looking at it, it in fact becomes a crisis."[4]

---

[1] *Time* (April 28, 1967), p. 88.

[2] Ibid., p. 88.

[3] Henry Fairlie, "Can You Believe Your Eyes," *Horizon* (Spring 1967), p. 27. © Copyright 1967 by American Heritage Publishing Co., Inc. Reprinted by permission.

[4] *Ibid.*, p. 27.

Fairlie objects to the motion picture's basic nature, which is like objecting to the zebra's stripes. Nor is the world always as patient and familiar as he would have it. But there is justice in his complaint. The attention of the audience is focused on the moment of high drama partly because television news turns its lens on it. The writer must consider the meaning of the event and convey that meaning as clearly as possible. Where the picture distorts, he must use counterpoint.

Historian Will Durant reports that Michelangelo "preferred drawing to writing—which is a corruption of drawing."[5] What else should a Michelangelo prefer but the medium of emotion over the medium of ideas? Writing can express concepts much more intricate than drawing, but the primitive art out of which hieroglyphics grew expressed the emotions of the artist far more powerfully. Writing is the realization of the abstract. And it is the concrete, not the abstract, that moves the heart.

In television we have both. The picture pulls at the heart, the words tease the mind. This counterpoint is the key to some of the best television writing.

Elements of Confusion

Euphemism The use of vague terms simply because they are inoffensive is the bane of good writing because it dilutes meaning. The good writer never calls a spade an entrenching tool, or a garbage collector a sanitary engineer. He considers it a journalistic misdemeanor to refer to rape as "criminal assault." The sugar-coating of euphemism is best left to those writers capable of believing that roses by any other name might stink.

Headline clichés These, too, have no place in television. They are born of the space limitations of newspaper columns, limitations which do not exist in television. The governor's opponent does not "rap" him, he criticizes him. Crime is never "curbed," although automobiles may be. Space scientists and surgeons "probe," but grand juries investigate. There is nothing inherently wrong with these metaphors except overuse, which is wrong enough.

Complex syntax If the writer's inclination is toward the more complex syntax of an Eric Sevareid, he should be sure that he is as much the master of the language as is Sevareid. Few writers are. If he prefers the

---

[5] Will Durant, *The Renaissance* (New York: Simon and Schuster, 1953), p. 464.

urbane style of a magazine like the *New Yorker*, he should forget television entirely; he will never cut the mustard.

Journalese and redundancy Restraint is always admirable in writing. The newspaper writer, sensitive to the dramatic limitations of his medium, is tempted toward journalese to compensate for its lack of emotion. Thus, the crowd "surges" forward, the auto crash is "grinding," the thundercloud "towers" (an inverse metaphor if ever there was one), the enemy fire is "withering," etc., etc., ad infinitum.

This would be terribly bad television writing. It is terribly bad newspaper writing too, but in television the effect, like everything else, is magnified. We do not need purple prose to enlarge the picture. The picture is usually its own clear statement of fact; and if an overly emotional description is laid on top of the visual statement, the result is redundancy. Redundancy breeds boredom.

In summary, good television news writing is simply good writing which also gives due consideration to the picture. It conforms to the principles of clarity, brevity, precision, philosophy, metaphor, and counterpoint. It would be considered good writing in any medium.

Helping the Air Man

In the interests of clarity and conversational quality the television news writer makes much use of abbreviations, and he writes in such a style that the air man can comprehend his meaning at a glance even when reading the script "cold," or without having seen it previously. In these respects the style of television news writing is largely derived from radio, and while styles vary in different news operations certain basic rules have become traditional.

Abbreviations Most abbreviations are written in capital letters separated by hyphens: "U-S-A," or "G-O-P" or "N-A-A-C-P." The purpose of the hyphens is to separate the letters and make it instantly clear to the air man that this is not a word to be pronounced but an abbreviation in which each letter is to be spoken separately. Where double letters occur in an abbreviation, some stylists prefer the form "N-double-A-C-P," but this is actually harder for the air man to comprehend quickly.

In the case of acronyms which are customarily pronounced as words rather than spelled out verbally, the writer omits the hyphens between letters: "HUD" for Department of Housing and Urban Development, "CORE" for Congress of Racial Equality.

Many abbreviations which are not acceptable in print, especially at the first mention of the subject, are quite acceptable in television. For example, there is no need to write "United States Steel Corporation" in reference to a company so well known; "U-S Steel" is enough. And especially in second references abbreviations such as "G-M," "U-S-S-R" and "N-B-C" are common.

Figures The general rule on the use of figures is that digits one to ten are spelled out, the cardinal figures are used for higher numbers.

Very large numbers, however, are written as combinations of words and figures. Ten thousand is written "10-thousand." $514,000,000 becomes "514-million dollars." Figures written in this manner can be grasped at a glance by the air man, who might have to pause for a second or two to take in a large figure written in conventional newspaper style.

Unless there is good reason to be specific, large numbers are also usually rounded off, lest the viewer get lost during the verbal delivery. A federal budget of, say, $121,395,428,991.28 is impossible to absorb by ear; by the time the air man gets to the "28 cents" the viewer will have forgotten how many billions are involved. It is much more meaningful to write "more than 121-billion dollars."

Unusual words When unusual words, such as scientific terms or uncommon foreign names, must be included in the script, the writer should supply both the correct spelling and a phonetic spelling for the benefit of the air man. The phonetic spelling is written in capital letters and enclosed in parentheses to set it off from the rest of the copy; syllabic emphasis is indicated by underlining: "France's former foreign minister Couve de Murville (KOOV-DUH-MIR-VEE-UH) was named premier today." The correct spelling is important for proper identification (which the phonetic spelling cannot supply) and also in case the air man happens to know how to pronounce the words; the phonetic spelling helps him if he does not know how.

The Declarative Sentence

Some of the best writing being done today is done for television news, but unfortunately some of today's worst writing is also on exhibit on television. Writing is a direct reflection of thought process. The newsman whose writing is flabby or confused is a man whose thinking is flabby or confused. Which brings us back to clarity.

If clarity is the first requisite of television news writing, the simple declarative sentence is the first requisite of clarity. Consider the following construction typical of newspaper writing:

"We shall fight it out on this line if it takes all summer," General Ulysses S. Grant, commander of the Army of the Potomac, said.

Now try to say it aloud; it cannot be done effectively, because no one *ever* speaks that way. It is literary language. The reverse order of construction (predicate first) creates anticlimax. But turn it around:

General Ulysses S. Grant, commander of the Army of the Potomac, said, "We shall fight it out on this line if it takes all summer."

Notice the flow of thought: the important thing is not that Grant said something, it is *what* he said. The sentence now builds to climax, not to anticlimax. The simple declarative sentence allows the point (what he said) to be emphasized with the vocal inflection.

The same objection applies to the following lead taken from a newspaper story:

The city's teachers have given overwhelming approval to the creation of a new association to replace two teacher organizations which have 18-thousand members. it was announced today.

For television purposes, the sentence could be improved by deleting "it was announced today." Details of the announcement could be supplied later in the story. The action that was taken is more important than the fact that it was announced.

Adherence to declarative construction means, perhaps above all else, the avoidance of dependent clauses, especially at the beginning of the sentence. The dependent clause represents a separate thought, and that thought is most forcefully expressed by putting it in a separate sentence. Consider:

Charging the company with violating the new contract, the strikers resumed their picketing at dawn, ignoring the pleas of union officials to return to work.

The same ideas gain impact in vocal delivery from the more direct declarative construction:

The strikers resumed their picketing at dawn. They charged the company with violating the new contract, and they ignored the pleas of union officials to return to work.

Examples

Other crimes committed against clarity in the name of television news are the same crimes that are committed in other media: incorrect antecedents, redundancies, use of the passive mood instead of the active mood, complex tenses where simple tenses will do the job, long and cumbersome titles preceding names instead of placed in the appositive, purple prose, lack of precision in the use of words, and improper emphasis. One of the best ways to discern the good is to study the bad. The following are examples of bad television news writing taken from actual broadcast scripts:

Example

More than half of the city's 625 police officers have gone on record demanding better pay and improved working conditions. A delegation of 75 off-duty officers went to the city council, complaining that the men were "angry and frustrated" because the council brushed off their spokesman when he went to the council last month.

Comment

The first sentence can be simplified considerably, and clarified in the process: *More than half of the city's 625 police officers today demanded better pay and working conditions.* Notice that the time is pinpointed by the word "today." The simple past tense is substituted for the present perfect. The redundancy of "better" and "improved" is eliminated. The phrase "gone on record," meaningless here, is also eliminated.

In the second sentence the dependent clause should be eliminated. The construction also "throws away" the fact that last month's brushoff involved only one spokesman; this diminishes the contrast between that incident and today's mass protest. Better: *In a mass protest, a delegation of 75 off-duty officers laid their demands before the city council. They said the men were "angry and frustrated" at the brushoff they received from the council last month, when they were represented by only a single spokesman.*

Example

An explosion at the Harvey Aluminum plant in Torrance that injured 13 persons is under investigation by arson investigators.

Comment

The antecedent may be clear on second thought, but there is no time for second thoughts in television. The mood is passive; it should be active. And instead of using the redundant "investigators," the writer should identify the specific agency or officers doing the investigating. Better: *Police are investigating the possibility of arson in an explosion that injured 13 persons at the Harvey Aluminum plant in Torrance.*

Example

Later, Kerr told a news conference he had high regard for former Central Intelligence Chief John McCone . . . who Governor-elect Ronald Reagan wants to head a blue-ribbon probe of the Berkeley campus.

Comment

The past tense ("had regard") should be carefully avoided in a case like this, where it implies that Kerr's high regard for McCone is a thing of the past; the writer must distinguish between actions which are completed and those which can reasonably be assumed to be continuing. The use of the long and cumbersome title preceding McCone's name is newspaperese, bad in print but worse when spoken; the title should be shortened or placed in an appositive phrase. The word "probe" is a cliché in the sense used here. The grammatically incorrect "who" is not necessarily bad since it conforms to widespread spoken usage, but it does offend some people and can easily be avoided. Better: *Later, Kerr told a news conference he has high regard for former C-I-A Director John McCone, the man Governor-elect Ronald Reagan wants to conduct a blue-ribbon investigation of the Berkeley campus.*

Example
Stiff winds pushed a fast-moving fire through a swank marina in Fort Lauderdale, Florida, during the night, destroying a fleet of luxury yachts valued at more than one-and-a-half million dollars.

Comment
The writer's desire to dramatize the story has overcome his better judgment; the result is purple prose, which sounds forced and pretentious (as it is) on television. The problem is excessive use of adjectives; "stiff," "fast-moving," "swank" and "luxury" all in the same breath leave the viewer breathless. The placement of "during the night" interrupts the flow of thought. The figure, written out, is difficult to read at a glance. Better: *Fire during the windy night raced through a marina at Fort Lauderdale, Florida, and destroyed yachts valued at more than 1½-million dollars.*

Example
The bonfire was kept a big secret from firemen until it was well under way.

Comment
Why a "big" secret? And who ever heard of a fire getting "under way"? Boats, yes; fires, no. Better: *The bonfire was kept a secret from firemen until it was burning fiercely.*

Example
The most valuable left arm in America—the great pitching arm of Sandy Koufax—is being retired from baseball.

Comment
The passive mood again, reducing the impact. Better: *The most valuable left arm in America—the great pitching arm of Sandy Koufax—will pitch no more.*

Example
At the Hidden Hills ranch where Don Drysdale lives with his wife and children, our reporter talked with the Dodgers' star right-hander about the retirement of Koufax.

Comment

The reference to Drysdale's family is irrelevant (they were not seen on the film) and therefore confusing. Better: *At Don Drysdale's ranch in Hidden Hills, our reporter talked with the Dodgers' star right-hander about Koufax's retirement and what it means to him.*

Example

The Labor Department—stymied by a backlog of 28 labor union elections in litigation—plans to ask the Supreme Court for help. The department will ask the high tribunal for a broader interpretation of the 1959 Landrum-Griffin law. The department is irked that illegally chosen union officers can perpetuate themselves in office, inasmuch as it takes years for a given case to wind its way through federal district courts . . . and the department's power to supervise a new election generally comes when the incumbents' term expires anyway.

Comment

Anyone who can listen to this and make sense of it is a genius. It is grossly overwritten, in terribly bad style. Ignoring the editorial implication of the phrase "illegally chosen" in reference to cases still in the courts, the air man gave it a hasty penciling in studio and it came out this way: *The Labor Department—annoyed by a backlog of 28 disputed union elections —plans to ask the Supreme Court for help. The department will ask the court to reinterpret the 1959 Landrum-Griffin law, under which illegally-elected union officers can retain their posts for years while their cases are fought through the courts.*

Example

The Reagan-backed proposal slipped quietly into effect at one minute past midnight, designed to raise 944-million dollars this year and more than one-billion dollars next year.

Comment

That mixed-up antecedent again. And why "slipped quietly"? The process was without subterfuge, and of necessity noiseless. Better: *The Reagan-backed proposal, designed to raise 944-million dollars this year and more than one-billion dollars next year, took effect at one minute past midnight.*

Example

Bottle-throwing Negroes rampaged through the nation's capitol. The small gangs roamed through a 25-block area, smashing windows, looting and setting several fires.

Comment

Separation of the "bottle-throwing" from the other activities gives it unwarranted emphasis and confuses the thought. The misspelling ("capitol" for "capital"), while it does not alter the pronunciation greatly, may confuse the air man. Better: *Small gangs of Negroes rampaged through a 25-block area of the nation's capital. They threw bottles, smashed windows, looted, and set several fires.*

Example

A security guard in a supermarket was wounded this morning in what otherwise was a botched-up robbery attempt by two bandits.

Comment

The writer of this one botched his work worse than the bandits did theirs. The "otherwise" makes the concluding clause a non sequitur. Better: *Two gunmen botched the robbery of a supermarket this morning, but they shot a security guard before they got away—with no money.*

Example

In the nation's capitol this morning, administration officials, congressmen and senators are straining to get the legislative machinery up to speed in time to put an end to the racial crisis sweeping the country . . . and to give the country some guarantees for a peaceful future.

Ardent civil rights advocates such as New York Senator Robert Kennedy and Senator Edward Brooke of Massachusetts talked tough at committee hearings on the crisis.

Comment

Seldom has so much been said to so little effect. Again the misspelled "capitol," the strained mixed metaphor, the confusion of thought (for example, the implicit assumption that the racial crisis can be solved by legislative action). The second paragraph contains the only facts; the first would never be missed, and its presence can only be deplored.

Story Structure

Television writing style involves more than merely the ability to use language effectively, although if that is lacking all else is surely lost. The writer who has a good command of language must also consider the structure of the news story, by which we mean the arrangement of facts within the story.

In this respect the demands of television news differ from those of other news media in the degree of their importance, but not in kind. Good writing structure in any medium is usually good writing structure in all media. Generally, however, less attention is paid to structure in newspaper writing than elsewhere, whereas television news writing *demands* more attention to structure than almost any other kind of news writing. The closest comparisons are found in news writing for radio and magazines, and even here there are significant differences. In comparison with news magazine writing, the differences are occasioned by the necessity of structuring the news broadcast, and all of its parts, in the form of a show; in comparison with radio news writing, which also requires some adherence to show structure, the differences are occasioned mainly by the addition of visual elements.

The television news story is not fully told until the last word is said and the last picture shown. It is never written to be trimmed if time catches us short, as the newspaper story may be written to be trimmed if space runs short in the type column.

This is primarily because the nature of television demands dramatic unity, and secondarily because the problem in the studio does not resemble the problem in the composing room. When adjustments must be made for time, it is easier and quicker to delete entire stories from the show than to trim out parts of stories. This process usually takes place in the last few minutes before air, or even after the show is on the air, and therefore speed is essential.

The television news story's Aristotelian unity is what makes it difficult to trim. It is not written to be cut off at the end, or anywhere else. It has a beginning, a middle and an end, and to delete any part of it makes it meaningless, just as omission of the last act of a well-written play makes the play meaningless. Further, this characteristic resistance to trimming is accentuated by the story's brevity; it is a lean, spare creature that leaves the viewer hungry for more; there is no fat on its bones.

Aristotle's own description of dramatic unity applies perfectly to the television news story: "The truth is that, just as in the other imitative arts one imitation is always of one thing, so in poetry the story, as an imitation of action, must represent one action, a complete whole, with its several incidents so closely connected that the transposal or withdrawal of any one of them will disjoin and dislocate the whole. For that which makes no perceptible difference by its presence or absence is no real part of the whole."[6]

This of course relates directly to our previous remarks on the relationship between brevity and meaning; both are achieved by adherence to the principle of dramatic unity. A full understanding of the meaning of dramatic unity can be obtained only by a study of its application in the structural design of a play; a glimpse of its meaning can be had by studying the structure of the magazine article or the radio news story, to which the television news story bears a closer affinity. Both studies are strongly recommended for the television news writer.

In the television news story, unlike the play, the climax is usually placed at or near the beginning. It is the action or event which causes a peripety, or reversal of fortune; it is what the newspaper man would normally select for the lead of his story. For television purposes it is more valuable to think of it in its dramatic sense, rather than as

---

[6] Aristotle, *Poetics*, trans. Ingram Bywater, in *The Rhetoric and The Poetics of Aristotle*, Modern Library Edition (New York: Random House, Inc., 1954), p. 234.

merely a lead, because viewing the event as a peripety forces the writer to view all of the related facts in dramatic terms, as causes or effects of the peripety. These two groups of facts then become clearly the other two major parts of the structure.

The causes correspond to the rising action of a play in which a convergence of forces leads inevitably to the peripety. But whereas if the play is divided into the same three parts, of which the rising action is the first, in the news story this part constitutes the middle. It is a recapitulation of the causative factors, and therefore an explanation of the peripety.

The last part of the news story corresponds to the denouement of the play. It states the effects, actual or probable, of the peripety. Here the news story differs from the play, however, since what is called the "extension" of the play is not, or should not be, staged. This extension, the implication of future events, goes beyond the scope of the dramatic action itself although that action contains the seeds of the extension. The audience leaves the theater imagining what happened after the curtain fell because further events were implicit in the climax. The news audience leaves the story imagining what may happen because the probabilities have been stated in the story.

We have thus a news story structure proceeding from climax to causes to effects. Not every story can follow this pattern, any more than every play follows a pattern of rising action, climax, and denouement. But an example or two may demonstrate how the pattern works.

The story of a highway accident begins with the statement, verbal or visual or both, of the climax: two autos collided at a certain place, such and such persons were killed. It continues with the causes, explaining how the accident happened. It concludes with the effects: two small children of the victims are orphaned, and a relative plans to take care of them for the time being, but their future is uncertain.

President Lyndon Johnson's surprise decision not to run for reelection, announced on television in the spring of 1968, was a peripety. It was a reversal of fortune for him and for all who aspired to his office. News stories began with the announcement itself, proceeded to discuss the probable reasons for the President's decision, and concluded with reports on the opinions of political leaders as to the probable effects on the presidential election, the war in Vietnam, domestic policies, and other matters of national interest.

Variations on the climax-cause-effect structure are more likely to be minor than significant. In the automobile accident story above, for example, the lead might mention that two children were orphaned by the accident, but the details of that portion of the story would be supplied in the concluding section. Similarly, the lead on the story of President Johnson's announcement might mention that he threw the presidential campaign into confusion. Actually such references to the import and extension of the story, when contained in the lead along with the climax, contribute to the effect of dramatic unity; the viewer is expecting some discussion of the early reference, however casual it may seem at the moment it is made, just as the theater audience is subconsciously expecting the climax and denouement to grow out of the rising action in the early part of the play. Thus the conclusion of the news story "ties it all up neatly," leaving no loose ends.

Summary

Clarity is the first essential of television news writing; its major elements are brevity, philosophy, metaphor, conversational quality, and counterpoint. Elements of confusion include euphemism, headline clichés, overly complex syntax, journalese, and redundancy. The declarative sentence is the most effective grammatical form for television.

Styles for abbreviations, figures, and unusual words are standardized in a manner to make easy reading for the air man.

The television news story demands Aristotelian unity of structure, most frequently following a three-part progression from climax to causes to effects.

Suggested Assignments

1. Rewrite a local newspaper story, at least one column in length, into a standup television story of no more than 30 seconds. (It is suggested that this be made a regular homework assignment for the remainder of the course, with variations—as long as one minute, as short as 10 seconds—in the length of the story.)

2. Monitor a television news show, at the same time recording the audio on an audio tape recorder (by simply placing the microphone of the recorder near the loudspeaker of the television receiver). From study of the show list an example of each of the following in the narrative writing: (a) brevity, (b) philosophy, (c) metaphor, (d) conversational quality, and (e) counterpoint with video. (Class discussion of this assignment is most valuable when the entire class is required to monitor the same show.)

3. From the same audio recording list an example of each of the following in the narrative writing: (a) euphemism, (b) headline cliché, (c) overly complex syntax, (d) journalese, and (e) statements so overly simplified that the meaning is unclear or distorted.

4. Discuss the reasons for the desirability of the simple declarative sentence in television news.

5. From a newspaper select any five sentences that could not be spoken aloud effectively, and in each case explain why and rewrite the sentence in broadcast form.

6. Discuss the reasons for Aristotelian unity in the television news story.

7. Monitor a television news show and from it select one story which is a good example of dramatic unity, and one which is not. In each case explain why. (Again, it is most desirable for the entire class to monitor the same show.)

8. Analyze a major visual story broadcast by a television station in terms of the climax-cause-effect structure. If it departs from this structure, discuss the probable reasons for such departure and the effectiveness of the resulting structure.

9. Analyze the same story as printed in a newspaper, with the same points in mind, including use of photographs.

10. From the audio tape recording (see Question 2 above) select a story which could be improved by the elimination of irrelevant information, and rewrite it in briefer form to clarify its meaning.

11. From the audio tape recording select a story which includes only a climax-cause structure, eliminating the effects portion of the structure, and explain why you think that portion was omitted.

12. Rewrite an assigned play (preferably a classic, such as *Hamlet* or *Oedipus Rex*) as a 1-minute standup television news story.

13. Discuss the significance of the television reporter's philosophy as it is reflected in his writing in terms of (a) his education, and (b) his relationship to society.

Chapter 7

The Logic
of the
Motion
Picture

The motion picture is what makes television unique among news media. Nothing else brings events directly into the living room of the viewer, nothing else projects their meaning so directly into his mind and heart. Which is to say no more than what the theatrical filmmaker has long known: the motion picture is the most powerful artistic force in human history. Its dramatic potential has excited film artists from D. W. Griffith to François Truffaut. No art presents a greater challenge to its masters, for the motion picture encompasses all of the other arts of man.

The Language of Emotion

Like all art forms, film has its own special logic. In particular, film is not subject to the logic of language. It does not respond effectively to the kind of objective thought process which derives from the printed or even the spoken word. Today, after nearly three quarters of a century of cinematic culture, this is still not widely understood. Too many film stories are merely "word stories" transposed onto film. But the magic of the word does not transmute into the magic of film, nor does the process operate in reverse.

Compared to language, film is a form of poetry, and it is as difficult to describe a film in words as it is to film a poem. The ultimate truth of all news media is the same, but they arrive at it by different routes.

The language of film is emotion; or, to paraphrase Marshall McLuhan, with film the effect is the affect.

At the 1960 Democratic National Convention the (then) governor of New Jersey, Robert Meyner, was asked a politically embarrassing question during a news conference. (The question itself is not important to our story.) He did not answer immediately. He looked down at the table, he picked up a fork and played with it, he studied the ceiling. The camera kept on rolling while he searched for an answer. Finally, after 20 seconds of hesitation, he found it.

The author happened to see the film of that incident five times, with five different groups of people. The reaction was as precise as clockwork. At 7 seconds someone chuckled. By 15 seconds every viewer was laughing aloud. At 20 seconds, when Meyner began to speak, his answer was drowned by the laughter of the audience.

This is the logic of film at work. The incident as reported in the newspapers was worth a mild chuckle at best. On radio that 20-second eternity of silence would have had the listener fiddling with the dial to determine whether he had lost the signal. But on film—and *only* on film—Meyner's political discomfiture was excruciatingly funny. The viewers, *feeling* his discomfiture with him but not forced to share it, enjoyed the luxury of being at once detached and empathic. The film triggered an emotional audience response which found its catharsis in laughter, and at the same time it conveyed accurately the import of the political situation in which Meyner was involved.

The important thing to notice is that it made its point indirectly, by creating emotion in the audience, whereas the newspaper men reporting the same incident were forced to fall back on logic by stating Meyner's position and reporting that he was reluctant to answer the embarrassing question about it. The conclusion reached by the television viewer is the same as the conclusion reached by the newspaper reader, but they do not arrive at that conclusion by the same path. The reason is that the language of film is emotion.

The television news writer, who works daily and intimately with motion pictures whether they originate on film or video, requires an understanding of this logic of emotion. He must develop a sense of the particular and peculiar values of film, and he must be able to discern them when the camera has captured them, and he must be able to extract them from the uncut film by editing. He must know how to use these values to transmit information accurately, because the most powerful and most effective stories he writes will transmit their information in this indirect manner. His final product, the finished story, cannot be conceived in terms of words; it must be conceived in terms of a succession of moving images interwoven with words and precalculated to evoke in the audience a specific affective response.

This method of news reporting is both the strength and the weakness of television. Its strength lies in stories which concern individuals and their problems directly and individually, especially when those problems contain implications for the news audience. Its weakness lies in stories involving abstract ideas, which television seldom can convey as well as print for the reason that abstractions cannot be filmed and seldom stir emotions.

The deeper meaning of television's reliance on visual values, then, is a reliance on emotional values which convey information. And this explains why many people object to news stories on television when they find little or no objection to the same stories in other media; the television story moves them to anger or fear or hatred which the other media cannot so easily generate. What they are really objecting to is not television or even the story, but its disturbing effect on themselves, the sharper realization of unpleasant facts of life.

In sum, what we call "writing" in television news is as much the evaluation and editing of motion pictures as it is writing in the traditional meaning of the word.

Sometimes, of course, luck plays into the writer's hands. The author once interviewed a mental hospital employee shortly after her arrest on a charge of mistreating patients—a charge later determined by the courts to be unfounded. The woman was stunned, ashamed, reluctant to talk, actually hiding her face from the camera. Finally, after some urging that she tell her side of the story, she jumped up so abruptly and in such white hot rage that it appeared she was going to strike me. Instead, for nearly four minutes, she poured out her pent-up feelings of outrage, disbelief, shame, determination, dedication, sorrow—the entire gamut of emotion. At one point, as she spoke softly in sorrow, an enormous tear rolled slowly down one cheek. And a great cameraman, Jack Leppert, shooting in almost impossible light, zoomed in until that tear completely filled the frame.

That interview was broadcast in its entirety by several stations, without one frame cut. The ultimate compliment was paid it by a woman viewer who described it as "just like soap opera, only this was *real!*"

But seldom does the film story thus fall into the writer's hands like a ripe fruit, needing only leaders to put it on the air. More often the writer must deliberately use the art of film to breathe life and meaning into the story. Much of that meaning is achieved in the shooting of the film, and this the writer must recognize when he sees it in the projection room. More of it he must create by his editing of the film. And for both purposes he must understand what causes film to generate emotion.

Involvement

Involvement is the essential element in film logic. The Meyner interview mentioned above made its point only because it caused the
audience to become involved in Meyner's predicament. Involvement
actually says all there is to say about the power of film; the audience
watches because it seeks desperately to find involvement.

To a great extent people watch television news out of the same
impulse that drives them into theaters where they become involved
vicariously in the affairs and problems of fictional people. Whether this
impulse is stronger today than in past generations is impossible to say;
today's opportunities for vicarious involvement are so much greater
because of the technological advances of the last century or so. However, those same technological advances, television among them, have
also increased the alienation of large segments of society which therefore have greater need of vicarious involvement in order to maintain a
sense of human contact.

Involvement vs. commitment   In any case, a distinction must be made
between involvement and commitment. The audience does not seek
commitment. Commitment implies active participation, involvement
implies detached empathy. The viewer wants to become involved vicariously in the problems of persons in the news without being committed
to their support. He wants to have his cake and eat it, too.

The "epic" theater of Bertolt Brecht was an attempt to convert
involvement into commitment—that is to say, into personal action—
and its dramatic weaknesses stem directly from this attempt. Epic
theater is unabashed propaganda theater, and this fact alone would be
reason enough for the newsman to reject any tendency to follow in
Brecht's footsteps by trying to utilize television for the purpose of
securing audience commitment. The television newsman's business is
not to propagandize, but to inform through the use of the motion
picture's capacity to generate involvement.

Sympathy vs. empathy   A distinction must also be made between sympathy and empathy. The latter generates involvement, the former does
not.

Consider, for example, a film which opens with a shot of a young
woman emerging from a taxicab and entering a courthouse. This shot
arouses only curiosity as to what her business with the courts may be.

But add a shot of a young prisoner being led into a visiting room
inside the courthouse, and immediately the viewer leaps to the conclusion that there is some connection between this young man and the
young woman he has just seen entering the courthouse. This conclu-

sion is automatic and inevitable, even though the viewer has as yet no idea what their connection may be. The viewer's leap to this conclusion is *solely the result of the juxtaposition of these two shots.*

Add a third shot in which the young woman enters the visiting room and rushes tearfully into the young prisoner's arms. Instantly the viewer experiences empathy; the film is beginning to do its work on him. He still does not know anything about this young couple except that they seem to have mutual affection. They may be lovers, or married, or brother and sister. The young man may be a vicious criminal, or a man unjustly accused. The woman may be his unsuspected accomplice in crime, or his lawyer-mistress, or the wife of a close friend. But at this point none of this matters to the viewer; he *cares* about the young couple, at least enough to want to know more. He empathizes; he is involved.

It is important to an understanding of involvement to recognize that the audience does *not* sympathize with the young couple. It feels *with* them in their predicament, but not *for* them. It does not yet know enough about them or the reasons for their predicament to feel any sympathy, and in any case sympathy has absolutely nothing to do with involvement.

The audience becomes involved solely because it lives through their experience with them. It identifies with their aim (which in this case is still not clear), but not with the still unexplained motives underlying that aim. The audience does not identify with a man because he is kind to dogs and helpful to the blind; it identifies with him because it identifies with his aims and his will to achieve them, even when it does not particularly admire those aims. Were this not true, the gangster movies of the 1930s would never have been successful, nor would the "anti-hero" movies of today find an audience. There is a lesson here for the producers of those television entertainment series in which the heroes have only noble motives, but the lesson has not been learned. Confusion of sympathy with empathy has produced more bad movies than any other error.

The identical error underlies those breaches of good taste which occur all too often in television news, as for example when the reporter, interviewing a grief-stricken mother whose son has just been killed in a robbery, asks her, "How do you feel?" The question of course elicits an emotional response: usually tears, occasionally anger and indignation. But it elicits no information that the audience does not already have; the audience already knows that the mother is grief-stricken. On informational grounds the question cannot be justified. What the reporter in his ignorance is trying to do is generate sympathy in the audience. He fails to realize that the audience is already empathic, since it knows the situation. And if, instead of sympathy, he generates contempt and irritation at his unwarranted intrusion into the privacy of the mother's sorrow, this is the mildest of the rebukes he should expect. He should expect a much sharper rebuke from the writer or producer who throws that portion of the film on the cutting room floor and stomps on it in rage.

Those who consciously seek sympathy never find it, in television news any more than in personal relations. What the writer must seek, as he views and edits film, is the empathy which creates involvement.

The Discovery Principle

A film report of a traveling musical production designed to entertain slum dwellers in Washington, D.C., began with a close shot of feet tapping to music. The camera panned up and pulled back to discover that the feet belonged to Hubert Humphrey, then the Vice President, obviously enjoying the show.

The key word here is "discover." The narrator did not explain whose feet were shown; he allowed the audience to make the same discovery the camera had made. The shot was all the more effective for his restraint. Words were not only unnecessary, they would have denied the audience its greatest desire: to become involved. Words would have negated the sensitive logic of the film by negating the discovery principle.

A television news report on a controversy surrounding a phonograph recording of Malvina Reynolds' "The Little Boxes" explained that the "ticky-tacky boxes" of the lyrics were the look-alike tract houses with which developers have defaced the San Francisco landscape. Over the music, film of the "ticky-tacky boxes" was shown. Viewers responded with hundreds of telephone calls, both complimentary and complaining. They could place themselves vicariously in the shoddy houses of the song (houses in which many of them actually lived), and also in the position of critics such as Mrs. Reynolds voicing lyrical contempt for the builders. The viewers had been touched by the oblique logic of film reinforced by music. They had discovered the meaning of the song.

Douglas Aircraft introduced its "stretched-out" Super DC-8 at the time the company was being purchased by McDonnell Aircraft. Television reporter Jim Brown devoted the largest part of his report to a retrospective film interview with the company's founder, Donald Douglas, Sr., taking a final and emotional bow as chairman of the board. The end of an industrial dynasty was far more moving than the birth of a new airliner, and the logic of the film took its inexorable effect. The audience discovered a touching personal story behind the more obvious but impersonal story of the plane.

Allowing the viewer to make his own discoveries in this way is one manner of achieving involvement. Given such a chance, the viewer seizes it eagerly. He delights in thus participating in the story, rather than functioning merely as a passive receiver of information. As any scientist well knows, the discovery part of the learning process is pleasurable; it is the reward for work and study. The viewer, too, likes to be rewarded and to savor the pleasure thereof.

Understanding this, the writer in viewing film looks for every opportunity to let the film make its own point, to let the viewer discover for himself its meaning. If the film shows an angry man, the writer need not explain in the script that the man is angry; the viewer prefers to discover that for himself. The script should never supply information which the film makes clear; to do so is redundant. Actually, the discovery principle is the obverse of the redundancy principle, which is anathema to every professional writer.

In each of the examples given above the discovery principle was used in a different way. In the first example, that of the traveling musical production, the effect was achieved entirely by the work of the cameraman, by the manner in which the camera moved to make its discovery. In the second example it was achieved by reinforcing the mental image which the lyrics created with the film image of the "ticky-tacky boxes" themselves; the effect was to make concrete the meaning of the lyrics, especially for those viewers who had only a vague mental image of their meaning. In the third example it was achieved by surprising the viewer with an unexpected story-beneath-the-story; the routine report suddenly took off tangentially. The ways in which the discovery principle may be utilized to create involvement are limited only by the materials at hand and the imagination of the newsman functioning as filmmaker.

Juxtaposition of Images

The writer's greatest opportunity to exercise his creative faculties to generate involvement occurs in the editing room. Here the writer most effectively uses his understanding that the power of film derives not from its physical motion, its simulation of life, but from the dramatic effect created by the juxtaposition in time of carefully selected images.

A shot of an opulent dinner party is, by itself, nothing more than that. The same can be said of a shot of starving slum children. But when by editing these two shots are juxtaposed, an entirely new meaning is created which could not be conveyed by either shot alone. It is a statement about the dynamics of a society, and its revelation of tensions within that society cannot help but create emotion in an audience composed of members of that same society. Willingly or unwillingly, they become involved, and this is true whether the individual's reaction is rejection or concern, anger or shame.

The meaning of the film is determined entirely by such juxtaposition of shots. Consider a shot of a man lying shot to death beside a lake; it has no further meaning without explanation. But suppose we place three other shots before it. The first shows a girl strolling along the edge of the lake; the second shows birds on the water suddenly taking flight; the third shows the girl, startled, staring out of the shot in horror; *then* we see the body. Suddenly we are in the presence of murder. We have heard a gunshot (even if the film is silent, the viewer hears it in his mind, which connects the sudden flight of the birds with the sound which startled them). The killer lurks nearby. The girl may be in danger. Meanings have multiplied far beyond the sum total of the meanings of the individual shots.

Now suppose we change only the third shot of this sequence; instead of looking off in horror, the girl smiles into the sky. The meanings have changed. The viewer did not hear a gunshot, the discovery of death is in the girl's future, there is no sure indication of imminent danger—all this changed by one shot. The girl's reaction is the clue to the meaning of the montage; it even changed the meaning of the previous shot, of the birds taking flight.

An example of film editing destructive of involvement was seen in a network report on Ronald Reagan's midnight inauguration as governor of California in 1967. The film showed Reagan's joking comment to his fellow actor-turned-politician, Senator George Murphy: "Well, George, here we are on the late show again." This was followed by a close shot of Murphy looking solemn, almost frowning. The effect was incongruous and disturbing. What had happened was that the shot of Murphy had been filmed at a different time during the ceremony; it had been inserted at this point in the film sequence by editing. If a laughing shot of Murphy was not available, it would have been better not to put in a reaction shot. The meaning of the montage became incredible; the incongruity of the reaction shot destroyed the logic of the film and shattered both the truth of the report and the viewer's involvement.

The diversity of the film (or video) stories which the news writer encounters is limitless, and the specific rules which apply to a particular story may never find application again. But in general terms the writer must realize that in its final form any film story is a work of art. Artistry in juxtaposing images by editing is not only desirable, it is unavoidable. The only question is whether the art is good or bad.

Summary

The logic of film is the logic of emotion rather than reason; it is created by generating involvement and empathy in the viewer. Efforts to generate commitment or sympathy are destructive of involvement and empathy. The discovery principle is an aid in creating involvement.

The meaning of film is determined primarily by the juxtaposition of images; that is to say, by editing.

Suggested Assignments

1. Monitor a television news show and from your observations prepare a brief paper on each of the following: (a) how a major visual story makes its point primarily by generating emotion in the audience, and whether it does so responsibly; (b) how a newspaper covers the same story, and whether its coverage is more or less responsible than the television coverage; (c) an example of the television reporter or writer confusing sympathy with empathy; (d) an example of the use of the discovery principle to generate involvement.

2. Analyze a television news story in terms of the manner in which it creates audience involvement or fails to do so. (This assignment might be made in advance of the broadcast by selecting, for example, the first film story to be used on a particular show on a specified night.)

3. After classroom viewing of one or more film stories (obtained by the instructor from a local station after they have been broadcast), explain to what extent each story uses emotion to make its point, and to what extent factual narration is used as counterpoint to restrain the emotional impact.

4. Report any example you can observe of the failure to distinguish between involvement and commitment in television news broadcasting.

5. Analyze the juxtaposition of shots in a film news story for the effectiveness of the editing in generating involvement and for the accuracy of the resulting report.

6. Explain your understanding of the relationship between audience involvement and television news reporting.

7. Explain why the visual element of television news increases its reliance on emotion to convey information, or whether in fact such is not the case.

8. Shoot a silent film story selected for its emotional potential, edit it, and script narration over. Defend your work against class criticism.

Chapter 8

Film
Basics

To work with film the writer or reporter must speak the jargon of film, the technical language used by cameramen and film editors. But he needs to be able to do more than merely converse intelligently about film; he also needs an understanding of the general types of film and film equipment and how they are used, and he must understand the physical structure of the film story, which was discussed in general terms in the last chapter. Knowledge of film story structure necessarily includes the ability to recognize and define the various types of shots which compose the story, and an understanding of the manner in which they relate to one another. Fortunately, almost all of these terms and all of this knowledge applies equally to the video picture, which has simply borrowed its jargon from film.

The Medium-within-the-Medium

Film is the medium-within-the-medium, without which much of television news would be little more than radio with a picture. This condition will prevail until the professional equipment for the production, recording, and transmission of video motion pictures is reduced in size and weight to a point where it can compete with film equipment.

The average mobile video unit at present is the size of a large truck or bus, carries tons of equipment, and may take hours to get into

Figure 8-1 Sam Greenwald, dean of the world's news cameramen (shooting news film since 1915), with the Bell and Howell Filmo, the camera most widely used for shooting silent news film. Because it is spring-driven, it cannot be used for shooting sound film, and in several other respects it is less versatile than many newer models. However, its ruggedness and dependability make it a favorite with news cameramen. CBS Photo.

operation. The only way to shoot video pictures of a fire, for example, would in most cases be to burn down the television studio.

On the other hand (almost literally) film equipment is easily portable. With less than 100 pounds of gear film can be shot under water, in space, at the North Pole, anywhere. It is this portability which gives film its present advantage over video for the roving, fast-moving newsman.

Sizes of film Film is manufactured in three sizes (widths) used by television: 8-, 16-, and 35-millimeter. The larger the film the better the picture resolution, or quality; unfortunately the cost increases in roughly geometrical ratio to size.

Most of the film used in television news is 16-millimeter, the optimum size considering quality, cost, and portability. The 8-millimeter film used by most amateurs does not provide satisfactory picture

Figure 8-2   Hand-held 400-foot modified Auricon camera films the author's dockside interview with television star Buddy Ebsen and yachtsman Patrick Dougan on plans for race between Ebsen's catamaran Polynesian Concept and Dougan's 12-meter Columbia, former holder of the America's Cup. Soundman (crouching, lower right) uses highly directional shotgun microphone to pick up all three voices. Zoom lens enables cameraman to take one-, two- or three-shot as desired, moving smoothly from one shot composition to another without interrupting continuity. In editing, transitional movements often are eliminated. (See also Figure 5-1, page 52.) Photo courtesy CBS Enterprises, Inc.

resolution, and the 35-millimeter film used by most theatrical and commercial film producers requires excessively heavy equipment and needlessly large crews.

The 16-millimeter film comes in three standard lengths: 100, 400, and 1,200 feet.

Equipment   Most film crews carry a hand camera for silent film, and a sound camera which may be carried on a shoulder-pod or placed on a tripod as the situation requires.

Figure 8-3 KMOX-TV cameraman uses 1200-foot camera to film airport interview in St. Louis. Camera is much larger, more complicated than 400-foot models, must be operated from tripod because of weight, can take a single shot of more than 30 minutes duration. Soundman (lower left) has chosen to use hand-held microphone (held by reporter, right) covered with wind-sock to reduce rumble caused by wind. Choice of interview setting is visually appropriate for story. W. F. Jud Photo, courtesy KMOX-TV.

The hand camera (Figure 8–1), which weighs 4 to 6 pounds, takes a 100-foot film roll, the equivalent of approximately 3 minutes of shooting time.

Most sound cameras are fitted to take a 400-foot film magazine (Figure 8–2). The combined weight of camera, zoom lens, loaded magazine, and shoulder pod is about 25 pounds. All sound cameras are electrically driven, either on conventional AC current or by a power pack. If the cameraman carries a portable light, a separate power pack for the light is needed, unless he can plug it into an AC source. If he has to carry both power packs, the total weight on his back may be 50 to 70 pounds.

For shooting certain events, such as lengthy hearings or football games, a larger sound camera which takes a 1,200-foot magazine is often used (Figure 8–3). This type of camera is too heavy to operate except on a tripod, but the greater length of film eliminates the need for frequent reloading at critical moments.

Recording of film sound requires a sound amplifier; the transistorized amplifier used most widely for news film weighs only 3 to 4 pounds. If the sound is recorded on a track separate from the picture track, a film or tape recorder is also required; this may weigh up to 25 pounds.

In addition, the well-equipped crew carries a variety of microphones, lights, cables, and related paraphernalia. The total weight of all the equipment may be 300 pounds; however, only a part of the equipment is ever used at any one time.

The Sound of Film

Film was born in silence, but like a precocious child it acquired the art of speech at an early age. (But even sound film *can* hold its tongue. In Hollywood studios sound film shot without sound is to this day called MOS, meaning "mitout sound." This is said to be our heritage from the late Erich von Stroheim, who spoke film better than English.) Film sound is produced by either of two means, one optical, the other magnetic. (See Figure 8–4.)

Optical sound This type of sound, abbreviated OPT, is made by varying the width or density (darkness) of the sound track; a "picture" of the sound is drawn on the film by a lamp which is excited electronically by the signal from the microphone.

Optical sound has the disadvantage of being tied to the chemical processing of the film. If the film is over- or underexposed, or if the laboratory makes a mistake in the processing speed, the sound track may be ruined.

Magnetic sound This type of sound, abbreviated MAG, is a more recent development. It is recorded on film coated with a magnetic oxide material similar to ordinary audio tape. The quality is superior to that of optical sound and does not depend on the processing of the film. MAG has the additional advantage of allowing for playback a fraction of a second after recording, so that the soundman can hear what is on the film and catch any flaws or errors on the spot.

Magnetic has replaced optical sound for almost all original recording, although a news crew with an optical recorder is still seen occasionally in the hinterlands. But the sound track on a finished film print, such as is exhibited in theaters, is nearly always optical (although a trend to magnetic is beginning). This is partly because the dubbing and

Optical   Balance   Magnetic
sound track   stripe   sound track

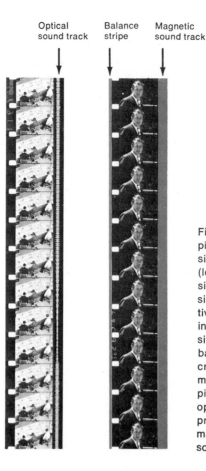

Figure 8-4 Single-system film carries picture and synchronized sound on a single strip of film. Optical sound track (left) varies in width (as here) or density. Magnetic sound track (right) consists of striping of magnetically sensitive oxide material similar to that used in audio tape; narrower stripe on opposite edge of film serves sole purpose of balancing film thickness to prevent crimping on reel. In 16-millimeter film, magnetic sound is 28 frames ahead of picture with which it is synchronized, optical sound is 26 frames ahead; in projection same distances must be maintained between picture gate and sound head.

processing of such prints is done under laboratory conditions, and under those conditions the optical sound can be of good quality.

Whether optical or magnetic (but from here on we shall be discussing only magnetic unless otherwise specified), sound film may be either single-system or double-system.

Single-system is the most widely used type of sound film for news. The television news team of reporter, cameraman, and soundman, linked by their electrical umbilicals, has become as common a sight as the newspaper man with his notebook and baggy pants. Ninety-nine times out of a hundred the film they are shooting is 16-millimeter MAG single-system.

The sound on single-system film is recorded on a track or stripe on one edge of the film, hence the abbreviation SOF (for "sound on film"). The arrangement permits a comparatively lightweight camera to record both sound and picture.

A major disadvantage of single-system is caused by the fact that the picture aperture and the sound-recording head cannot occupy the same place inside the camera. This is because the film must stop at every frame for picture recording, while it must move at a constant speed for sound recording. The result is that the sound corresponding to a given picture frame is not directly opposite that frame. In 16-millimeter optical film the sound is 26 frames ahead of its corresponding picture; in magnetic it is 28 frames ahead. This distance corresponds to slightly more than 1 second of time, since 16-millimeter film is run at a constant speed of 24 frames per second.

In projection of the film this separation is compensated by having the projector gate and the sound pickup head the same distance apart, so that sound and picture are reproduced in sync. The disadvantage of the separation becomes evident only when the film is edited—a matter which we shall discuss later.

Double-system consists of two separate film tracks, one carrying only the picture, the other carrying only the sound. They are recorded in precise synchronization and must of course be replayed in sync.

Double-system increases the flexibility of editing, but is more difficult to reproduce on television. It requires two film chains rather than one, and the two chains must have an electronic interlock (not found at most stations) to insure synchronized projection. (See Figure 8–5.)

Double-system also requires more editing than single-system, and this involves more time than the television newsman can usually afford. Unless the additional quality which it affords is essential to the story, news is best shot single-system.

However, double-system is the principal type of film used in shooting documentaries, commercials, theatrical pictures, and television entertainment series. Most films of this type go through a complicated production process, beginning with the negative film shot by the camera and proceeding through a master positive film, a duplicate negative (dupe neg), and finally a release print for actual showing. The main reason for this complicated procedure is to protect and preserve the original negative, which in the case of theatrical pictures may represent an investment of millions of dollars.

For television news, and for most television documentaries, this process is unnecessarily expensive and prohibitively time-consuming. Therefore these productions, whether single-system or double-system, are usually shot on *reversal print* film which produces a print directly from the camera; this print is edited and used on the air.

A relatively recent development in double-system which is occasionally used in news or documentaries consists of a tape recorder kept in synchronization with the camera by means of an electronic *sync pulse*. This makes possible the shooting of double-system film with an audio tape recorder rather than the heavier, bulkier film sound recorders.

Figure 8-5 Double-system film consists of two film tracks, one (left) carrying only the picture, the other (right) carrying only the sound. Full-coat sound track is film stock coated with magnetic oxide material; sound is usually dubbed from original recording on audio tape synchronized with picture. Wild track sound film is identical to sound track shown except that it is not synchronized with picture. Air use of double-system film requires two film chains; and since the two tracks must be projected in precise synchronization, the chains must be controlled by an electronic interlock.

However, the tape audio is customarily dubbed onto 16-millimeter film, so that what the film editor actually works with is double-system film.

Color vs. Black and White

Little can be said about color in television news except that it is more realistic than black and white, from the journalistic point of view. Many if not most news broadcasts are now in color, and eventually black and white probably will disappear from the air. Some holdout producers are still heard to argue that certain types of material "belong" in black and white. This is nonsense; the world is in color, and the news of it should also be in color.

The shooting of color film presents few difficulties for the newsman as compared with black and white. Color film speeds are extremely fast—so fast that street scenes can be shot at night with available light. And even faster color films can be obtained on special order.

One disadvantage of color film is the muddy green hue it picks up under the fluorescent lights so widely used for interior illumination. But this is a mild disadvantage compared to the realism that color adds to the news.

In the days of black and white many news operations shot negative film; for broadcast purposes the film polarity can be reversed electronically to present a positive image. This cannot be done with color film; reversing the polarity merely makes the picture unintelligible.

Motion Picture Structure

Motion picture film consists of a series of still pictures, called *frames*, each of which depicts a single stage of a continuous action. When run at the proper speed, the series of frames gives the optical illusion of motion.

The frames recorded on a strip of film from the instant the camera starts until the instant it stops constitute a *shot*. The same term is applied to any portion of the original shot used in the edited film.

The film story consists of a *montage* or *sequence* of shots, one after another, connected by *transition devices*.

The theoretical minimum length of a shot is one frame, a subliminal shot. The theoretical maximum is determined by the amount of film the camera can hold. In practice, action shots tend to be fairly short— a few seconds in length—while talk shots, as in a speech or interview, may run up to several minutes long.

Shots Shots are identified by at least 6 systems of nomenclature, all of which are intermixed without any apparent recognition that the systems are different. This confusion, probably a result of the haphazard way in which the motion picture industry developed, is often puzzling to the novice, for whom a classification of the systems may be helpful.

1. Shots are classified according to the proportion of the subject encompassed by the frame.

The *wide shot* (WS) or *wide angle* is a shot in which we see the entire subject in relation to its surroundings: two men seated in a room, a group of students gathered around a teacher in a classroom, a building with portions of the neighboring structures and streets.

The wide shot may also be called a *long shot* (LS). The terms are virtually indistinguishable; if there is a difference, it is usually in the subject itself, or in its distance from the camera—i.e., a subjective difference. It might be a wide shot of a fat man, a long shot of a tall man; or a wide shot of a building, a long shot of a distant ship.

If the camera moves closer to the subject, framing, say, a man so that his body nearly fills the frame, that is a *medium shot* (MS). Still closer, framing only the face, we get a *close shot* (CS) or *closeup* (CU). Framing only the eyes and lips, we get an *extreme closeup* (ECU).

These definitions are always loose, and there are as many combinations and variations on the theme as there are movie makers; anyone can be an expert and call for *medium closeups, extreme long shots,* or whatever suits his fancy. Bing Crosby once added a new one to the author's list during a street corner interview, when an amateurish news cameraman shot Crosby's face from a distance of no more than two inches. Crosby looked cross-eyed into the lens in some puzzlement and inquired, "What is that—a *nostril shot?*"

2. Shots may be characterized by the number of people in the frame: *one-shot* (for one person), *two-shot, group-shot, crowd-shot,* etc. Curiously, mathematical shot designations higher than *four-shot* are seldom encountered, which may indicate the arithmetical limitations of the early movie makers.

3. Shots are classified by the movement, or apparent movement, of the camera.

Every television viewer is familiar with the *zoom shot,* in which the framing changes from LS to CS, or vice versa, during the shot. This is accomplished not by moving the camera but by changing the focal length of the lens while the camera remains stationary; the shot requires, rather obviously, a lens of variable focal length, commonly called a zoom lens.

The *dolly shot* resembles a zoom, but the viewer who watches closely will detect a difference. The dolly is accomplished by moving the camera closer to the subject (dolly in) or farther away (dolly out). In studios the camera is rolled around on a wheeled truck called a dolly, from which the shot derives its name.

In a dolly shot the perspective changes, in a zoom shot it does not; in the zoom the point of view (POV) remains the same, since the camera does not move. The dolly shot is seldom used in news because few news cameramen include a dolly with their equipment, and if they do they have few opportunities to use it. The dolly is useful only on a very smooth surface; for theatrical and, sometimes, for documentary productions a special track is built for the dolly, but this is almost never possible in shooting news film, for reasons of time and cost.

The news cameraman can obtain an approximation of a dolly shot by walking with the portable camera, but this is usually referred to as a *walking shot;* the movement is not as smooth as that of a dolly shot, and the camera does not make the automatic interpretation of that movement which the human eye-brain system does, nor is the eye-brain system trained to make the same interpretation of such a shot projected from film. Briefly, the walking shot is often too rough in its motion to use.

The *panoramic shot,* or *pan,* is accomplished when the cameraman, remaining in one position, "pans" or sweeps or rotates the camera slowly across a panoramic view, or from one subject to another. The movement can be horizontal or vertical, or even diagonal, although this last usually has a vertiginous effect on the viewer. Some precisionists insist on calling a vertical pan a *tilt shot.*

If the panning movement is so fast that the picture blurs, the result is a *swishpan.* The swishpan is generally undesirable (the viewer cannot distinguish objects in the picture, and the effect is dizzying). However, it is sometimes used to indicate a change of scene, in which case it is not so much a part of a montage as it is a transition device (of which more later).

When the camera moves to follow a moving subject, as when it holds in frame the ball carrier on a football play, the shot is most appropriately called a *moving shot.* The difference between the pan shot and the moving shot lies not in the movement of the camera, but in the intent of the cameraman. In the moving shot the intent is to keep the subject in frame no matter how it moves; in the pan shot the subject is too big to frame without moving the camera, or the subject changes as the camera moves.

If the camera follows behind a moving subject wherever it goes, like a man following a pretty girl, keeping the subject in approximately the same range throughout the shot, it is called a *following shot.*

If the camera, in fixed position, is moved past a series of subjects (as when the cameraman films a row of houses while being driven along a street), the result is called a *running shot* or a *trucking shot.*

The newsman will seldom, if ever, have the luxury of a camera crane or cherrypicker, a device commonly used in theatrical production to move the camera in three dimensions so that it can swoop down on its subject or soar away from it in a *crane shot.* However, cameraman Jim Wilson once captured a reasonable facsimile of a crane shot for the author by shooting from a huge cement bucket swung aloft by a convenient construction crane. We suppose that should be called a *bucket shot;* anyway, it was better than a nostril shot.

4. Shots may also be classified by the movement of the subject with respect to the frame.

If the camera remains motionless, and an automobile drives through the frame, that is a *run-through shot*. Similarly, there are *walk-through shots, fall-through shots*, etc.

5. Another system of shot classification depends on the position of the camera with respect to the subject.

If the camera is positioned low, looking up at the subject, the result is a *low-angle shot*. Looking down at the subject, it is a *high-angle shot*. Shooting from a plane or helicopter produces an *aerial shot*.

6. Still another way to classify shots is by their function in the cinematic sequence.

A shot which establishes the general scene of the action in the mind of the viewer is an *establishing shot*. Usually this is also a wide shot.

Many sequences involve the use of a *master shot*. This is a shot of the entire action from a single point of view; it is usually a wide shot, but not necessarily so. If at the same time other cameras are shooting the same action from other angles, usually closer, or if parts of the action are later re-enacted and shot from other angles, these various shots can then be substituted for portions of the master shot to present a variety of angles, emphasize specific points (by close shots), or merely to avoid visual monotony. This is essentially the way all theatrical films are made.

In filming news events it is seldom practicable to hold a single shot throughout an action. There is usually only one camera to record the action, and it can be in only one place at a time. And it is usually impossible to have the action repeated time and again, as is done in studio productions employing actors and scripts. For this reason the zoom lens is widely used in filming news events; by zooming in or out, the cameraman provides visual variety and emphasizes specific points. But the principle remains the same: this varying shot of the subject, with all its zooms, is the master shot.

The *insert shot* pinpoints a detail which the master shot fails to emphasize or make clear. If during an interview, for example, the interviewee picks up a map and discusses it, the cameraman later shoots a close shot of the map in approximately the same position that the interviewee held it during the master shot. In editing, this shot is "inserted" into the sequence so that the viewer sees the map in close detail while hearing the interviewee discuss it.

The *point of view shot*, or *POV shot*, explains what the person seen in the previous shot was looking at. (We see a man. He hears a gunshot. He looks at something out of the frame, or out of shot—OS. Cut to what he sees, shot from his point of view.) Naturally, every shot has to be taken from some point of view, but the POV shot becomes significant only in the context of the sequence. The function is always explanatory of the last previous action.

The *reverse shot*, as its name implies, is a shot taken from the reverse of the angle of the master shot. In the customary interview the master shot concentrates on the face of the interviewee, while the reporter has his back to the camera. In the reverse the camera concentrates on the reporter's face, while the interviewee has his back to the camera.

The *cutaway shot* takes the picture away from the master shot to avoid a *jump-cut*. A jump-cut is a visual non sequitur. For example, assume that the editor wishes to splice together two nonconsecutive portions of the master shot of an interview. In the first of these two shots the interviewee is smoking a cigarette; in the second the cigarette is gone. The effect of splicing these two shots together is to make the cigarette vanish as if by magic; this is a jump-cut. Any such abrupt change in the position of the same subject is a jump-cut.

The film *Gigi*, which won an Academy Award for film editing, contained a jump-cut, at least in the version seen by the author. Actor Louis Jourdain stood up and buttoned his coat; instantly, on the next shot, the coat was open again and he buttoned it again. As in this case, the effect of the jump-cut is a comic or shock effect because what we see is impossible in life. Therefore the jump-cut should not be used unless such an effect is intended, which seldom happens in news.

To avoid the jump-cut, all that is necessary is to splice a cutaway shot between the two shots which otherwise create the jump-cut. The picture "cuts away" to something else—anything else, as long as it has been established and thus does not confuse the viewer. When it cuts back to the master shot, a change in position is never noticed; the viewer automatically assumes that the change occurred while he was looking at the cutaway shot, no matter how unreasonable such an assumption may seem upon detailed examination. The viewer believes what he sees, as long as what he sees appears to make sense in terms of human experience.

Frequently used news film cutaways include shots of interested bystanders, a close shot of the reporter, a shot of the reporter's hand writing notes, or a shot of a photographer or TV cameraman (several, if more than one are present) shooting the subject. If the change in the subject's position is not too great, a long shot may serve as a cutaway; especially if the long shot is taken from a slightly different angle than the master shot, any small change in the subject's position will pass unnoticed. (See Figure 8–6.)

A San Francisco news cameraman once shot a few feet of an interesting face in a crowd in Union Square. The cameraman liked the face so well that he had several hundred feet of it reproduced in the laboratory, and for years his station used this film for "stock" cutaways. The face in the Union Square crowd seemed to attend almost every news event in San Francisco for many years.

The Washington, D.C., bureau of a national news film syndication

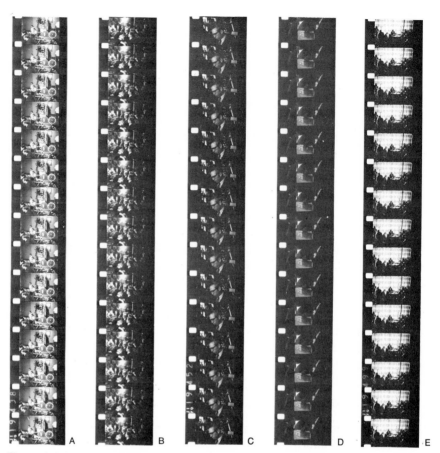

Figure 8-6 These typical cutaway shots were all filmed during the same news conference for possible use in story covered by KNXT newsman Howard Gingold: (A) cameras filming story, (B) newsmen covering story, (C) medium close shot of reporter Gingold, useful in identifying him for the audience, (D) close shot of reporter's hand taking notes, (E) long shot of conference (also useful as establishing lead-in shot). Note that lip movements of speaker cannot be seen clearly in E; cutter need concern himself only with position of speaker's head and hands. KNXT films.

company once shot 400 feet of film of a cameraman supposedly shooting a subject. Whenever a stock cutaway was needed, the film editor would simply splice a section of this stock cutaway film into his story without even bothering to look at it. Unhappily, the cameraman who was himself the subject of this charade tired of it all near the end of the film, turned toward the other camera—the camera shooting him—and thumbed his nose at it. Thus he achieved the distinction of being perhaps the only man who ever thumbed his nose at the entire United States.

The cutaway is usually very brief—1 or 2 seconds. But it can run longer if the cutaway shot is interesting in itself. It can also be used to shorten a master shot that runs too long. A 7-second cutaway of cameramen tracking the takeoff of an experimental plane at Edwards Air Force Base accomplished both purposes in one shot.

The reverse shot is sometimes used as a cutaway. But there is a sharp distinction between the two. The cutaway is not necessarily a reverse; it may be from a completely different angle. And the reverse may serve a totally different purpose, unrelated to the jump-cut; for example, it may be used simply to break the monotony of the master shot, or it may serve the purpose of re-establishing the presence of the reporter on the scene and thereby enhancing his authority.

The *reaction shot* is also sometimes a reverse, but it is not limited to the reverse angle and it performs a far different and, often, more important function. Its function is to show someone's reaction to the previous shot: the crowd laughing at the comedian's joke, the politician's anger at the accusation of bribery, the accused murderer's relief on being acquitted, the mother's agony on learning of her son's death.

Most filmmakers consider the reaction shot the most important shot of all. In a context that is already established (there must be action before there can be reaction), the reaction shot cuts closest to the semantic heart of the motion picture precisely because its purpose is to reveal emotion. The stronger the action, the deeper the emotion, the more powerful the effect on the viewer.

Transition devices There are several ways to connect one shot to the next, and one sequence to the next. All, however, are simply film *conventions* whose meaning is established largely by usage and tradition and is not necessarily inherent. For news film purposes only the most basic need be considered. The same transitions are used for the same purposes in the video picture, which has inherited all of the film traditions. Each transition device has a distinctive effect and is used deliberately to achieve that effect.

The most common transition device is the *direct cut*, or simply *cut*. The film cut is accomplished by splicing the last frame of a shot directly to the first frame of the next shot, so that the picture changes instantly and abruptly. The cut is normally used to connect a series of shots, all of which depict various aspects of the same continuing action; it implies simultaneity or consecutiveness.

The cut is also used to move back and forth between two or more simultaneous and related lines of action. When so used, the convention is termed *intercutting* or *crosscutting*.

The *fade* is used to begin or end a sequence or a series of sequences, where each sequence depicts a separate action or a separate phase of a continuing action. The fade always marks a definite break or pause in the continuity of action or thought.

In the *dissolve*, two shots overlap for several frames, the last shot fading out as the next shot fades in. The *lap dissolve* is the same thing, although sometimes this term is used to indicate a dissolve of longer duration than normal. The dissolve usually indicates a change of place, time, or subject matter, but at the same time it indicates that there is a relationship between the two actions depicted. The break in continuity is not as great as with the fade.

In its effect the *wipe* is comparable to the dissolve, but it has a greater tendency to call attention to itself; it is more self-conscious. It is therefore used more sparingly, and with the intent that it be noticed. In current cinema fashion its effect is often comic, but it need not be so.

The *superimposition*, or *super*, in which two shots are both seen full screen for a considerable time, is likely to produce only confusion unless very carefully handled. Properly handled, it creates a remarkable, subjective, dreamlike effect. It is seldom seen in news film because of its subjective quality and because of production problems; there is, however, one notable exception: the use of the superslide to convey readable information visually. Strictly speaking the super is a transition device only in that it displays a connection between two shots; but that connection is not sequential, as with other transition devices.

The *swishpan*, while currently out of fashion, is a very effective device for making transitions from one to another in a series of somewhat related stories or actions, as for instance several fires occurring on the same day. The swishpan indicates a change of scene; it is much like saying, "Meanwhile, back at the ranch . . ."

Leaders News film stories are usually assembled on a single film reel, two or more reels if the show runs an hour or longer. (This designation of show reels is not to be confused with the designation of A-reel and B-reel used for double-chain projection stories. For such stories, the primary show reel normally but not necessarily is also the A-reel.) The stories on the show reel are separated by short lengths of opaque film stock called *leaders*. Leaders are not intended to be seen; they simply provide a spatial separation between stories so that the film reel can be stopped and recued without running over into the next story.

Leaders are also used for those portions of the film not intended to be seen within multiple-chain projection stories, where the picture cuts or dissolves from one chain to another. While the A-reel picture is being shown, for example, the B-reel runs off leader.

A special type of leader known as *Academy leader* is used to cue the film at the beginning of each story (Figure 8–7). The name derives

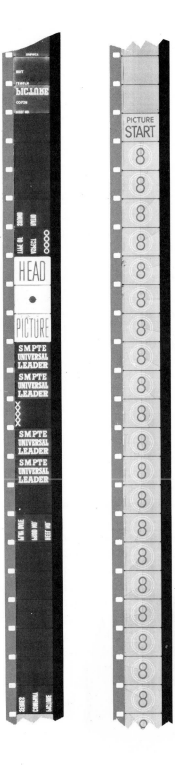

Figure 8-7 Academy leader is used to establish film roll and take cues. Head of leader provides spaces for film editor to write in information needed by projectionist (aspect ratio of picture, and type of sound) and by producer (reel and production number, and play date, production company, picture title and series title), but these are seldom used in news. Picture start frame is 8 seconds before picture, but film is normally cued for shorter roll (as short as 3 seconds). Leader shown is marked with "C" cut-out (to indicate color film) 3¾ seconds before film should be taken. Numbered frames end at 2 seconds because sound film should be allowed minimum of 2 seconds to achieve speed; cue time for both sound and silent film is normally the same, but differs at different stations.

from the Academy of Motion Picture Arts and Sciences, under whose auspices this type of leader was developed at the time sound film first came into general use.

Sound film cannot be cued to start rolling at the first picture frame because the film requires a second or two to attain the proper speed to eliminate wow in the sound reproduction. The Academy leader commonly used in television has numbered frames beginning at 192 frames, or 8 seconds, before the first picture frame. The frame numbers correspond to the number of seconds before picture should appear; there are, for example, 24 frames numbered 6. Each frame also contains a clocklike shading indicating its position within that second. The frame numbers stop and the leader goes blank at 2 seconds. By glancing at the cued frame on the preview monitor in the control room, the director can tell to the 24th of a second how long the film will roll before the picture appears.

Thus the film may be cued to run off 2 to 8 seconds of leader before picture. The number of seconds "in the cue" varies from one television station to another, but it is standardized at each station. The shorter the time in cue, the less likely it is that the air man, reading script while the Academy leader rolls off, will "upcut" sound film by talking too long.

Sequence and montage   The terms *sequence* and *montage* are normally used interchangeably; occasionally the word *scene* is used for the same purpose, but it has other rather definite meanings which merely confuse the issue, and we shall not use it. Further, to indicate the two basic types of sequence or montage, we shall make a purely arbitrary distinction between these two terms.

The sequence is a series of shots depicting the details of an event in their approximate chronological order of occurrence. This is the most typical news film story.

The montage is a series of shots not necessarily related in time or space, the totality of which is designed to create a specific effect.

A montage of shots of paintings in an art gallery may give the over-all impression of the exhibition, but for film purposes the only significant relationship among the shots is the physical connection given them by the film editor. The paintings may bear no relationship whatever to one another except that they happen, at the moment, to be hanging in the same gallery; their relationship, in any case, is a relationship *outside* the meaning of the film. Cause, effect, time, continuity are not involved. The purpose of the montage might be to catch a glimpse of the mind of Andrew Wyeth.

A montage of shots of children at play may convey the idea of innocence and happiness, even though the shots were filmed years and continents apart under totally dissimilar conditions.

A montage of trash cans, rats, leaking plumbing, falling plaster, and jobless men idling outside a bar may convey the reality of the urban ghetto—*any* ghetto—no matter where or when the shots were taken. Not one of the shots need have any connection whatsoever with any other, except that philosophical connection created by their cinematic juxtaposition.

The principal difference between the sequence and the montage, then, is that the sequence depicts a specific occurrence in a specific time-space continuum, whereas the montage depicts a selection of people, things, or actions which are related only by a philosophical commonality imposed by the film editor.

When demonstrations against the war in Vietnam took place on the same day in the United States and several European countries, the CBS news coverage consisted of a montage of sequences. Each sequence was a report on the happenings in a different city; the whole was a montage which provided a world view of anti-war sentiment and action.

While the sequence is more typical of news film, the montage is more common than might be assumed at first thought. Consider the film report of a traffic accident. The cameraman usually arrives on the scene too late to film the accident in progress; he can film only its results: a montage of wrecked automobiles, dazed and injured victims awaiting the ambulance, the dead, stalled traffic, police setting out flares, tow trucks arriving. There is only a hint of chronological continuity here; certainly the chronological continuity is not the significant element. What we really have is a montage of the scene of an accident. However, the time and place are specific, and the montage often concludes with a definitely sequential shot: the departure of the ambulance with the victims. Sometimes our arbitrary distinction becomes blurred.

The montage may be used to create the effect of action speeding up or slowing down, simply by shortening or lengthening the successive shots. Some viewers may recall a washing machine commercial (and, content aside, the best use of film techniques is often found in commercials) in which a number of people were shown picking lint off their clothing. As the montage progressed, the shots grew shorter and shorter and closer and closer, until the final shots were almost subliminal glimpses of fingers snatching at lint. The impression was one of a hilariously frenzied nation of lint pickers; had not the pace quickened, both the hilarity and the frenzy would have been absent.

In general, then, the montage conveys an impression created purely by the artistic assemblage of the shots, whereas the sequence is matter-of-fact and chronological. They speak the same language, but the sequence is prose; the montage is poetry.

Summary

Because of its advantage in portability over video equipment, film equipment is used for shooting most news stories in the field. The standard film used in news is 16-millimeter.

Film sound may be optical or magnetic, but almost all original film recordings are magnetic. Sound film may be single-system or double-system; most news stories are shot on single-system film.

The news film picture track is usually shot on reversal print stock rather than negative; this master film is not duplicated, but is edited and used directly on the air.

The film story consists of a series of pictures, or frames, constituting a shot, and a series of shots constituting a sequence or montage. Shots may be characterized in six different classifications, but shots of different character are intermixed. The shots in a sequence are connected by any of several transition devices, each with its own meaning and purpose.

Leaders are used to connect film stories on the same reel, and for rollthrus where the film is not to be aired while running. Academy leaders are used to establish the roll cue for each film story.

The terms *sequence* and *montage,* ordinarily considered synonymous, are used herein to distinguish between a series of shots depicting the chronology of an action (sequence) and a series of shots designed to create an artistic effect not necessarily representing a particular time-space continuum (montage).

Suggested Assignments

1. Define each of the following: (a) single-system film, (b) double-system film, (c) reversal print, (d) sync pulse, and (e) MOS.

2. Describe the physical structure of the motion picture film story.

3. Explain the differences between each of the following: (a) wide shot and establishing shot, (b) zoom shot and dolly shot, (c) pan shot and moving shot, (d) trucking shot and run-through shot, (e) high-angle shot and crane shot.

4. Define a master shot and explain how it is used.

5. Explain the difference between a cutaway shot and a reverse shot.

6. Explain why many filmmakers consider the reaction shot the most important shot of all.

7. Explain the basic functions and meaning of each of the following: (a) cut, (b) intercut, (c) dissolve, (d) wipe, (e) superimposition.

8. Discuss the difference between the sequence and the montage, as the terms are used in this work, and cite an example of each from a television news show.

Suggested Class Discussions

1. Invite a local television film cameraman to address the class on his work and demonstrate the equipment he uses. Discuss.

2. View news film clips from a local station and discuss the various shots and their functions. (For this purpose a reversible projector is best, so that each story can be rerun quickly as many times as desired.)

Chapter 9

Film
Editing
for the
Writer

The art of film, as was previously indicated, lies more in the editing than in the shooting. Significantly, many of the most successful directors and producers of theatrical films began their careers in the editing room, where they learned and mastered the techniques of building the film story. Contrarily, the trouble with most home movies made by amateurs is that they are not edited; not enough of the film ends on the cutting room floor. It is often the face on the cutting-room floor that makes the picture a work of art.

The television news writer, working under time, technical, and cost restrictions much more severe than those which limit theatrical or documentary filmmakers, can seldom achieve the finesse in his editing which they do. But still he can never allow his editing to descend to the level of crudity and amateurishness of the home movie maker; his work should display consistent professional polish.

Working with the Editor

In the news film editing room the writer is boss. The editor makes the purely technical decisions, or at least argues for them, but the writer makes the more important editorial decisions which frequently override technical considerations.

The wise writer of course listens carefully to the suggestions of the experienced editor, who is likely to see cinematic possibilities which the writer can easily overlook. A talented cutter can sometimes save a badly shot story by clever editing, although if the story has been shot with too great a disregard for the problems of the editor it may be unusable. But cutting film is always a cooperative task, and unless that cooperation is a two-way street it is only too likely to be a dead-end.

An example of how this cooperation works is frequently encountered in the jump-cut. Editors consider the jump-cut little short of a felony, because their main interest is in the technical cinematic perfection of the film. But the writer is more concerned with the continuity and flow of thought of the story itself, and if the jump-cut is not too distracting he may prefer to use it for the sake of keeping the *story* moving smoothly rather than to interrupt story continuity with a bridge or cutaway simply to keep the *picture* moving smoothly. In such a case the writer, after taking into account the editor's objections, may exercise his editorial prerogative and order the jump-cut used.

On the other hand, the writer is well advised to heed the editor on the length of silent shots and sequences where the cinematic possibilities should be the dominant consideration. It is easier to "squeeze" or "stretch" narration over the film in scripting than it is to squeeze or stretch the film to some arbitrarily predetermined length. And the editor's cinematic perception is apt to be sharper than the writer's. For example, if a story is planned to run, say, 30 seconds, that should be considered not as a rigid goal but as an approximate aim. It may be a better film story at 20 seconds, or at 40 seconds; on this the editor's advice should be taken.

Transitions

In news film the direct cut is the *only* transition device that can be achieved in the cutting room; others are accomplished electronically in the control room, just as in theatrical films they are accomplished photochemically in the optical effects laboratory.

Therefore any optical effect involving two film picture sources requires multiple-chain projection. A fade can be created by fading in or out the film picture originating with a single film chain; but a dissolve or wipe or superimposition, or any type of matte or key shot, can be created only by a mix of the pictures originating with separate film chains (assuming, of course, that both picture sources are films).

Thus the first decision the writer may have to make in the editing room is whether to edit the story for single-chain or double-chain projection. If the story has been shot for single-chain, he may have no choice. But if the choice is debatable, the writer's decision involves the value to the story of the desired optical effects, the amount of time remaining for editing before deadline, and the number of film chains available for the story.

Assuming the chains are available, the mood value of the story may determine the value of optical effects. The abruptness of a cut tends to break a delicate mood, whereas dissolving from one shot to the next may sustain or even intensify the desired mood. Dissolves may also be needed to indicate changes in time or locale.

If the hour of broadcast is near, time may be an extremely important factor in the decision, because double-chain almost doubles the work of the film editor, who must assemble two film sequences for the one story. Even if the editing can be completed in time for air, it may be too late to include the story in the regular film reels; then it becomes a question of whether additional film chains are available to project the story. In any event, double-chain projection increases the complexity of the work in the control room, thereby increasing the ever-present possibility of error in broadcast.

Thus, the writer's decision must be based on a rapid evaluation of technical factors, in addition to the artistic values he wishes to inject into the story by means of transition devices.

Rollthru

The rollthru is used whenever it is desired to let the film continue rolling but neither picture nor sound is to be used. It consists of the proper length of leader.

Between film stories The rollthru is used to avoid recuing the film for the next story, especially where the time between stories is insufficient for the technicians in telecine to recue the film. During the rollthru a picture of something else is taken: a shot of the air man in studio, or perhaps a shot of a still. The timing of scripted narration during rollthru must be precise, because the length of the rollthru is predetermined. Rollthrus should not be used when there is time for a recue, because the possibility of mistiming the narration, either in writing or in delivery, increases in proportion to the length of the rollthru. A recue should require no more than 15 to 20 seconds.

Within film stories The rollthru may be used where it is desired to cut away to another picture source. The second picture source may be a studio shot, but the most common use of the rollthru within a story is in the case of multiple-chain film projection: the picture from one film chain is shown while the film reel on the second chain runs off leader. The separate reels of a multiple-chain story are given letter designations: A-reel, B-reel, C-reel.

Editing the Sequence

In editing a sequence the primary consideration is to let the film tell as much of the story as it can. The chronology dictates the order of shots. Consider a hypothetical sequence depicting a fire and rescue:

We see flames shooting from a building. Firemen pour water on the blaze. The gathering crowd watches in excitement. Someone points upward. A man waves for help from an upper window. His wife pushes forward out of the crowd, looking upward in fear. The firemen raise a ladder. The man crawls out on a ledge to escape the flames. Agony is written on the woman's face. A fireman climbs the rising ladder. The man waves again, urging him to hurry. The woman turns her head away, unable to watch. The ladder touches the ledge, and the fireman helps the trapped man onto the ladder. Great spouts of steam rise from the fire as more hoses are turned on it. A wall collapses. The rescued man reaches the ground and rushes into the arms of his tearful wife. The flames subside. The rescued man shakes hands with his rescuer, and his wife impulsively kisses the fireman. The fireman grins in embarrassment. Final shot of the smoking embers.

Each sentence in this paragraph represents a shot. The paragraph is a sequence. It is, to be sure, a sequence of a completeness we are not likely to see very often. Usually the film crew arrives on the scene too late to shoot the beginning of the story as we have described it, the cameraman misses some shots while he is reloading, and too much is happening at once for half a dozen cameramen to shoot it all. But this hypothetical sequence will serve to demonstrate how the chronological film story is told.

Each sentence not only describes a shot; it also indicates what type of shot it is.

The first sentence, "We see flames shooting from a building," is an establishing shot; it shows where we are and what is happening. It is also necessarily a wide shot, else it could not show what the sentence says it shows.

"Firemen pour water on the blaze" continues the establishing process by placing firemen on the scene; it is also necessarily a wide shot because the information contained in the sentence cannot be contained on the film in any closer shot. The same factors apply to the third sentence.

"Someone points upward" is a medium shot: too close, and we cannot see him point; too wide, and he is lost in the crowd.

"A man waves for help from an upper window" might be a long shot zooming into medium.

The final shot of the sequence is a wide shot. Notice that the story both begins and ends with a wide shot. This is not a rule to be followed, but it illustrates one principle of film: successively closer shots lead the viewer into the story, successively wider shots lead him out of it. Successively closer shots increase involvement, successively wider shots increase detachment.

Further study of the paragraph will reveal that as the progression of events becomes more firmly established, the proportion of reaction shots increases, although not by any fixed ratio. "Agony is written on the woman's face" is a reaction shot; it also must be a close shot. "The man waves again, urging him to hurry" is both action and reaction shot; it is a medium shot. "The woman turns her head away, unable to watch" is pure reaction shot. "The rescued man shakes hands with his rescuer, and his wife impulsively kisses the fireman" is entirely reaction. So is "The fireman grins in embarrassment," a close shot.

In accordance with the logic of film, this increase in the proportion of reaction shots means a buildup in the film's emotional content, and therefore an increase in audience involvement. This, it should also be noted, is achieved by selection of shots which concentrate more and more on the *people* and less and less on the fire; people are more interesting than fires. The burning of the building may provide spectacular action footage, but that event is primarily of interest to the building's owner and his insurance agent. The rescue adds the element of human drama which deepens the cinematic meaning, and it is this *emotional* action, not the physical action, which gives this film story its greatest value. That value is most sharply impressed upon the viewer by the reaction shots.

There is an apparent contradiction here, but it is more apparent than real. Emotion is an abstraction, and abstractions cannot be filmed; film is limited to the depiction of physical reality. But this apparent contradiction is actually the source of film's great power, and in this rather ordinary tale of a fire and rescue we see exactly how it works.

We see it especially through the wife of the rescued man. Her anxiety, her fear, her relief and gratitude are all abstractions which we cannot film. But we *can* film the actions which betray these emotions: her face distorting in fear, the turn of her head away from the unbearable, her cathartic tears when the suspense is ended, the kiss of gratitude she gives the rescuer. The shots of the fire itself, the physical action shots, serve primarily to establish the validity of her emotional reactions; they set up the viewer for the reaction shots. And the viewer does not merely witness these reactions; he empathizes with the wife. He actually *feels* the identical emotions that she feels; he *lives through* the experience with her.

By selecting out of the footage the cameraman has shot those particular shots which focus on the human drama, and by arranging them chronologically to carry the viewer through the action while constantly deepening that focus, the writer of this story has created involvement.

Time Compression

However real the chronology of this fire sequence may seem to be, it is false. The fire may have taken an hour in actual occurrence and filming, but the edited film report may tell the story in a minute or two. Obviously, then, the editing process has compressed time artificially.

Time compression is familiar to anyone who has seen a news film report of, say, a baseball game. All the long dull stretches are eliminated; only the high spots and dramatic moments of the game are shown. The shots of the crucial plays are connected by cutaway shots, usually of crowd reaction; a two-second cutaway may cover five innings of dull, indecisive baseball, but when the picture returns to the game something important is happening.

Thus the cutaway shot may be thought of as a time-bridging transition device. However, in the baseball example the process might equally be viewed as intercutting the game and the crowd reaction. Examination of the fire and rescue story will reveal examples of intercutting, between the rescue action itself and the wife's reaction; in this case, the time-bridging shots are not cutaways but essential portions of the action itself. In either case the purpose is to eliminate action which does not contribute to the progression of the story, and this process of elimination, or selectivity of shots, necessarily compresses the chronology artificially.

An understanding of this artificiality of cinematic time, a full consciousness that the writer is working with unreal time to create the impression of real time, is essential to effective film editing. In particular it demands of the writer the ability to distinguish relevant from irrelevant action, and that distinction derives from the writer's original concept of the story. The uncut film of the fire story above might have contained much visually interesting footage of the fire-fighting action which was never used; it was the writer's choice to focus his story on the rescue, and that decision enabled him to determine which shots were relevant to his concept and which were not. By discarding all other footage, he was able to compress the apparent time of the event into a real film time short enough to fit into a news show.

In this case the decision may seem obvious and the point somewhat labored, but nearly every film story imposes on the writer the necessity of making a time compression which is directly related to his conceptual approach to the story. That conceptual approach is determined by his judgment of both news values and cinematic values.

Editing the Montage

The need for artistry in cutting is most obvious in the montage, where the chronological order of events may give no clue to the editing concept. Frequently, though not always, the montage is distinguished by three characteristics which differ from those of the typical sequence:

1. Lack of time compression. The montage in its pure form often is characterized by timelessness, a total lack of any time continuum. There is no time relationship whatever among the shots of the various montages mentioned in the previous chapter: the paintings in the gallery, the shots of children at play, the shots of ghetto life.

2. Lack of progression. Similarly, there is no story progression in these same montages. There are no beginning, middle, and end to the story, no development of a line of action, no climax and denouement. It is not so much that nothing happens as that the montage ends as it began, and nothing has changed.

3. Monotony of shots. Variation in the pattern of shots is an inherent characteristic of the film sequence; we do not ordinarily encounter a long sequence of close shots unrelieved by wider angles, or vice versa. Such a calculated monotony would have a specific artistic purpose; for example, a montage of wide shots of the Kansas plains would have the effect of emphasizing the flatness, the emptiness, the "big sky" quality of that area. This type of montage is perhaps the least frequently encountered, but it is typical of the montage in its purest form.

It should be remembered that our distinction between sequence and montage is quite arbitrary, and that in practice almost every sequence will share to some degree the characteristics of the montage, and vice versa. The dividing line between them is extremely hazy. We make the distinction to make a point, and the examples we have chosen are chosen for the purpose of exaggerating the differences in order to make that point, which is that the writer should know what he is about before he begins to edit the story.

Is he trying to show the progression of an event? Then he will construct a sequence.

Is he trying to state a theme, to demonstrate a condition, to establish a mood? Then he will construct a montage.

The montage is essentially editorial in nature, since the selection of shots is predetermined not by events, but by the concept which the writer wishes to express in visual terms. The montage is an event in itself, an event which would not have occurred had not the writer willed it to occur. And because the montage is an editorial statement, the writer must be sure of his ground before he makes that statement. He must not let himself be so carried away by the emotional possibilities of his material that he loses his sense of responsibility to the public. He must ask himself whether the theme stated by the montage is an accurate reflection of a condition involving the public interest.

This use of montage in news film is not frequent, but where it is appropriate it can be strikingly effective because of the capacity of the montage for creating mood and involvement and thereby altering public opinion.

A film story concerning a proposed reduction in state funding for the training of handicapped children in California public schools employed a montage of shots of children struggling, with the aid of their specially trained teachers, to overcome their handicaps. So emotionally effective was the story, so overwhelming the public response, that the state administration quietly shelved the proposal.

It is very easy to generate viewer empathy, even commitment, with film of handicapped children. But this story also involved matters of fiscal policy and priorities, as well as political ideology, which the writer had to appraise before he could responsibly proceed to stir the public's emotions in such a manner.

The power which the writer can wield from the darkness of the editing room is awesome, and he can never allow himself to forget that while events may dictate the editing of the sequence, in the montage the editing literally creates the event.

Narration over Film

Most film reports require narration to fill out the story. In the fire and rescue sequence mentioned above, narration is required to supply information about the exact location of the fire, its cause, the identities of the people involved, and the amount of damage; none of this information is supplied by the film. This information is written in script form, to be delivered by the air man in studio, and to the extent possible it should be keyed to the film shots.

Keying narration to film For example, the building and its location should be established by narration over the establishing film shots, because such narration is also establishing in nature. The narration at the first moment the wife is seen should identify her, to enable the audience to understand her emotional reaction to the situation. Such emotionally noninvolving information as the amount of the damage could well be delivered over the closing shot. If the narration is scripted in this manner, by keying it to the shots, it supplements and reinforces the visual image, even to the extent of increasing viewer detachment at the close of the story by supplying noninvolving information over the closing wide shot which itself is selected to increase viewer detachment.

Redundancy between film and script In no case should the narration duplicate information on the film. The shot of "a wall collapses" should not be accompanied by the statement that a wall collapsed. The shot of the wife kissing her husband's rescuer should not be accompanied by a statement that she did this; if any explanation is scripted for this shot, it should be oblique: "Mrs. Jones impulsively showed her gratitude to Fireman Smith." The oblique reference does not insult the viewer by telling him what he is seeing, but it may supply needed information if the viewer has lost the context of the film (if, for example, he has not previously seen Fireman Smith on a close enough shot to be able to identify him in this shot and therefore understand why Mrs. Jones is kissing this particular fireman).

In other words, the function of the narration is limited to supplementary information. Redundancies between picture and script are worse than redundancies in print, because the impact of film is greater; film exaggerates both the good and the bad.

Fitting copy to film Not every second of film need be covered by copy, and here is where the writer must consider the problem of the air man. If the air man has to race through the copy, he can give it little inflection or meaning in his delivery; it is easier for him to stretch copy that is too short than to try to squeeze in too much talk. Often a pause in narration is more meaningful than any words. And a competent air man can always ad lib a few additional words if the copy is extremely short. Therefore, in scripting copy over film, the writer should always lean toward the short side.

Film domination of script Allowing the film to tell its own story in its own way implies that the writer should, in most cases, tailor the narration to the film rather than vice versa. That is, he should first cut the film with the cinematic possibilities, rather than the narration, as his first concern.

As was mentioned earlier, it is equally wise for the writer not to specify the exact length of shots and sequences unless the time consideration is of overriding importance; such decisions are better left to the film editor with his more acute sense of visual continuity. This is especially true of all types of moving shots (pan, trucking, dolly, zoom, etc.), which tend to define their own time because most desirably they both begin and end in static position; therefore the time required for the movement determines the length of the shot. If the writer is forced to enter or leave a moving shot in mid-movement, the best transition for the purpose is a dissolve, not a cut.

Bridges The most frequent exception to this general rule is narration over a film bridge—a shot or sequence of either silent or sound-under film connecting, in most cases, two sequences of sound film. In the bridge the necessary narration may be more important than the film itself, and the length of the required narration therefore determines the length of the bridge, even if that length exhausts the purely filmic considerations.

Lead-ins The silent lead-in to sound film, with narration over, is frequently used to establish the scene. Here the writer has much more flexibility than with the bridge because narration may precede the film as well as continue over the lead-in.

If possible, lead-in narration should be keyed to the film shots; if the final shot of the lead-in is a shot of the reporter who conducted the interview, appropriate narration at that point would identify the reporter and state the nature of his question, the answer to which is coming up immediately afterward on the sound film.

But while the principles of establishing film shots apply to the lead-in, the keying of narration to shots is perhaps less important here than in any other type of narration over film. If the best film lead-in requires, say, 12 seconds, but the required narration cannot be delivered in less than 20 seconds, the writer simply scripts the opening film cue at 12 seconds before sound film, leaving the preceding 8 seconds for standup copy.

It might be added that, as this example shows, the writer cannot work without a stop watch.

Some consideration should be given to the *backup lead-in* to sound film. This is where several seconds of the sound take immediately preceding the sound to be used are "blooped" (that is, the sound is removed by degaussing or neutralizing the magnetic field of the sound track) and used as a silent lead-in with voice over. This sometimes provides an excellent establishing shot (if, for example, it is a two-shot leading into an interview) with very smooth, in fact unbroken, visual continuity leading into the sound sequence.

But the backup lead-in can be dangerous because it may lead to an upcut or an overlong pause between studio narration and film sound. The problem becomes evident only in studio, where the air man times his lead-in delivery partly by watching the film picture on monitor. Unless the field reporter is using a hand mike, which the air man can see moving toward the interviewee as the reporter finishes his blooped question, the air man has no visual cue indicating when the film sound is about to begin. (We are discussing a time span of no more than half a second.) After several seconds of film lead-in, and especially if the director errs slightly in cuing the film roll or in taking the film shot, or if the writer has mistimed the lead-in narration, the result may be unprofessional.

The more satisfactory lead-in provides the air man with a brief final shot in the lead-in sequence which constitutes a visual cue. For example, after a 4-second wide shot of reporter and interviewee, a 2-second close shot of the reporter on a reverse angle is an excellent visual cue for upcoming sound, especially if it is indicated in the script for the air man's guidance. It might be noted that this brief lead-in sequence also establishes the scene and identifies the field reporter visually, while at the same time the reverse of the field reporter eliminates any possible jump-cut between lead-in and sound film; the reverse therefore functions as a cutaway.

Editing to Time Restrictions

The time allotted to the story by the producer is a major factor in determining how the film is to be edited. Most television news writers chafe under time restrictions, just as newspaper writers chafe under space restrictions. But this is merely one of the limitations which force the writer to improve his abilities. This particular restriction forces him to search the uncut film carefully for the most meaningful shots, and to be ruthless in discarding film which does not advance the main story line.

If we return again to our fire and rescue film story, and if we suppose that the time allotment is too brief to allow the film to include all of the shots in the original edited version, we quickly see several shots which could be eliminated to shorten the film. The basic story could be told with only the following shots:

The man crawls out on a ledge to escape the flames. Agony is written on the woman's face. A fireman climbs the rising ladder. The woman turns her head away, unable to watch. The ladder touches the ledge, and the fireman helps the trapped man onto the ladder. A wall collapses. The rescued man reaches the ground and rushes into the arms of his tearful wife.

We have eliminated 13 of the original 20 edited shots, and still we have managed to retain the heart of the story, the rescue and the wife's reaction. This final cut is not as satisfying, and part of the broader picture is missing, to be sure. But a great many more shots were missing from our original cut; it is only a question of degree. And by paring the film to the bone we have at least halved the time it takes to tell the story.

Editing to time, if we may repeat our refrain, amounts to no more than reducing the story to its most relevant shots. Or, to put it another way, the writer's concept is determined in part by his time allotment.

However, there comes a point where the writer must stand in defense of his story. If the time allotment is so severe that even the seven shots listed above cannot all be included, it begins to be difficult to tell the story adequately. For example, if shot number six is eliminated from this seven-shot story, it begins to disintegrate cinematically because of the resulting jump-cut. The jump-cut calls attention to itself and thereby turns the viewer's attention away from the story line. At such a point the writer must either argue for adequate time or recommend that the story be dropped from the show; he may lose on both counts in this argument with the producer, but at least the fault, from that moment on, lies with the producer and not with the writer.

Sound Film

To this point only peripheral attention has been given to the problems and opportunities presented by the addition of sound to the film. All of the editing principles stated thus far apply equally to sound and silent film. But the addition of sound creates new problems and offers new opportunities. Two types of sound are recorded on film: natural sound and voice sound.

Natural sound Because sound as well as sight is part of our environmental experience, the addition of natural sound to film increases its effectiveness enormously. It is "natural" to hear the growl of gears as the truck accelerates, the clang of steel as hammer hits anvil, or (in the case of our much-used fire and rescue story) the howl of sirens and the crash of falling walls. These are natural sounds, as the filmmaker uses the term.

In an earlier era in which the shooting of news sound film was reserved almost entirely for voice sound, Edward R. Murrow insisted that his film crews shoot sound film rather than silent film of actuality whenever possible. The effectiveness of that insistence is evident today when screening stock historical footage; Murrow's film is instantly identifiable. The projection room viewer, watching thousands of feet of film, mostly silent, shot by crews of many different producers, suddenly feels the past "come alive" as Murrow's film speaks to him. The Korean War becomes real and present, not shadowy and historical, as the viewer hears the unmistakable crunch of boots on ice in subzero cold, or the ominous thunder of distant artillery. Sound film is more trouble to shoot and more trouble to edit, but the results certainly justify the effort.

Natural sound makes the work of both writer and air man easier, because it so intensifies the impact of the film that it can "carry" the story with little or no narration. We are so conditioned to the presence of sound that long periods of silence, even over film, make us uncomfortable; the writer feels the need to inject at least a few words of narration now and then. But when the film speaks with its own voice, uttering all the sounds of life and activity which we simultaneously see, narration sometimes becomes superfluous. The best news film simply lets the viewer see and hear what happened, without comment by the writer.

Where narration is necessary over film of actuality, much of the natural sound's effectiveness can be retained by running it under (at a lower level than) the narrator's voice. This adds "presence" to the film.

If the narration originates live in studio, the writer sometimes must include narration cues in his script because the air man cannot hear the film sound; it cannot be fed to the studio loudspeakers and broadcast at the same time because the sound in studio would "feed back" into the audio system through the air man's open microphone. However, inclusion of such cues in the script—cues keyed to the natural sound on the film—is important only if the narration is keyed to the film sound more than to the picture; the air man can see the picture on his monitor.

Voice sound The editing of film for voice sound is primarily a matter of selecting content rather than searching for cinematic effects. One of the hardest lessons the print-oriented writer has to learn is that a speech, statement, or interview cannot be edited in film as it can in copy. The newspaper writer can pick a dozen widely scattered significant quotations out of any statement and string them together in print as if they had been delivered in sequence. On film this produces a choppy, jerky, annoying visual effect which destroys the viewer's ability to absorb the content. The picture dominates, and the film must be edited with due respect for that domination.

Thus the television news writer must select reasonably long, uninterrupted shots, and only two or perhaps three of them at most for the typical news story. These shots may include much unwanted content, because few people speak concisely; they ramble, pause, digress, and repeat. These takes will, however, reveal the personality of the speaker much more clearly than any printed account of what he says. Whatever is important that the writer could not cover with film, he can cover with copy.

Whatever the sound cut chosen, the speaker's voice should drop as he concludes. That is the way we are accustomed to hearing people speak. To end a sound take on a rising or suspended inflection gives the impression that the speaker has been cut off in mid-sentence; this irritates the viewer, who naturally assumes that he has been prevented from hearing something of significance. In other words, the viewer becomes aware of the editing process, and this distracts his attention from the content.

There are a few people who never drop their voices to a concluding inflection, and they are the despair of film editors. Fortunately such people are seldom of public prominence, perhaps because they cannot think well, and thus they are not frequently encountered on news film. When they are, there is no really satisfactory solution to the editing problem.

Lip-flap In single-system film the 28-frame offset between sound and corresponding picture creates an editing problem. Since cutting the film at the desired first frame of picture would eliminate the sound which goes with that picture, the film *must* be cut at the sound, 28 frames ahead of the picture. But this leaves the film editor with slightly more than one second of picture which he does not want, but which he must use.

There is no problem if, for example, the desired sound take begins with the answer to a reporter's question; during the question an interviewee's lips are motionless while he listens, and most questions take more than a second or so to ask. But suppose the writer wishes to use, say, 1 minute out of the middle of a 3-minute SOF take during which the speaker never pauses for a second between words or sentences. At the beginning of this 1-minute take the speaker's lips will be seen silently forming the words he spoke during that last second before the first word of the desired take was recorded. This lip-flap, as it is commonly called, is undesirable for purely artistic reasons and also because the viewer is distracted; he cannot help wondering what sound has been omitted from the film, what it is that he did not hear.

The film editor, as always more concerned with technical perfection than with content, will usually prefer to cut into the speech where the speaker pauses long enough to avoid lip-flap. However, the writer may feel that the editorial content is more important than any other consideration; again, the decision is the writer's.

It is sometimes possible to avoid lip-flap with a *sound overlap*, but only where there is no jump-cut. If the two sound takes to be spliced together are of totally different subjects (such as a natural-sound wide shot of a crowd followed by a close shot of the speaker addressing the crowd), there is no jump-cut. But if two separate takes of the speaker himself are to be spliced together, there is nearly always a jump-cut unless the camera view of the subject changes considerably (as from a wide shot to a close shot, or vice versa); two successive close shots of the same person almost always produce a jump-cut, however minute the "jump."

If there is no jump-cut, an overlap is possible because the 28 frames of lip-flap at the beginning of the second take can now be covered by the sound at the end of the first take. Figure 9–1 illustrates the difference between a normal single-system splice and an overlap splice.

In the overlap the viewer *sees* the speaker mouthing the last words of Take 1 while he *hears* the speaker saying the first words of Take 2. There is usually some discrepancy in lip movement, but it is seldom so noticeable as to call attention to itself and it lasts for only a second. The overlap, where possible, is always better than its two alternatives, which are lip-flap or a cutaway shot.

Another solution to the lip-flap problem is the SOF transposer, which unfortunately is not widely used. One reason is the cost; a better one is the time required for transposing the sound track. The transposer, a device sold under various trade names, transposes the sound track 28 frames so that the sound is directly opposite its corresponding picture. (This, of course, cannot be done with optical sound tracks.) Once the sound track is transposed, the film can be cut at the picture. After the film is edited, it must be run through the transposer again to reestablish the 28-frame separation for projection purposes.

Intercutting

Intercutting, sometimes called *cross-cutting*, is one of the most basic arts of the film story. Everyone is familiar with its use in the movie western, where the film intercuts shots of the wagon train fighting off the Indians and shots of the cavalry riding to the rescue. But this technique can be put to many uses besides the winning of the West.

Arguments on two sides of a public issue are frequently presented by intercutting the statements of opposing advocates. Spokesmen for the two sides may be interviewed at different times in different places, but instead of editing each interview separately the writer intercuts them so that each speaker seems to reply to the other's arguments. Not only

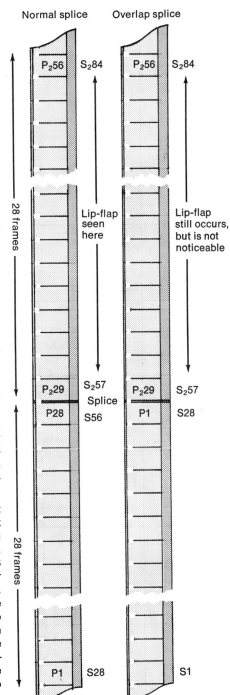

Normal splice   Overlap splice

$P_2 56$ $S_2 84$ $P_2 56$ $S_2 84$

Lip-flap
seen
here

Lip-flap
still occurs,
but is not
noticeable

28 frames

$P_2 29$ $S_2 57$ $P_2 29$ $S_2 57$
P28   Splice   P1   S28
         S56

28 frames

P1   S28   S1

Figure 9-1 Frames in Figure 9-1 are numbered sequentially for ease of identification, and the sound corresponding to each frame is given the same number. Thus S28 should be heard while seeing frame P28.

Lip-flap occurs during the first 28 frames of the second shot ($P_2 29$ to $P_2 56$) unless the speaker has paused for the equivalent of 28 frames immediately preceding $P_2 29$. But since the first desired sound of the second shot begins at $S_2 57$, these frames cannot be eliminated.

In the overlap splice the cut is made at the last desired sound of the first shot (S28) rather than at its corresponding picture (P28) as in the normal splice. Thus the viewer hears the sound S1–S28 while seeing the picture $P_2 29$–$P_2 56$, for which there is no corresponding sound. Two visual considerations limit the use of the overlap splice: there must be no jump-cut, and the lip movements seen in $P_2 29$–$P_2 56$ must roughly match the words heard on the sound track S1–S28. In practice the splice may be made anywhere between P1 and P28 to achieve the best simulation of lip-sync.

are the opposing positions directly juxtaposed, almost as in a debate, but the pace of the story is quickened.

A story concerning a municipally-sponsored project to find jobs for ghetto residents was shot entirely in an office where project employees telephoned various industrial firms, explained the project, and asked company personnel executives to offer job commitments to the project. But telephone conversations of any kind contain long, dull sections in which the caller is merely listening and no information is conveyed to anyone watching. In this case the writer edited the film by intercutting the various telephone calls, using only the "action" portions and eliminating all the dull, noninformative sections. This form of editing was a way of achieving time compression by intercutting. Story progression was accomplished by selecting the shots so that each one conveyed new information to the viewer. Shot 1 showed a caller making the initial contact, Shot 2 explained the project, Shot 3 demonstrated the "sales pitch" (explaining the advantages of the project to society in general and the executive's company in particular), Shot 4 showed the conclusion of a losing (no sale) conversation, Shot 5 showed a winner. The entire story (almost) was told by intercutting actuality shots; only a small amount of additional narration was needed to round out the viewer's understanding of what was happening.

Another way of using the intercut technique to compress time was demonstrated by the editing of a story on a telephone wiretap or "bugging" device. The story began by showing the reporter and the bug's manufacturer in the latter's office; the manufacturer showed the bug to the reporter (and thus to the camera), then installed it in his own telephone—a process which took only a few seconds. The two men then discussed the bug: how it worked, its various uses, and its social and political implications. Meanwhile, in another room nearby, a second official of the company dialed the number of the bugged telephone and blew a special whistle; the interview in progress in the manufacturer's office had just explained that this process activated the bug and prevented the bugged telephone from ringing. Thus two actions were now in progress at the same time: (1) an explanatory interview in the first office, and (2) surreptitious listening in the second office. By intercutting these two lines of action, the writer enabled the viewer to listen in at both ends of the line; at the same time that the viewer heard the interview (which explained what was going on, and why, and how), he saw a demonstration of the subject of the interview. With one stone the writer here killed three birds: time compression, depiction of two simultaneous and related lines of action in two separate locales, and reportage by depiction of actuality.

(For a discussion of the technique of shooting this particular story, see page 180.)

Multiple-Chain Projection

To this point our discussion has assumed almost exclusively the use of single-chain projection of single-system film. The use of two or, occasionally, even more film chains expands the horizon. Some news stories simply cannot be told adequately without the simultaneous use of two or more film chains.

Double-system film The simplest type of double-chain projection involves double-system film; the picture track is run on one chain, the sound track on another. The chains must be synchronized by an electronic interlock.

Double-system frees the writer of the problem of lip-flap and increases the flexibility of editing in other ways, but from the purely journalistic point of view there is little if any difference between double-system and single-system film; it amounts to no more than a single film which comes in two pieces.

Double-chain, single-system The significant advantage obtained by projecting single-system film on two chains simultaneously is that sound *and* picture can originate with *either* chain, or with *both* simultaneously. This *multiplies by nine* the possible combinations of double-chain projection of double-system film. And no interlock is needed.

In practical terms, double-chain projection of single-system film makes possible almost all types of optical effects, such as supers, dissolves, and wipes. Similarly, it makes possible the sound *segue*, which is to sound what the dissolve is to picture. And it makes possible any combination of optical effects and segues. In other words, it gives the television newsman almost as much flexibility in production as the theatrical filmmaker.

Perhaps the most typical use of double-chain single-system is the self-contained film story complete with both actuality and on-scene narration, in which the actuality film runs on one chain, the narration on the other. The story usually (but by no means always) opens with an A-reel shot of the reporter who by narration establishes the story. Then picture and sound move to the second chain (B-reel) to show actuality, the actuality picture sometimes being bridged at some points by the sound of narration on the A-reel. At the conclusion both picture and sound move back to the A-reel for the closing narration.

The same technique is often used to illustrate an interview. We see the reporter interviewing the highway engineer about the problems encountered in building the highway. As they talk, the scene dissolves to what they are talking about: the earth-moving machines, the surveyors, the trucks hauling ready-mixed concrete. But over the sounds of these activities, the interview goes on.

Subliminal effects are best accomplished in television news by the use of double-chain single-system. Theoretically subliminal shots are possible with single-chain single-system, but the insertion of the subliminal shots (only perhaps two to four frames in length) interrupts the single-system sound track, and the close proximity of the splices causes the film to jump annoyingly as it runs through the projector. It is better to run the subliminal shots on a second chain, scripting cues to direct the TD to cut to the second chain as briefly as possible; the effect is not as precise as can be obtained in a film processing laboratory, but it will do considering the time, cost, and technical restrictions under which the news writer must work.

Where music is an integral part of a story the double-chain single-system technique is often highly effective. A story on a theatrical group formed by members of a farm workers' union opened on a shot of two members of the group performing a musical number from their repertoire; this was on the A-reel. After one verse and chorus, the music was faded under a narrative bridge on the B-reel, while the picture held on the A-reel. The narrative bridge led into an interview with the director of the group, on the B-reel; where the bridge ended and the interview began, the picture dissolved to the B-reel. The music continued under the entire interview. When the interview ended, the picture again dissolved to the A-reel, the music was brought up full for a final chorus, and the story ended on a fade-out. The effect was as if the musical number was continuing in the background throughout the interview, providing a continuity which the story would not have had without it.

The interview portion of this story actually had no music in the background, else it could not have been edited; editing the film would have destroyed the musical continuity. Therefore the music had to be recorded separately and mixed with the interview sound by running the two tracks simultaneously on separate film chains. By the same technique the music of a band might run throughout a film report on a parade, the music on one reel and edited shots of the parade on another.

Similar use of A- and B-reels to achieve an artistic effect within a meaningful social context was demonstrated by a story on a proposal for residential and recreational development of the last tidal marshlands in Southern California, in upper Newport Bay. The proposal triggered opposition from conservationists; in particular, a small group of biologists at the nearby University of California at Irvine objected, pointing out that the salt marshlands were the only remaining habitat within hundreds of miles for more than a hundred species of waterfowl and many marine species as well. The film report began with aerial shots of the bay leading into a reporter's bayside interview with one of the biologists. After the interview was well under way, the scene dissolved into a montage of SOF shots of the birds on the B-reel, while the interview continued on the A-reel. Even after the interview ended, the montage continued for several seconds before fade-out, thus, in effect, letting the birds plead their own cause and giving them the last "word."

A more sophisticated technique, involving triple-chain projection, was used in a news documentary report on efforts of college students to help the disadvantaged in ghetto tutorial projects, in prison, and in a summer camp for diabetic children. The A-reel and B-reel carried montages of actuality, showing the students engaged in their projects. The C-reel carried interviews with the same students, in which they expressed their motivation; this reel was used for sound only, the interviewer's questions were edited out, and a slight echo was laid on the sound to give it a rather ethereal quality. The A- and B-reels were used to dissolve from one locale to another; narration was supplied voice over in studio. When the nature of each student's activity was thus suitably established, the natural sound from the first two reels was faded under and the ethereal C-reel sound was brought in over. The effect was as if the viewer were hearing the thoughts of the students while seeing them engaged in their projects. The action continued throughout; it was not brought to a halt for conventional film interviews, but the motivational information which such interviews could have contributed was conveyed in a much more cinematic fashion.

It is especially in stories of this type, utilizing all of the possibilities offered by multiple-chain projection of single-system film, that the writer has the greatest opportunity to achieve the unique potential of television. His challenge is not simply to present an event recorded on film, but to use the art of film to convey the style, the substance and the meaning of an event.

In the typical multiple-chain story, two lines of action (or information) are in progress simultaneously, each reinforcing and explaining the other; the sound and picture of actuality are reinforced by the sound of explanatory narration or interview. Nothing like this is possible in any other medium, and this possibility drastically alters the structure of the news story as compared with the structure of that same story in any other medium. The more artistically (in the cinematic sense) the story is told, the greater the difference in structure is likely to be. Yet most stories will, in general, follow the structural progression of climax-cause-effect outlined in Chapter 6.

Consider the story of the farm workers' theatrical group mentioned above. It begins not with a statement of the climax (the performance), but with the actual performance itself, in which both style and substance are inherent and self-evident. Such explanatory information as is necessary is provided by the narrative bridge without interruption of the climax, which actually continues throughout the story. The interview, during which this continuing climax is subordinated, explains first the cause and then the hoped-for effect: the group's motivational origins in the depressed conditions of the farm workers, and the hope that their status and pride can be elevated by carrying their message to the public by theatrical performance. Thus meaning, significance, and social context are made apparent to the viewer. The two lines of action, performance (climax) and interview (cause and effect), are simultaneous. At the end of the story the climax, subordinated in mid-structure, rises to dominance again as at the beginning, this final reprise giving the total structure something of Aristotle's unity.

Special Devices

Many television news stories can be improved by the use of special devices which are so varied in character that, as a group, they fall into no particular category.

Film loop The film loop is just what its name indicates: a length of film spliced to itself to form an endless loop. Since it is endless, it can be projected for an indefinite length of time. It can be used for picture (provided there is no jump-cut at the splice) or for sound.

One story called for repeated dissolves to a shot of an American flag waving in the breeze. The solution was the film loop, to which the story could dissolve at any time; the flag was always waving.

More commonly the film loop is used for natural sound to accompany the picture projected by another chain. The loop is always a wild track; no sync with picture is possible.

ET The ET, or audio tape (to which the same term is often loosely applied), also makes a useful wild track. It may be in the station's sound library, or it may be purchased from a professional sound library; in either case it adds a sound dimension to film without the necessity of shooting film for the purpose.

A story in point involved in-flight shots of aircraft used in an airline pilot training program. It was desired to intercut interior SOF shots of the training plane, in which the instructor and student gave and received orders, with exterior silent shots of the same plane in flight (the latter shot from another plane alongside). But to make the silent shots longer than the briefest cutaways and thus preserve their cinematic value would have involved losing all sound for the duration of each silent shot; this would have distracted the viewer and ruined the story. The solution was an ET of a comparable plane in flight. The ET was run throughout the sequence; when the film cut to the interior SOF, the louder film sound completely drowned the ET (in part because the SOF naturally included sound of the plane in which it was shot, sound with a very close presence). Over the silent shots the ET maintained a realistic distant sound presence.

Studio picture with film sound Occasionally—very occasionally—a story presents an opportunity to mix studio picture with film sound. For example, a film report on the teaching of a unique type of music (*Orffschulwerk*) ended with a close shot of a hammer hitting a large cymbal. The sound rang on and on. And as its reverberations continued, the film picture at the school dissolved to a video shot of the narrator in studio, listening, and the sound continued to reverberate. If the writer views this transition in the light of noncinematic logic, it makes no sense. But where the material lends itself to such an effect in good taste, the result can be delightfully whimsical.

Beep-tape The beep-tape, an adhesive magnetic oxide tape on which a constant "beep" is prerecorded, can be laid over a word or phrase on a film sound track with interesting results. The author recalls a film story about a baseball park rhubarb involving Leo Durocher and a fan. A formal hearing resulted, and the hearing resolved itself into a spirited discussion of whether the fan had called Durocher a "son of a bitch." The phrase came up so often that it could not be edited out of the story without destroying the story; it was *the* central point of the story. But the constant repetition of this particular phrase might have offended many viewers.

The solution was beep-tape, laid over the sound track every time the offensive phrase was spoken. The television viewer could see the words being mouthed, but all he could hear was the beep. Nothing was removed except the objectionable phrase, which every adult viewer could easily deduce. The result was even more hilarious than the reality, and there were no complaints—not even from lip readers.

Such special devices cannot and should not be used too often, but they are justified where they contribute to the impression of reality. This is especially true where the lack of such a device destroys that impression and thereby destroys involvement by causing the viewer to become aware of the technique (or lack of it) employed by the writer. And where the issue is not too grave, they are justified purely for the fun of it. The viewer delights in this sort of thing as long as he understands that he is not being deceived about something of importance. The writer, too, should delight in playing such games; if his work cannot be fun at least part of the time, he really should be doing something else.

Editing VTR

Anyone who can edit film can easily edit VTR. All of the basic principles are the same, and the basic nomenclature for shots, sequences, and optical effects is identical. The principal difference is that VTR is always edited by an engineer or technician, not a newsman, although the newsman selects the takes to be edited.

VTR is edited in either of two ways: (1) by actually cutting and splicing the tape or (2) by dubbing the desired takes from one tape onto another, which is called electronic editing.

Editing by splicing is time-consuming (it may take from 5 to 20 minutes to make a single splice, as compared with a few seconds for a film splice), and if the cut is not made with extreme precision a disturbing "rollover" of the video picture results. Electronic editing is preferable because it is faster and more accurate, but it requires two VTR machines plus a device called an electronic editor; the latest electronic editors are computerized and provide extremely rapid, precise editing. Because of cost, not all stations have the necessary equipment for electronic editing.

Unless the editing is to be done electronically, it is often best to edit "in the black" if possible—that is, to take an entire video segment from fade-in to fade-out. Any rollover which occurs in the black will not be noticeable.

With electronic editors VTR may be dubbed on the frame, just as film is spliced. The term "frame" is customarily used although there are, strictly speaking, no frames in VTR; it provides a continuous picture in the same sense that a sound track provides a continuous sound, and only when it is moving across the video recording head at its designed speed (15 inches per second in the case of the 2-inch tape most widely used in television).

Slow-motion and stop-motion (frozen frame) shots are possible with many of the newer VTR machines. These effects are created by running the tape at slower than normal speed, or by stopping it, while the recording head rotates at an appropriate speed to simulate the proper movement of the tape. If such effects are desired in a sequence of otherwise normal shots, they must be dubbed in by electronic editing so that the resulting edited tape can be run throughout the sequence at normal speed. The sound is unusable.

There is very little problem with lip-flap in VTR (which is essentially similar to single-system film in that both sound and picture are recorded on the same tape) because sound and picture are only about half a second apart. It is not difficult to find pauses of this length for editing purposes.

In general, then, VTR editing follows all of the principles of film editing, the only differences being those technical differences occasioned by the difference in the recording method.

Summary

Chronology dictates the order of shots in the sequence, which is characterized by variety of shots. The proportion of reaction shots (and therefore the degree of emotional involvement) increases as the sequence progresses. Successively closer shots lead the viewer into the story and increase his involvement; successively wider shots lead him out of it and increase his detachment. Almost all film stories are characterized by time compression achieved by careful shot selection in editing.

The editing concept alone determines the order of shots in the montage, which in its purest form is characterized by lack of time compression, lack of story progression, and monotony of shots. The montage is therefore essentially editorial in nature; rather than depicting an event, it constitutes an event in itself.

Narration over film should be keyed to the film shots, should avoid redundancy between film and script, should be shorter rather than longer than the film it covers, and should allow the film rather than the narration to dominate the story where possible.

Natural sound adds realism to the film story, sometimes enabling the film to carry the story without narration. Voice sound must be edited for content, but with due consideration for the effect created by the edited picture. In single-system film the problem of lip-flap may be resolved by a cutaway shot or an overlap splice.

The elementary film art of intercutting different but related lines of action is frequently used in news film. It depicts the relationship of the lines of action in cinematic terms, and usually accomplishes time compression as well.

Multiple-chain projection of single-system film is used in television news to accomplish most of the optical and sound effects achieved by laboratory processes in theatrical films. It is a common form of the self-contained film story.

Video tape editing follows the principles of film editing in general; it is best accomplished by a computerized electronic process.

Suggested Assignments

1. If uncut, unused news film can be obtained from a local station, and editing equipment is available, project the film in class and assign editing teams to cut it.

2. Analyze one or more news film stories in terms of the following: (a) transitions, (b) avoidance of jump-cuts, (c) time compression, (d) use of montage, and (e) story structure.

3. Analyze a news film montage in terms of the following characteristics: (a) lack of time compression, (b) lack of progression of action, and (c) shot monotony.

4. Analyze a news film script (obtained from a local station) in the following respects: (a) narration keyed to film, (b) redundancy between film and script, (c) length of lead-in and bridge narration in comparison with film time, and (d) editing of lead-ins and bridges for visual effect.

5. Explain how a news film clip shown in the classroom might be trimmed for time without destroying the story.

6. Using a newspaper story as an example, and given specific hypothetical film coverage, explain how the film should be edited with particular reference to single- or double-chain projection.

7. Reduce a newspaper story to a single paragraph in which each sentence represents a hypothetical film shot, and explain the choice of each shot.

8. Define climax, cause, and effect in a double-chain news film story.

9. Given 100 feet of silent film, shoot, edit, and script a story of your own selection, no more than 30 seconds in length.

10. Given 400 feet of sound film, shoot, edit, and script a story of your own selection, no more than 3 minutes in length.

Chapter 10

The
Script

There are several basic formats for television news scripts, and innumerable minor variations are found at different stations and networks. Some stations seem to have no set policy on script format; at others the writer is expected to follow the "local rules." In general, however, the various formats reduce to three: CBS, NBC, and syndication.

Basic Script Formats

The NBC format uses typewritten lines running the full width of the page. In the CBS format the page is divided, with video directions (cues) on the left, audio directions and narration on the right. The syndication format is similar to the CBS format except that, in addition, it usually provides a column describing each shot, and sometimes other columns listing the length of each shot and the total running time to that point. In all three formats video and audio cues are usually written in capital letters, narration in caps and lower case. In this discussion we shall use the CBS format for three reasons: it is easier to follow at a glance, it is more widely used, and the author prefers it.

Scripts are typed double-spaced or, preferably, triple-spaced on copy "books" of five or more pages. The original goes to the narrator because it is the most readable. Other copies go to the director, audio mixer, stage manager, and usually the producer. In some shops the

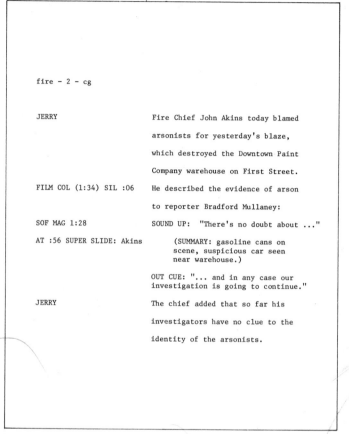

```
fire - 2 - cg


JERRY                              Fire Chief John Akins today blamed

                                   arsonists for yesterday's blaze,

                                   which destroyed the Downtown Paint

                                   Company warehouse on First Street.
FILM COL (1:34) SIL :06            He described the evidence of arson

                                   to reporter Bradford Mullaney:
SOF MAG 1:28                       SOUND UP:  "There's no doubt about ..."
AT :56 SUPER SLIDE: Akins               (SUMMARY: gasoline cans on
                                        scene, suspicious car seen
                                        near warehouse.)

                                   OUT CUE:  "... and in any case our
                                   investigation is going to continue."
JERRY                              The chief added that so far his

                                   investigators have no clue to the

                                   identity of the arsonists.
```

Figure 10-1. Sample news script.

colors of the various pages are different, providing a color code to identify the ultimate user.

The writer *never* pencils the script except to the extent absolutely necessary in editing the copy. If much penciling is done, the page should always be retyped. Clean copy pages are extremely important not only for readability, but also because each of the various users customarily marks his copy in a different manner for his own purposes, and any additional marks of any kind made by the writer may cause confusion and error under the time pressure of broadcasting.

Figure 10–1 shows a sample CBS-style script page for a story involving studio narration at the beginning, the narration continuing over a 6-second silent film lead-in to single-system sound film 1 minute 28 seconds in length, and the story concluding with a live narrative "tag."

At the top, the page is identified by a story slug, a page number, and the writer's name or initials. The video cues on the left are the concern of the technical director, the audio cues on the right are the concern of the audio mixer, and the director is of course concerned with both.

Cues

Video cues   Taking the video cues in Figure 10–1 from the top, the first cue (JERRY) identifies the air man. The name, usually the first name, is the simplest identification, and it avoids confusion if there are several air men on the show. Shot directions are usually left to the director.

The second cue is a direction to take film at the instant the air man begins the line of narration directly opposite. It also gives the total length of the film (1:34) and indicates that the first 6 seconds are silent. The cue for color (COL) is necessary because much film, especially old movies, is still in black and white, and if the film chain is not set for color the picture will be black and white.

No cue is scripted for the director to order the film roll. He himself will select a word in the lead-in standup narration which is 3 seconds, say, before the film "take" cue. The selection of the roll cue depends on the air man's speed of delivery, with which the director should be more familiar than the writer.

The third video cue (SOF MAG 1:28) indicates the beginning of a single-system sound take.

The fourth cue orders a superslide identifying the fire chief precisely at 56 seconds into the film. The location of the superslide should be selected in the editing room for several reasons: it should be over a close shot, so that there can be no confusion as to who is identified, as there might be on a two-shot; if possible it should be over a shot in which the lower part of the frame is fairly dark, so that the super can be read clearly; it should not be over a reverse or cutaway of the reporter, which would only confuse the audience; and since the chief has been identified by narration leading into the film, the super here serves to reidentify him and therefore should not be placed too early in the sound take. The super is held for only a few seconds.

The fifth cue indicates that the video picture returns to a studio shot of the air man after the film ends.

From Figure 10–1 it can be seen that video cues are written as briefly as possible, and that they contain no unnecessary information; a clutter of needless data only causes confusion in the control room. However, the cues must contain *all* of the information the control room needs.

For example, if the film in Figure 10–1 is black and white with optical sound, and of 35-millimeter size, the cue should be scripted: FILM 35 MM B&W (1:34) SIL :06; and the sound take cue should read: SOF OPT 1:28. It is seldom necessary to specify film size unless it is of a size not ordinarily used.

Audio cues The audio in Figure 10–1 begins with live narration copy for the air man. The first cue indicates where the audio mixer should bring up the film sound, and to help identify the sound the cue includes the first few words of SOF.

The summary in parentheses within the film audio portion of the script is not a cue, but a summary of the film *content* for the benefit of the air man. This will be discussed in more detail below.

The second audio cue is for the end of the film sound, and here the last few words of that sound are much more important than at the beginning. If the film has not been properly timed, for example, the audio out-cue gives both director and audio mixer an accurate indication as to when to go back to the studio with both video and audio. Theoretically the film timing as read off the counter in the editing room should be absolutely accurate, but somehow even with the best of effort it does not always turn out that way, or perhaps it is the director's stop watch (with which he is timing the film) that is inaccurate. In either case, a few seconds of closing wording is essential for polished production effect. It is the duty of the writer to take down those words and include them in the script.

SOF Summary

The SOF summary is seldom seen in news scripts, and yet it can be the most valuable part of the script if anything goes wrong. If the film breaks while it is being broadcast, or if the film video is lost for any other of a thousand technical reasons, the director has nowhere to "go" but back to the air man; this is the only shot he can take.

But unless the air man is also the reporter who covered that particular story, he may know nothing about it except what he can read in the script. The typical script of Figure 10–1 shows how little indeed that is likely to be. Here the summary at least provides him with a modicum of information with which he can ad lib while the director struggles frantically in the control room to restructure the remainder of the show. If the air man knows more about the story, so much the better, but at least he can tell the audience that the fire chief's investigators found gasoline cans at the scene of the fire, and that a suspicious car was seen near the warehouse, and he should recall enough about the previous day's story (the fire itself) to ad lib some detail about that. The air man's ability to fill in the audience on details in this manner makes him appear more credible and more authoritative as a newsman.

However, at the moment that is the least of his (and the show's) problems. What he is really doing is killing time until the director can determine what to do next, and how. Since the film stories are usually assembled on a single reel, when the film breaks or is lost for any other reason the critical problem becomes the time required to repair the damage, and thus to get on with the show as prepared by the producer. If the film chain has failed electronically, the reel may be placed on another chain; the usual practice is to abandon that story and recue it for the next, and this takes time. If the film itself has broken, it must be respliced, replaced on the chain, and recued; this also takes time. The director is busy finding out what happened and estimating how long it will take to get the show back on the track; meanwhile the air man is killing time. And *his* problem is what to kill it with.

Now suppose the script contains only 15 seconds of standup copy between the lost film story and the next film story, but it takes a full minute to recue the film for that next story. If the air man cannot stall for a minute, he must go on to something else—anything else, as long as it gives him something to say. He may have to start rummaging through the script for any other standup copy he can find, or he may have to ad lib about anything he can think of until the stage manager cues him to resume script. But a chain reaction which can cause the loss of several stories has been set in motion. The author has known shows to lose 7 or 8 minutes of planned production in precisely this manner; he himself was once forced to ad lib for nearly 5 minutes while the director reassembled the show, but in that case the air man was also the field reporter and knew enough about the story to fill the time. The point is that much grief and embarrassment can be saved by a simple, brief SOF summary, and it is the writer who must think of it.

Pad Copy

In addition to the SOF summary, the writer should always provide 2 or 3 minutes of pad copy, often called fill copy, and for exactly the same reason. (This applies, of course, to the writer of a complete show, not necessarily to a writer who handles only certain stories or a package.) Pad copy is copy intended purely for padding the show if needed; it is usually copy which is not intended for use except in such emergencies.

Other Script Formats

Figure 10–1 was an example of a news story involving only live studio narration and single-chain projection of single-system film. But many stories involve many more elements and far more complicated use of video and audio techniques. The writer should be familiar with the script formats suitable for such techniques, even to the point of being able to develop his own new formats for new problems which he may encounter. (It should always be remembered that script formats are not so calcified, in fact are still so amorphous, that it is impossible to lay down any more than the most general rules. Hopefully this condition will continue for a long time; it is only in the early stages of development of a medium, during which the "rules" are still being made, that imagination has free rein and the creative mind can explore its capacities.) At this point a brief sampling of a few other possibilities may be in order.

Double-chain SOF with VTR and live video   Figure 10–2 illustrates one of many possible combinations of these elements, using a slightly different style of cues. For reasons of space we have eliminated the SOF summary.

The story begins with a (necessarily) wide shot of the air man in studio, standing beside an FP screen which displays a still photograph of the president on the scene of the disaster. Midway in the standup lead-in (at the cue CHANGE FP AND ZOOM IN) the FP changes to a close-shot still of the president in his helicopter, and the video camera zooms in tight on the FP, thus removing the air man from the frame.

From this shot the picture dissolves to a VTR showing the president's helicopter landing at Brownsville and his conversations with some of the people there.

At :53 the picture dissolves from VTR into a double-chain SOF sequence showing details of the devastation and including a reporter's narration. Notice that 3 seconds at the end of the VTR (and, obviously, an equal time at the beginning of the film) must be allowed for the dissolve. This is slightly more than is needed, but it is wise to allow the director some leeway in such a dissolve; there are two possibilities of error in timing, first in the timing of the VTR, second in the timing of the film roll cue.

Since the film is double-chain, the cues must include instructions as to which reel to take, and when, for both video and audio. The first film cue, for example, instructs the director to take the silent picture off the A-reel, and the sound from the B-reel. In this case the A-reel shows

```
flood - 1 - chas.


BEN - (FP of LBJ)          President Johnson today made a quick

                           helicopter tour of the south Texas area

                           devastated by Hurricane Beulah and

                           declared it a disaster area--which

                           qualifies it for federal aid.

CHANGE FP AND ZOOM IN      At Brownsville the President got a

                           first-hand account of the devastation

                           from residents driven from their homes

                           by flood waters of the Rio Grande:

DISS. TO VTR :56           SOUND UP: (helicopter noise)

AT :53 DISS. TO FILM COL   OUT CUE:  "... your government will take
DBL.-CHAIN 1:48            action to help you."
TAKE A-VID SIL AND
B-SOF MAG                  B-VID IN CUE: "... Before the President
                           arrived in Texas ..."

AT : 33 DISS. TO B-VID

AT :45 SUPER SLIDE: Jones

AT 1:03 DISS. TO A-VID     BRING A-AUD UNDER: (rushing water)

AT 1:48 FILM ENDS          B-AUD OUT CUE: "... whether help can
                           arrive in time.  This is Jack
                           Jones reporting from Harlingen,
                           Texas."
```

Figure 10-2. Sample script, using live video, FP, VTR, double-chain SOF.

action footage of the flooding, and the B-reel contains the reporter's narration.

At :33 into the film (which, it should be noted, is timed separately from the VTR), the picture dissolves to the reporter, and at :45 he is identified by superslide. At 1:03 the picture dissolves back to the action footage on the A-reel, while the reporter's narration continues on the B-reel; at the same time natural sound from the A-reel is brought in under the narration.

Frozen frame with double-chain SOF Figure 10–3 illustrates the scripting of a somewhat unusual but, where appropriate, extremely effective use of the frozen frame both to establish personality visually and to convey emotion. It also illustrates the flexibility of double-chain projec-

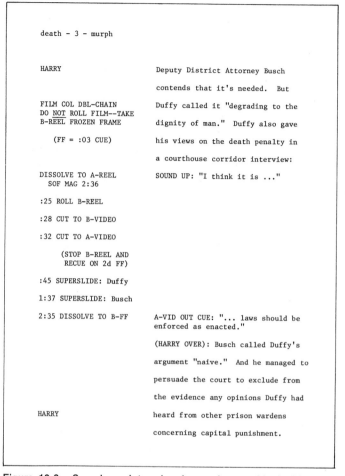

```
death - 3 - murph


HARRY                              Deputy District Attorney Busch

                                   contends that it's needed.  But

FILM COL DBL-CHAIN                 Duffy called it "degrading to the
DO NOT ROLL FILM--TAKE
B-REEL FROZEN FRAME                dignity of man."  Duffy also gave

       (FF = :03 CUE)              his views on the death penalty in

                                   a courthouse corridor interview:

DISSOLVE TO A-REEL                 SOUND UP: "I think it is ..."
   SOF MAG 2:36

:25 ROLL B-REEL

:28 CUT TO B-VIDEO

:32 CUT TO A-VIDEO

     (STOP B-REEL AND
      RECUE ON 2d FF)

:45 SUPERSLIDE: Duffy

1:37 SUPERSLIDE: Busch

2:35 DISSOLVE TO B-FF               A-VID OUT CUE: "... laws should be
                                    enforced as enacted."

                                    (HARRY OVER): Busch called Duffy's

                                    argument "naive."  And he managed to

                                    persuade the court to exclude from

                                    the evidence any opinions Duffy had

HARRY                               heard from other prison wardens

                                    concerning capital punishment.
```

Figure 10-3. Sample script, using frozen frame with double-chain SOF.

tion if the writer is willing to use his visual imagination and refuses to be bound by any arbitrary rules.

The story involves a formal court hearing on the constitutionality of the death penalty, a hearing in which the prosecutor finds himself opposed by Clinton Duffy, the former warden of San Quentin Prison. (It should be mentioned that this script was taken from an actual broadcast by KNXT in Los Angeles.) Because the court proceedings could not be filmed, the television reporter who covered the story was reduced to interviewing these two antagonists in a courtroom corridor. We pick up the script in mid-story, at its most significant point (for our purposes).

A script of this type is so unusual that the writer must consult with the director personally to be sure that he can follow it; to include all of the necessary cue details in the script would make it too cumbersome. This rule—personal consultation with the director—should always be followed by the writer when his script is out of the ordinary.

Briefly, the film scripted in Figure 10-3 involved the use of the B-reel for three purposes: (1) a frozen frame at the top of the reel, (2) a four-second cutaway shot in the middle, and (3) a second frozen frame at the end. The A-reel consisted of a sequence of edited film interviews with Duffy and Busch, in that order.

The writer's reasoning for using this unusual structure must be explained. The expression on the prosecutor's face as he finished the desired SOF take was so interesting that the writer felt the viewer should have a chance to get a good look at it. But the expression was fleeting; it lasted only about three frames, and those frames were needed to complete the sound. However, the writer was persistent; he explored the uncut film further, and in it discovered the identical expression at the end of another sound take which he did not plan to use; the second frozen frame was taken from this part of the film, and it provided precisely the effect that the writer desired.

But now, to balance the coverage of the two opposing points of view, the writer felt that Duffy deserved similar exposure. This could come only at the beginning of the film sequence unless it were to destroy the continuity; at the beginning it could be justified as establishing. Thus the film sequence began with a frozen frame establishing Duffy, and it ended with a frozen frame reprising the prosecutor. This structure, not entirely incidentally, gave the story Aristotelian unity in the visual sense.

Having thus determined the story structure, the writer incorporated two other factors in his editing of the film, one that improved the visual film continuity, and another that simplified the work in the control room. The first was the use of the B-reel for a 4-second cutaway shot to cover a jump-cut; the cutaway was interesting in itself, and its length gave the audience time to appreciate it, however unconsciously. The second was the placement of the first frozen frame in the 3-second frame of the Academy leader; thus when the frame was frozen, the film was already cued for its normal roll.

With this explanation (the same explanation that was given to the director personally), the script in Figure 10-3 should be self-explanatory. From standup narration the picture cuts to the frozen frame of Duffy and holds this shot for approximately 8 seconds while the narration continues. Here the B-reel remains motionless. At 5 seconds into the narration over frozen frame, the A-reel is rolled; at 8 seconds the picture dissolves to the A-reel and the viewer sees and hears Duffy's opinion.

For lack of film the cutaway shot was necessarily brief; thus it was

```
France - 1 - bt


FILM - FROZEN FRAME -        French President Charles de Gaulle
  FRANK IN KEY
                            again demanded a return to the gold

                            standard, and again he spurned

ROLL FILM 2:12 SOF MAG      Britain's efforts to join the European
  (HOLD SOUND OUT FOR :10)
                            Common Market.  De Gaulle spoke at

                            his semiannual news conference.

                            Correspondent Charles Collins reports

                            from Paris:

AT :10 DISS. OUT FRANK      SOUND UP: "Under no circumstances ..."

AT 1:15 ROLLTHRU :05        OUT CUE: "... the part it has played in
  (CUT TO FRANK)            rearming the Arab states."

                            (FRANK): In Washington, the reaction

                            was more sorrow than anger, as

                            Joseph Horn reports:

AT 1:20 TAKE FILM           IN CUE: "Not since the days ..."

AT 2:12 FILM ENDS           OUT CUE: "... this is Joseph Horn
                            reporting from the nation's
                            capital."
```

Figure 10-4. Sample script, using frozen frame with narrator in key.

necessary to include in the script both roll and take cues for the B-reel
cutaway. Once the cutaway was used, the B-reel was stopped and
recued on the second frozen frame, to which the picture dissolved as
the A-reel ended. This frozen frame was held over the tag narration for
approximately 8 seconds.

Frozen frame with narrator in key In Figure 10–4 the frozen frame is
not isolated, as in Figure 10–3, but is the first frame of the film
sequence.

Here the story begins with the narrator keyed into the frozen film
frame so that he appears to be standing in front of a large still of De
Gaulle. In such a shot the film frame and the position of the narrator
must be so selected that the narrator does not block a significant
portion of the film picture; in this case he should be on the side
opposite from De Gaulle.

At the roll cue the still picture suddenly begins to move; the narrator
remains keyed in. At :10 into film the narrator is dissolved out and
only the film picture remains; at the same time the voice of the Paris
correspondent is heard beginning his report.

Between 1:15 and 1:20 a rollthru is used to cover the transition from Paris to Washington, which is narrated on camera by the studio air man. This is a fairly typical if unimaginative use of the rollthru.

Syndication script Figure 10–5 is an example of a typical syndication script. At this point it should require no explanation.

Video-Shot Considerations

In scripting video shots for the studio cameras, the writer must consider the camera problems of movement and focusing which his script demands. This is not a major problem in most news shows, in which the shots are usually static and standardized, but every show contains a few such considerations. The writer should be aware that his script may read well and call for an apparently logical sequence of shots, yet make difficult if not impossible demands of the studio crew.

Figure 10–6 diagrams one common stage arrangement for two video cameras and two or more air men. Camera 1 can shoot an air man at Podium 1, or by panning it can shoot a still or graphic on Still Board 1. Similarly, Camera 2 can shoot either Podium 2 or Still Board 2. In neither case can shots be taken during the panning motion between the podium and the still board, for two reasons: (1) the pan traverses a section of stage background not designed to be seen (a portion not covered by the backdrop), and (2) the camera must be refocused after such a movement and the zoom setting readjusted. No backdrop is needed behind the still boards because shots of stills are always close shots, framing only the still itself and eliminating its supporting board and the stage background.

In this stage setting assume that the anchor position is at Podium 1. The other air men use Podium 2. This allows the director to cut between the anchormen and the other air men. The positioning of stills on the boards is determined not by the writer, but by the director or stage manager. However, the writer must consider their problems in scripting. Assume a script calling for the following sequence of shots:

1. Anchorman
2. Still
3. Second air man
4. Anchorman

In this sequence Shot 1 is on Camera 1. Therefore Shot 2 must be on Camera 2, Shot 3 on Camera 1, and Shot 4 on Camera 2. But this means that either the cameras or the air men must exchange positions, and in either case the director will demand a change in the script. For example, if the air men move, the second air man will be taken by

⟨NTN⟩ National Television News   560 WEST EIGHT MILE ROAD ● DETROIT, MICHIGAN 48220 ● TELEPHONE (313) 541-1440

FOR IMMEDIATE USE
Distribution Date: July 25, 1968

MIAMI BEACH RUSHES PREPARATIONS FOR G. O. P. CONVENTION

(Suggested introduction before film)

While Richard Nixon and Nelson Rockefeller continue their battle for delegates around the country, at Miami Beach final preparations are being made for the first national political convention to be staged south of the Mason-Dixon line, the biggest ever held, and the first to be televised in color . . .

(SCENES)	(SUGGESTED NARRATION)
LS HOTEL ROW LS CREW DIGGING MS CREW DIGGING (15 Seconds)	Miami Beach hotels are all set for the onslaught of fifty thousand G. O. P. delegates, visitors and newsmen. Communications workers have been getting ready too. 250 thousand miles of cable have been laid, enough to reach from Miami Beach to the moon.

LS CONVENTION HALL
LS GIRL AT BOOTH
MS GIRL AT BOOTH
CU GIRL WORKING
CU SIGN
CU MEN INSTALLING
CU HAND IN WIRING
CU INSTALLER, TILT
       TO PHONE
LS EQUIPMENT
CU INSTALLER
MS CLOSES RACK
     (25 Seconds)
	At Convention Hall, where most of the action will be, and at other
	points along the Beach, more than six thousand new telephones
	are being installed. Portable phone booths have been set up.
	Engineers, technicians and installers from Western Electric and
	Southern Bell have joined forces to accomplish in ten months a
	job that would normally take two years. Telephone and
	teletypewriter equipment is checked out and will be in operation
	as needed.

LS ARENA FLOOR
MS MAN SAWING
LS CARRYING WOOD
MS UNREELS CABLE
MS UNCOILING CABLE
LS TV OPERATIONS
CU SCOPE
CU PATCH PANEL
CU MAN
CU PATCH PANEL
LS CONTROL ROOM
LS MICROWAVE TOWER
LS TOWER, ANOTHER
       ANGLE
     (26 Seconds)
	Inside the huge arena, as construction work proceeds, more cables
	are strung so that each delegation will have a direct phone line to
	the podium. Equipment permitting live tv coverage from anywhere
	in the Miami area is being tested. The result of all this effort will
	mean instant communications from the Republican convention, so
	that the winning candidate will be known in Saigon or Somaliland at
	the same moment he's chosen at Miami Beach.
	(TOTAL RUNNING TIME: 66 SECONDS)

Contact: Jack Carter
News Service Manager
American Telephone and Telegraph Company
195 Broadway, New York, New York 10007
Telephone: (212) 393-3528

Figure 10-5. Sample syndication script.

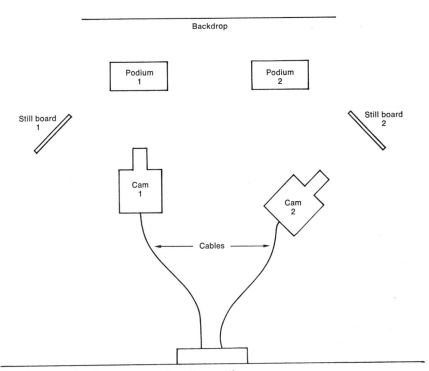

Figure 10-6. Studio camera and podium setting.

Camera 1 on Shot 3, and the anchorman will meanwhile have to move to Podium 2, dragging his script with him, to be ready for Camera 2 on Shot 4. If the air men remain at their original positions, the cameras must exchange positions, which means that one camera must cross the other's cables. All this is needless and confusing nonsense. But the solution is simple:

1. Anchorman (Cam 1)
2. Still (Cam 2)
3. Anchorman (Cam 1)
4. Second air man (Cam 2)
5. Anchorman (Cam 1)

Now both cameras remain in their original positions, the air men do not have to switch podiums, and the director is not angry with the writer. All the writer has to do is find a reason to come back to the anchorman before he goes to the second air man, and allow enough time between Shots 3 and 4 for Camera 2 to get off the still and refocus on the second air man.

If the show has three cameras, the solution is even simpler:

1. Anchorman (Cam 1)
2. Still (Cam 3)

3. Second air man (Cam 2)

4. Anchorman (Cam 1)

Another solution is to have a slide made of the still. This has the effect of adding another camera (in this case a film-slide chain camera) to the facilities, and the sequence is as follows:

1. Anchorman (Cam 1)

2. Slide (film chain camera)

3. Second air man (Cam 2)

4. Anchorman (Cam 1)

It is impossible to anticipate all of the possible problems the writer may encounter in scripting for video shots, but the essential thing to remember is that the video portion of the show is shot and aired in real time, and the possible sequences of shots are limited by the available video facilities. The writer must work within these limitations; he is not a pitcher hired to throw "curves" at the director.

Summary

Script formats vary considerably in detail. The most popular (CBS) format uses the left side of the page for video cues, the right side of the page for narration and audio cues. Cues are written in capital letters, narration in caps and lower case.

The script must specify the precise timing of each change of or alteration in video and audio source.

The SOF summary can prevent disaster to the show in the event of technical difficulties. Pad copy should be supplied to the air man for the same reason.

All shows must be scripted with proper consideration for the technical means available for switching from one picture or sound source to another.

Suggested Assignments

1. Given a news script obtained from a television station, explain the meaning of each video cue and each audio cue.

2. Write the script of one or more stories in the current news, assuming the availability of specific technical facilities, and that portions of the story involve film, VTR, graphics, and live video and audio.

3. Explain how you would remove a studio air man from a key shot matted into film, and why you would choose that particular method of doing so.

4. Shoot, edit, and script a double-chain SOF story, using one chain for narration and the other for actuality.

5. Name two methods by which still photographs might be used in a one-camera news show.

6. List the considerations involved in scripting the following succession of shots for a two-camera show: (1) anchorman, (2) still, (3) graphic, (4) still, (5) second air man, (6) third air man, (7) anchorman. If the sequence proves impossible or impractical, select alternatives which do not involve eliminating any of the elements listed.

Part Three

The
Television
Reporter

Chapter 11

The Film Reporter

Reporters who gather news at the source for television are generally called "field reporters," to distinguish them from reporters who merely read the news in the studio. The networks call them "correspondents." Whatever their titles, these reporters and their film crews constitute the visible "working press" of television.

In most of the larger localities the crew consists of a cameraman and soundman. Union rules in certain places, such as New York City, require the inclusion of an electrician. There are many operations, especially in smaller towns and cities, where one man is both reporter and crew. And sometimes, as for documentary production, the reporter may be accompanied by any or all of several additional persons: director, producer, assistant cameraman, grips, chauffeur, even a "gopher." (The "gopher" is a type of paid hanger-on peculiar to certain aspects of television and motion picture production; he exists in other businesses, but not by the same unofficial name. He is a person of no particular talent whose principal job is to "go for" a ham sandwich, an order of coffee, or whatever personal or business needs may arise. Therefore he is a "gopher.")

As a rule of thumb, the more people involved the longer it takes to accomplish anything. The optimum unit is the familiar trio of reporter, cameraman, and soundman. Here each man has a specific function which, to be performed properly, requires his full attention; at the same time none of the three is hampered by unneeded helpers. In a fast-moving situation an experienced trio can function almost as one man, backstopping one another with coordination so smooth that the job looks easy, which it isn't.

The Reporter as
Producer-Director

The reporter is the boss of the unit. He decides, within the limitations of the assignment, what is to be covered and how. He must be not only a journalist (which is to say, a reporter and writer), but also a performer for the camera, a director who determines the style of coverage, and a producer who can assemble all of the elements of the story into a completed package ready for broadcast. He must know the technical capacities and limitations of the camera and sound equipment, and he must anticipate every problem of the film editor.

Working with the crew   If he is wise, the reporter will lean heavily on his crew. They are usually much more than skilled technicians. Many are truly artists, and good newsmen as well. All are proud. Certain decisions should be left to them, depending on the reporter's judgment of their abilities; other decisions *must* be left to them.

The reporter cannot, for example, direct the shooting of film while he is performing for the camera by conducting an interview. Here the cameraman perforce becomes the director; he decides when to zoom in or out or, if he is using a portable camera, when and where to move around to obtain different shots and angles. If before the interview starts the reporter attempts to predirect it by ordering the cameraman how to shoot, he will wind up with film that at best has less variety than it should, and at worst is uneditable.

The reporter should not tell the cameraman which lens or exposure to use, or the soundman which microphone. There may be technical considerations in which they are far more expert than he; it is their business to know more about the equipment than the reporter has time to learn. What the reporter *should* do is explain his approach to the story, his concept, what effects he wants and why, what problems he can foresee. He may suggest; he should consult. If he anticipates unusual sound or lighting problems, these should be talked over with the crew before setting out on the story; special equipment may be needed, and once on location it may be difficult or impossible to obtain.

When the reporter treats his crew with this consideration and respect, they will produce results that will amaze and delight him. A good news film crew is a creative production unit whose capacities often exceed those of its more famous but tradition-bound Hollywood studio counterparts. A single example may illustrate the point.

The story was a feature report on a rustic mountain retreat for artists, writers, and composers. The reporter completed his film interviews and then, for lack of time, had to depart before the shooting of the silent film which was to depict the sylvan beauty of the place. He simply told cameraman Jack Leppert what he wanted. Days later, in the projection room, the reporter and the film editor watched beautiful shot after beautiful shot unreel. Finally the editor, a veteran in the business, turned to the reporter in awe and inquired, "Is this film of paintings or is it film of something real?"

When the reporter knows enough about camera work to shoot that kind of film himself, he may presume to give the cameraman specific orders. Even then he will not win friends, but that is another matter.

Shooting the right amount Always in the back of the reporter's mind should be the thought that the show can use only what he shoots. The building cannot be shown if he neglects to get a shot of it, and the interview he fails to shoot cannot be aired.

Always the shots should be longer than the shots that are likely to be used on the air. If the editor needs 5 seconds, give him 15 and thereby give him something to work with if it turns out that he needs 10 seconds. If the shots are too short, the editor has no freedom to edit, and film is the cheapest of the reporter's tools.

Conversely, too much film can drown the editor. It all has to be viewed; if the reporter shoots 1,600 feet of film, someone is going to have to spend three quarters of an hour just looking at it before it can be edited. If that film reaches the editing bench half an hour before air time, it may never get beyond the bench.

There is no general rule on how much film a story requires. One story might demand 4,000 feet, another might be shot in less than 100 feet. A double-chain story usually requires more film (and more editing) than a single-chain story. It all depends on the story. Lengthy public hearings, for example, may require the shooting of hundreds or even thousands of feet of film; the high spots, the dramatic or meaningful exchanges, can sometimes be anticipated but more often come unexpectedly, and if the camera is not running when that big moment comes that moment is not on film.

One method of easing the editor's problem is to note where the best parts of the film occur. These locations can be read off the footage counter on the camera. Thus, if the editor can be told that the best film segment is 225 feet into magazine number two, he can find it quickly without having to run through everything that was shot.

Logistics and deadlines At all times the reporter must keep logistics in mind. Which news show is he trying to make? How long will it take to get the film to the station, and to process and edit it? What means of transportation are available? And on the basis of all this, what is his deadline for completing shooting? Logistics are far less important to the newspaper or radio reporter who can phone in his story than to the television reporter.

When the film goes to the newsroom it should be accompanied by a *shot list* detailing everything on it, identifying every person, and pinpointing by magazine and footage exactly where the best segments can be found. This is particularly important when the reporter himself will not supervise the film editing; to a writer who was not present during shooting, the uncut film may be an impossible puzzle without a shot list.

Planning the Story

Single- or double-chain   The first decision the reporter must make is how he envisions the final product. Shall he merely shoot the basic story and assume that live studio copy will lead into and out of it, or shall he shoot a self-contained film story, including all the narration on film? What he decides here makes a difference in how the story is shot; the decision cannot always be made afterward.

For simplicity of editing and to reduce the possibility of technical error in the control room, the story should be shot for single-chain projection if possible. But if many camera setups are required, and especially if their locations are widely separated, shooting for double-chain projection will save much time. In such a case the film narration would all be shot at a single location, the rest of the story—the actuality—perhaps covered by shooting silent film with the hand camera.

The reporter's decision is also affected by his knowledge of the story. If his information is incomplete at the time of shooting, it may be impossible for him to shoot adequate narration. It may be possible, however, for him to shoot a generalized opening and closing, and to complete his narration voice-over later, either on a film sound track or live in studio.

In summary, the reporter's decision to shoot only basic coverage or to shoot a self-contained film story depends on the logistics, the filmic values, and his information at the time of shooting.

Actuality vs. staged event   The filmic values are likely to be the determining factor unless negated by one of the other considerations. And the filmic values themselves are frequently determined by whether the story involves actuality or whether it is what might be termed a "staged" event.

By actuality we mean film of an event as it happens: rioting, fires, a military attack, picketing during a strike, a parade, a political campaign speech. It may be noted that many such events (the parade, for one) are themselves staged or prearranged. But in the journalistic sense we are filming actuality when we film them as they happen. *We* did not stage them.

When the reporter himself intervenes in the event, it becomes staged in the meaning we intend. Any filmed interview, for example, is by this definition a staged event; it would not have occurred had not the reporter sought the interview. If the reporter steps into the picket line to interview the leader of the strike, what we are filming becomes a combination of actuality (the pickets marching) and staged event (the interview). Staging an event in this sense is not engaging in deception; it is a method of capturing the truth on film.

A film report on a poverty war project is an example of how actuality can be staged to give the film an insight unobtainable by other means. Young workers in the project were canvassing a neighborhood, trying to involve the residents in community affairs. A reporter and camera crew accompanied one of the canvassing teams as they visited one home. In the film we saw the canvassers walk up to the house and knock on the door, the housewife answering, and the ensuing conversation. All of the participants of course were aware that they were, for the moment, actors in a little film drama; their cooperation had to be obtained, they had to be warned to ignore the camera, and they had to repeat parts of their conversation while the camera shot from different angles.

But what they said and did was precisely what they were saying and doing when the camera was not present. The camera became the public's proxy, enabling the television audience to accompany the canvassers and see what they were doing and how they were going about it. The effect, although the event was staged, was actuality. This staged actuality film was followed by a film interview with the director of the project, who explained its purpose and its relevance for the community. This abstract, intellectual discussion was meaningful only because the audience had already seen the project in operation; they had seen the concrete, therefore the abstract was interesting. No other medium can so involve the public in events or provide so direct an insight into their significance.

In short, actuality, whether real or staged, is the natural way of telling the story on film, and it should be used wherever possible.

Film Narration

The more the actuality film tells the story, the less narration required of the reporter. Such narration as is essential to complete the story can be done either on film or voice-over in studio, or it may be in the form of standup copy preceding or following the film. Film narration may be delivered over the actuality, it may be a separate narration track, or it may be a combination of the two.

Narration over actuality Narration laid on the film sound track as the actuality is being shot is sometimes very effective, but it has its hazards. It makes natural sound of the event useless unless the narration is also used, because the two cannot be separated. Thus if by the time the film is aired the narration is outdated, the film can only be used MOS. However, it puts the reporter on the scene verbally and its very immediacy gives it impact, as for example when we see the reporter explaining what the police are doing while we see them shooting it out with the robbery suspect. In many such cases, unhappily, it merely stresses the reporter's courage (or foolhardiness) and ability to ad lib under pressure, while at the same stroke it presents the editor with a problem, if all he wants is natural sound.

Separate track narration The double-chain story, using one film track for actuality and the second for narration, obviates this problem. The separate narration track may employ a usable picture, as of the reporter addressing the camera, or it may be a wild track with no picture at all or a picture not intended for use. The usable picture method is preferable in the event technical difficulties make the actuality track unusable during broadcast. If by the time the story is aired the film narration is outdated, the writer can throw away the narration track and script fresh narration to be delivered over the actuality film by the air man.

Narration in studio If the field reporter plans to use a combination of film narration and voice-over in studio, he should try to structure the story so that the two types of narration do not abut. The reason for this is the change in sound quality; his voice in studio will sound quite different than it does on the film. But this difference will not be especially noticeable if the film and studio narration are separated by segments of other sound, such as natural sound or the voice of someone being interviewed.

SOF narration   In narrating on single-system film the reporter must keep in mind the editing difficulties posed by the 28-frame separation of sound and picture. There are several tricks he can use to minimize the effect of this lag.

In beginning any narrative take in which he is seen on camera (that is, a presentational take) the reporter must pause for about 2 seconds before saying anything. At the opening of the narration this pause, which can be cut to slightly more than 1 second in editing, is noticeably awkward; the closer the shot, the more noticeable the pause. But the effect can be minimized by opening on a wide shot, after which the camera zooms in closer. It can be eliminated completely by opening on a shot with the reporter out of frame, then panning to discover him.

On closing narration or bridges, where the edited film is to cut back to a picture of the reporter, the awkwardness of the necessary 1-second pause is reduced if the reporter begins speaking with his face turned away from the camera, as if looking out of frame at whatever was seen last. (This sequence, it might be noted, is the reverse of the two-shot sequence described in the discussion of the POV shot; the psychological effect works either way, whether the POV shot precedes or follows the other shot.) Even where no sound overlap with the preceding shot is possible, the reporter's contemplative attitude makes a pause seem natural; often an overlap is possible because the reporter's lips cannot be seen at the beginning of the shot.

Frequently the narration is filmed in several takes, each on a different shot (wide, medium, close) to lend visual variety to a lengthy presentational sequence. On each such shot the last sentence or two of both the preceding and the following shot should be included in the narration, so that the film editor can overlap the sound track to avoid pauses. The lip movements will of course match perfectly, because the same words are spoken on both shots being overlapped.

Film narration structure   Many film stories begin with an opening narration in which the reporter, speaking directly to the camera, establishes the scene and the action to follow. Next comes the actuality film, and finally another shot of the reporter summing up the story in closing narration. The center (actuality) section may contain narrative bridges where necessary, usually over actuality film rather than pictorially presentational. This is the most common structure of the self-contained film report.

But seldom is the narration simply a straightforward account of what happened, as in a newspaper story. As much of the event as possible is told by the actuality film and interviews; the narration merely fills in the cracks in this information, and serves to put the story into perspective. It supplements rather than dominates the actuality. Because the function of the narration is supplementary, the narrative structure may differ greatly from the format described above.

For example, a report on a turbulent state political convention might well begin with a montage of shots of the noisy delegates in action, *followed* by the opening narration explaining the setting and the meaning of all this sound and fury. This might be followed by segments of key speeches, any interviews the reporter considers essential, and perhaps a closing narration covered by shots of the delegates leaving the convention hall. Such a report, differing vastly in structure from the customary newspaper report of the same convention, takes advantage of the film's ability to establish scene and involve the viewer without the aid of narration.

Consider, also, how the reporter must approach the job of filming this convention story. In all probability he first shoots the actuality. Meanwhile he does his leg work like any other newsman, finding out what the key issues are and who can influence the outcome. He corners delegates in corridors and ferrets out activity behind the scenes. He tracks down the men he wants to interview and persuades them to come before his camera. Once he feels he has the story in hand, knowing what portions of his film he wants to use, he finally gets around to shooting his narration. He anticipates the editing problems involving transitions between the various elements of the story, and if narrative bridges are needed he shoots them. If he has time he may write his narration and work from script, or the narration may be entirely ad lib.

Interviews

The interview is one of the easiest of all stories to film, and one of the most common. Curiously, it is often done rather badly, even though most of the pitfalls are transparent.

Miscellaneous problems   Among the minor problems which make a difference in the quality of the film is the location of the microphone. Many producers object to seeing it in the picture. The hand-held mike is the worst offender because it calls attention to itself by its movement; the reporter brings it close to himself to ask a question, then thrusts it toward the interviewee to get the answer. As William Corrigan of NBC says, "It's like an ice cream cone: first I lick it, then you lick it."

The "ice cream cone" effect can be minimized if the reporter holds the mike motionless about midway between himself and interviewee. If the interviewee is soft-spoken, the mike should favor him; presumably the reporter can project his voice to balance the sound levels of the two voices. However, if the location is noisy it may be necessary to move the mike back and forth to get acceptable sound quality.

In any case the mike should be held in the hand away from the camera. When it is held in the hand toward the camera, the reporter's outthrust arm blocks more of the camera's view of the interviewee.

In many situations the mike can be hidden beneath the clothing or behind an object in the picture, such as a vase on a desk. The lavalier mike concealed beneath the clothing is especially desirable for a woman, because a mike hanging in front of her dress spoils the style effect she has taken so much care to create. However, clothing may muffle the sound, in which case a decision must be made as to whether sound quality or visual quality is more important.

The reporter's position and movements on camera can add to or detract from the quality of the interview. Generally the reporter should present his back or side to the camera, so that it shoots past him or over his shoulder to obtain a good view of the interviewee's face, which is what the audience wants to see. Certain sports reporters, who seem to be more interested in getting their own faces on camera than in getting good interviews, are notable violators of this rule. If the reporter sits facing the camera and beside the interviewee, the latter tends to turn toward him when talking, thus presenting a profile view to the camera.

If the reporter and/or interviewee move during the shot, the movement should always be with the face toward the camera if possible. To turn away from the camera (except as mentioned in the paragraph preceding) conveys a feeling of finality, or of transition to another scene, and this movement should be used only where such an effect is desired. In crossing or changing positions with the interviewee, the reporter should cross behind the interviewee, not in front of him.

If the identity of the interviewee cannot be revealed, as sometimes happens, the normal rule on the reporter's position must be broken deliberately. The reporter might face the camera while the interviewee sits or stands in the foreground, back to camera and face hidden. If the interviewee is also in comparative darkness, he will be visible only as a silhouette. Another possibility is to arrange the setting and the lighting in such a manner that the interviewee's silhouette is thrown against a wall although he himself is out of frame; this arrangement will usually present a profile view of the reporter.

Pipe and cigarette smokers always present a film editing problem. In one shot the inverviewee has cigarette in mouth, in another the cigarette is out, in a third he is lighting up again, in a fourth he gestures with cigarette in hand. Obviously it is going to be difficult to avoid jump-cuts in editing. If he cannot be persuaded to give up smoking while the film is shot, suitable cutaways must be shot to cover the possible jump-cuts: shots of the interviewee lighting a cigarette, stubbing it out, etc.

In shooting a telephone film interview, in which each of the two participants is shot simultaneously by different film crews in different locations, it is necessary to coordinate the shooting angles so that each is a false reverse of the other. Otherwise, when the film shot by the two cameras is intercut, the participants will appear to be looking away from each other, rather than toward each other. That may actually have been the case, but it is extremely important that it not *appear* to have been the case. (The false reverse is explained later in this chapter.)

Choosing the setting   Beyond these rather obvious problems, the difficulty with the film interview lies in its lack of movement; it is pictorially static. Its strength is in its content. Most interviews concern abstractions which cannot be filmed directly, such as opposing points of view which can be captured visually only by filming the disputants expressing their points of view. But the alert reporter is always on the lookout for an appropriate means of enhancing the value of the interview cinematically, which means he must cultivate his visual imagination.

KNXT's Jim Brown used visual imagination to convert an otherwise ordinary news conference concerning the earthquake resistance of high-rise buildings into a film report with good cinematic value. The setting was a common one for a news conference: a downtown hotel conference room. After shooting part of the proceedings in the room (establishing the scene and participants), Brown moved his camera to a balcony off the room. While the news conference continued, the camera roamed the subject itself, focusing on one after another of the tall buildings giving vertical definition to the once horizontal Los Angeles skyline.

Where a choice of location is possible, the choice may be made to improve the visual quality of the interview. But the choice must be made in relation to the content. A law office, its walls lined with legal books, may be an appropriate location for a discussion of the effects of a Supreme Court ruling on a nonvisual subject. But if the ruling affects, say, bicycle riders, an interview conducted while cycling through a park may add point to the story. An interview with a college professor on the subject of academic pay might be set appropriately in the college disbursing office, with calculating machines clattering away in the background. An interview with an adventurer setting off on a transcontinental horseback ride was conducted on horseback, its closing shot showing the interviewee clopping off into the rising sun. An interview concerning the late President Kennedy's physical fitness program was conducted with the world champion walker, Bill Mihalo, whose ability to walk faster than the television reporter could run made the improbable setting even more enjoyable for the audience.

Some of these things would be silly things for a newspaper man to do, but in television they make sense. They also make it advisable for the field reporter to keep in good physical condition.

How much the mere choice of location can add to a static interview was demonstrated by Sam Zelman of CBS in his coverage of a water rights dispute in Phoenix, Arizona. Indians at the headwaters of Salt Creek, a major water source for the Phoenix area, had dammed the creek to create a lake on their reservation; they hoped to make the lake a recreational and tourist attraction. Farmers and citizens in the valley below, fearing loss of their water rights, had obtained a court order for the destruction of the dam. But the Indians held off the sheriff's bulldozers at gunpoint. Zelman filmed the dam and its defending Indians, the miserable hovels in which they lived, the fertile fields of the white men in the valley. He interviewed both sides, and his last interview was with a suburban Phoenix resident who was clearly outraged at the impudence of the Indians. The man, wearing bathing trunks, was irrigating the sunken lawn of his modern home in the customary Phoenix manner, by flooding it with water. Zelman, trousers rolled to his knees, conducted the interview standing in the two feet of water flooding the lawn. The contrast in the conditions of the opposing sides was all the more devastating for its visual truth.

Reverses Nearly all film interviews include reverse questions. For these the reporter merely repeats some or all of the questions he asked during the interview, while the camera shoots from the reverse of the master shot angle (that is, the camera shoots the face of the reporter, not that of the interviewee). The purpose of the reverse question is to provide greater flexibility in film editing.

In shooting the reverse the reporter has two problems: "matching" it to his original question on the master shot, and making sure that the reverse angle is correct.

To make the reverse questions match the reporter must remember the questions he asked on the master track, and if possible the precise wording. Some reporters rely on memory, others take notes, a few prefer to record their questions on an audio tape recorder; the last is most desirable for a lengthy interview which may require the shooting of many reverse questions. A recorder with a convenient start-stop switch on the microphone enables the reporter to record only his questions; he need not run through the entire interview to find them. Further, with the recorder the reporter can hear not only his exact words, but also his inflection, which helps him match the reverse to the original not merely in wording but also in tone and manner of delivery. With reverses so perfectly matching, the film editor can cut from master shot to reverse shot in mid-sentence, giving single-system film the "feel" of double-system.

When memory and all else fail, the reporter can still fall back on the ubiquitous, all-purpose cutaway line: "Now let me ask you this question . . ." Using this as a reverse and cutting back immediately to the original master shot question, the film editor always has a detour around the jump-cut.

As far as camera position is concerned, the reverse may be either real or false; the viewer does not know the difference. In a genuine reverse, reporter and interviewee remain in position after the interview ends, and the camera is moved to shoot the reverses. The false reverse, while it looks like the genuine article, is faked from another angle, and sometimes (but very rarely) even in a totally different location.

The reason for the false reverse may be merely to save time, or to avoid inconveniencing a lazy cameraman. Sometimes it is necessary, as for example where the interview is shot in a room too small for the cameraman to move to the real reverse position.

The background of the false reverse must match the master shot as to both picture and sound. It is not absolutely necessary that it be shot, for example, in the same room where the interview was conducted, but it is desirable. At least the room must look like the same room, although this may be a minor consideration if the shot is held close on the reporter so that the background does not show very clearly. For audio purposes the location is a major consideration because the sound "presence" of rooms varies greatly; the same voice does not sound the same when recorded in different rooms. If the interview was shot in a noisy restaurant, the false reverse cannot be shot in a quiet library. It cannot be patently false.

Wherever the false reverse is shot, it *must* comply with the *rule of 180 degrees*. In this, oddly enough, the reporter cannot always depend on the cameraman to advise him correctly; it is therefore wise to set the rule firmly in mind.

The purpose of the false reverse is to convey the impression that the scene was shot with two cameras, one on the reporter, the other on the interviewee, whereas in fact only one camera was used. Consider, then, the interview or master shot setup with the luxury of two cameras, as shown in Figure 11–1.

Camera 1, looking over the reporter's left shoulder, shoots the mas-

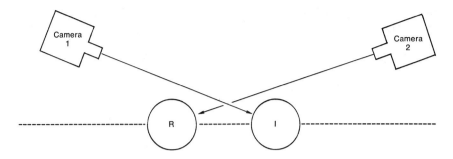

Figure 11-1. Interview setting with two cameras.

ter shot. Camera 2, looking over the interviewee's right shoulder, shoots the reverses. The imaginary line I-R between reporter and interviewee is extended infinitely. *Both* cameras *must* be on the same side of that line. It does not matter which side, but for both cameras it must be the same side, and this rule is unbreakable. If the cameras are on different sides of the line I-R, intercutting their shots will give the viewer the impression that reporter and interviewee are inexplicably looking away from one another rather than toward one another, and this unnatural impression will destroy the continuity of the film.

The viewer's impression is entirely subjective. It is only his interpretation of what he sees, and his interpretation may not correspond at all with reality. But our concern is to make his interpretation correspond with reality, and to do so we must take into account the *limitations of the camera eye*, of which the reverse shot is perhaps the perfect example.

Unlike the human eye, the camera does not roam the entire scene, automatically calculating the physical relationships of what it sees on the basis of human experience. The camera has only an eye; it has no brain, no experience, no memory, no means of relating what it sees to anything else. And when the human eye looks through the camera eye, a strange, subjective thing happens: its vision of the world becomes similarly limited.

The camera sees only what the cameraman selects for it to see, and its world is bounded by the frame of the film. Nothing exists beyond the frame, unless something happens within the frame to indicate its existence. And whatever happens within the frame is accepted by the mind as real, no matter how ridiculous or transparently fraudulent it may be upon examination.

This world-within-the-frame is unlike anything in human experience. No onlooker, for example, can jump instantly from the position of Camera 1 to that of Camera 2, and back again in the next instant. Yet that is exactly what the onlooker will do when he views the master shot into which the reverse shot is edited. This instantaneous transition from one point of view to another is a convention which we accept because we accept the world-within-the-frame unquestioningly, even if we have never experienced anything like it.

Look again at Figure 11–1 and assume that reporter and interviewee are looking at each other along the line I-R, as is usually the case. Notice that to *each* camera the reporter seems to be looking to camera left, the interviewee to camera right. Thus, if we intercut shots taken by the two cameras, the two men will appear to be looking *at* each other, as they really are.

But if either camera is moved across the line I-R, the men will appear to be looking *away* from each other. This appearance is false, but the viewer will accept it as true because he accepts the world-within-the-frame; he *sees* quite clearly that they are looking away from each other.

If both cameras are moved across the line I-R, the men will again appear to be looking at each other, but their positions will appear to be reversed. That is, the reporter, who was looking to camera left in the previous setup, now is looking to camera right; the interviewee, who was looking to camera right, now looks to camera left. Actually the men have not moved, but the cameras have.

In the two-camera setup of Figure 11–1 the shot taken by Camera 2 is a real reverse. The reporter, who except in rare circumstances has only one camera to work with, must have Camera 1 moved to the position of Camera 2 to shoot his real reverses.

If he shoots false reverses, they must follow the same rule: Camera 1 must be moved to a position which corresponds, in the false reverse setup, to the position of Camera 2 in the real reverse setup. The easiest way for the reporter to determine whether his false reverse setup is correct is for him to remember which side of his face was visible to the camera on the master shot. If it was the left side, that is the side of his face he must present to the camera on the false reverse; therefore he must look to the right of the camera. Or vice versa.

The importance of point of view in relation to camera position was not recognized in the early days of film. The camera was set up in one position to record, say, the action of a stage play. It was simply a recording device, and its point of view was fixed, like that of a member of the theater audience. Only when the early filmmakers began to move the camera during the action did they begin to comprehend that the camera's world was unlike the human world, that it was bounded by the film frame. The mobility of the camera created problems which the filmmaker must recognize and to which he must adapt; it also converted film from a recording device to an art form.

If all this seems like much ado about very little, consider the fact that an incorrectly shot reverse cannot be used under any circumstances. Shooting film is rather like making love: it is easier to do than to explain. But if the reporter cannot do it satisfactorily, he has a serious problem.

The interview technique Every reporter has to use psychology in the treatment of interviewees, but the television reporter has to use more of it than most. Many people become extremely nervous and inarticulate in front of the camera. Some even "freeze" and can say nothing. It is the reporter's job to put the interviewee at ease, so that he can obtain from him the necessary information on film. Casual conversation, a small joke or two, may help to ease the tension. It also helps to explain a little of the workings of the camera and sound gear; the more familiar they are, the less frightening. The interviewee who fears he may say the wrong thing is reassured if he is told that the errors can be reshot or edited out of the film.

Most people who have anything to say (and if they don't, why interview them?) tend to forget the camera after a short time, loosen up, and begin to speak effectively. Thus it sometimes solves the problem to shoot a magazine of film which may not be used. After 10 or 11 minutes the camera's eye is no longer so baleful, and the reporter may get what he wants on the second magazine.

Once in a while the reporter encounters an interviewee who is so inarticulate, for one reason or another, that the film is not usable. He may be a man with a speech impediment, someone who hems and haws constantly, or an elderly person whose senility is reflected in his speech. To show such handicaps to the world is unkind; unless the interview is imperative, it is better to search for another way to cover the story.

The *subject matter* of the interview is largely determined by the nature, activities, and interests of the interviewee. Presumably the reporter has a reason for interviewing him, whether the interview was his own idea or was assigned to him. The interviewee has done something, said something, or become involved in something that is of interest to the public; he can hopefully shed some light on the subject. Therefore the interview was sought in the first place as the result of a judgment of news values.

That judgment, made prior to the interview, predetermines the reporter's line of questioning. Time and the cost of film forbid rambling digressions unless, during the interview, the reporter stumbles unexpectedly upon a subject or point of view that is of interest. Of course, if the interview uncovers such an unexpected news bonus, it should be pursued.

But since in general the information sought is somewhat predictable, the reporter should plan his questions in advance—even write them down if his memory is faulty. He should do his homework beforehand. He should know the interviewee's probable positions on the issues to be discussed, and his probable reasons for taking those positions, based upon his background and previous activities. Estimating the interviewee's candor, the reporter should be able to anticipate roughly what the answers to each question will be, and whether he should be ready with a pertinent follow-up question. For example, if the reporter anticipates that the interviewee will at first deny any connection with the current city hall scandal, but the reporter is forearmed with evidence indicating the contrary, his follow-up question after the denial is a statement of his evidence and a request for an alternative explanation of its meaning. The news is most likely to be elicited by this follow-up question, planned in advance.

In other words, interviewing is in many cases a form of verbal fencing in which the reporter plans his attack in the hope of eliciting information which the interviewee may not wish to give. Even a reluctant interviewee will often reveal more than he plans to if pushed into a corner by adroit, persistent questioning. Even if he does not give a satisfactory answer, its very unsatisfactory quality may convey a great deal of information to the audience unless he can suitably explain his obvious reluctance.

A firm distinction must be made here between persistence in following a line of questioning and being argumentative. The reporter does not argue with the interviewee, he does not accuse; he merely inquires. But his inquiries follow the style of a well-informed devil's advocate; he asks the hard questions, the embarrassing questions, the opposing side's questions, the questions which either elicit a satisfactory answer or which, for lack of an answer, leave the interviewee visibly less than candid.

There are many interviews, of course, in which the information sought is freely and willingly given. But even with a fully cooperative interviewee, it is the reporter's duty to ask questions which force the interviewee to defend his point of view, not questions which merely give him an opportunity to make a speech of his own choosing. Only by such questioning is the heart of the matter uncovered.

The devil's advocate type of question is much more valuable to the television reporter than to reporters for other media, because the camera more fully exposes the weakness of a weak answer or a weak argument. Weakness may be revealed by the interviewee's manner, which no other medium can show, or by his hesitation and tone of voice, which only radio among the other media can fully transmit. These reactions, along with the words themselves, are part of the news; a "nonanswer" is sometimes more newsworthy than an answer. And in reporting the nonanswer television is supreme.

Sound

Sound is unquestionably the most neglected aspect of television news, despite the fact that the airwaves are full of it. The picture hypnotizes us to the extent that we forget that it is a *sound*-picture. The silent picture no longer exists. Even in the era of the silent screen the picture was supplemented by the sound of the piano player or organist in the movie theater. In today's television news all pictures are accompanied by sound, whether it is natural film sound, voice, music, narration, or a combination of these. At any moment some television news producer is likely to win acclaim for avant-garde originality by putting on the air that rarest of all news stories, a truly silent film. But for the purpose of this discussion we must accept the compulsion for sound and consider how to deal with it.

Natural sound In the field the reporter's most aggravating problem is likely to be natural sound. There is *always* natural sound: cars drive by, dogs bark, birds sing, the wind creates a rumble in the mike, and all of this goes onto the sound track. Sometimes natural sound overwhelms the desired sound; a jet liner taking off will completely drown the voices of an interview taking place near the runway, and a retake of that portion of the sound will be necessary.

In any case, sound must be explained if its source is not clearly evident. In a streetside interview the sound of passing cars is explained if the viewer sees them, if only in a silent lead-in. If noisy construction work is going on nearby, a brief shot of that work is usually explanation enough. If it is not, the shot may be coupled with a narrative reference to the source of the noise.

During an interview with actress Angela Lansbury at her seaside home in Malibu, it was necessary to explain the sound of the surf, which was only a few feet away but out of frame because of the camera angle dictated by other considerations. Miss Lansbury, bless her, solved the reporter's problem herself as only an understanding trouper could; during the filmed conversation she flung out an arm toward the invisible surf and explained, in perfect context with the interview, that the surf was one reason she loved living there. That kind of cooperation makes the newsman's job a delight.

The rumbling sound which wind makes in a microphone is like nothing on earth but the rumbling sound which wind makes in a microphone. It certainly does not sound like wind. If it cannot be avoided, it must be explained, and the explanation is inevitably an apology for shooting bad sound. The answer may be to cover the microphone with a wind sock, shield it under a coat, or move to a less windy location.

Music presents a particularly annoying problem when it is the background sound. Imagine an interview conducted in an office saturated with the omnipresent background music that is piped throughout so many modern buildings. If nonconsecutive portions of the master shot are used, the music will be only too audibly nonconsecutive too. Later, when reverses are shot, the tune has changed again. The musical mélange created by editing for voice content only makes it obvious to the viewer that tricks are being played; the viewer, having no knowledge of the technical problems involved, can only begin to suspect that the news coverage is tricky. If the music cannot be turned off, another location is advisable.

The same principle of matching sound applies for traffic, crowd, and other background noises. If the master shot has traffic noise, so must the reverses. If a plane flies over during the interview, any reverse to be used at that point should be shot, if possible, when a plane is flying over.

It is even necessary to match silence. Film sound, even when the background seems to be silent, carries a sound "presence" which differs according to the locality. For example, the sound presence of different rooms may vary greatly. The sound quality of a room depends on its size, shape, and furnishings; on the materials of which the room surfaces are made; on the number, size, and placement of windows and doors; and even on the number of people present, whether or not they make any noise. The same voice will not sound quite the same in different rooms, nor will a sound track recording of the silence in those rooms. Reverses should of course be shot in the same room in which the interview was conducted, if at all possible; certainly, if the interview was shot in a large auditorium, the reverses should not be shot in a telephone booth. But even silent cutaway shots may be unsatisfactory because of the total sound dropout on silent film; therefore cutaways should be shot on sound film for best results, so that the sound track can carry the sound presence of the location.

The presence of interior and exterior sound is obviously different, even to the untrained ear. Thus if a narration track is to cover film which moves from an exterior to an interior location, the narration should be shot in both places; the film editor will cut from exterior to interior narration at the point where the picture goes inside.

It is also necessary to make sure that *all* of the significant background sound is recorded. The story of ground-breaking ceremonies for a new office building was misleading because of this omission. The dedication speaker delivered some humorous remarks which brought laughter from the crowd. But the soundman was using only one microphone, at the speaker's platform, and it was set to pick up the speaker's voice; the laughter of the crowd, which was some little distance away, was completely lost to the sound track. The result was a deceptive film which made it appear that the speaker's humorous remarks were not well received, when exactly the opposite was the case. The fault was the reporter's; he should have foreseen the problem and ordered the soundman to use a second microphone to pick up crowd reaction.

Voice sound The ordinary interview usually presents no great difficulties in recording sound, but special problems are often encountered in filming public hearings and other large gatherings. The solution is often an unsatisfactory compromise dictated by the limitations of television news film equipment. The amplifier most widely used to record sound on film accepts two inputs; that is, it is designed to mix the sound originating from two microphones. But at a public hearing the reporter may wish to pick up the voices of several persons on the platform, others at a witness table, and still others scattered throughout the audience.

The number of inputs may be increased in several ways. One way is for the soundman to install "Y" connections in the input lines; one "Y" connection allows two microphones to feed into the same sound control "pot." However, adjustment of the gain control cannot differentiate between these microphones, and the soundman may have difficulty balancing these two inputs. (The only way he can do so is by moving the microphones.) A somewhat better solution is to add a sound mixer to the system; depending on its capacities, more inputs can be properly balanced. However, both solutions cause a reduction in signal strength, with a resultant increase in background noise and electronic distortion because of the higher gain, or volume, required. In other words, the more microphones used, the poorer the sound quality.

Some hearing rooms are equipped with loudspeaker systems incorporating provisions for additional sound pickups into which the news soundman can plug his equipment. A similar portable system, usually called a "presidential patch" because it was first used in a presidential campaign, can also be used by several camera crews at once. (The act of connecting into the system is known as "patching.") However, if too many crews patch into a system, it may become overloaded, with consequent debasement of sound quality.

The "boom" mike is often helpful for picking up sound from a group of people. It is a microphone suspended from a boom, or pole, extending over the heads of the group just out of the camera frame. News crews seldom carry a boom, but a boom mike can easily be jury-rigged with any kind of pole.

Another sometimes helpful device is the "shotgun" mike, a highly directional microphone with which sounds can be isolated and picked up from a considerable distance. The mike is aimed directly at the person speaking; its unidirectional quality tends to eliminate sounds originating elsewhere. But still, the farther the speaker, the worse the sound quality. And it is less useful indoors than out because of echoes bouncing off the walls of the room.

For picking up sound from a great distance, or from a moving vehicle, the wireless mike may be the answer. This is, as its name implies, a microphone which broadcasts its signal to a receiver and amplifier at a distance. In some circumstances it cannot be used because of radio interference.

It is not so much the reporter's job to decide precisely how the sound is to be recorded, as it is to anticipate and understand the general problems encountered. If unusual recording problems can be anticipated, he should advise the soundman of their nature before setting out on the story; thus advised, the soundman can pick up any equipment which he may need and which he does not normally carry.

Special sound problems   Artifice is sometimes the only way to achieve reality in sound. For example, certain sounds cannot be recorded directly with a single microphone. The sound of rain broken by loud crashes of thunder cannot easily be recorded because there is too much difference in the loudness of rain and thunder. Each must be recorded separately, then mixed, either in the amplifier-mixer or in the station control room.

In shooting the story of the telephone bug described on page 134, it was desirable to have "filtered" sound of the interview as heard by the eavesdropper listening on the bugged telephone line. Filtered sound is sound to which an effect is applied to alter its character; in this case it had to have the tinny sound characteristic of a telephone receiver. It would have been simple to tape a microphone to the receiver held by the listener, but the microphone would have been visible to the camera and its presence would have raised questions in the viewer's mind.

The solution was very simple. Two telephones were used; one was connected to the bugged line, the other was a dummy. The eavesdropper stood behind a counter (as viewed by the camera). The cradle of the bug-line phone was placed in sight on the counter; its receiver was placed out of sight below the counter, with the microphone taped to it. The cradle of the dummy phone was also placed below the counter, and its receiver was placed in the cradle of the bug-line phone. Thus when the eavesdropper picked up the dummy receiver to listen to the interview being conducted in the other room, he actually could hear nothing; he was "listening" on the dummy receiver. But the television audience could see him apparently listening, and it could hear (through the other receiver) the bugged conversation. What the audience saw and heard was, in the real sense, illusory, but the illusion was necessary to reconstruct reality on film.

Picture Problems

To bring back usable film with which his story can be told effectively, the reporter must make sure that the film is shot in a way to circumvent the limitations of the camera eye and the technical limitations of his camera equipment. These two categories cover a broad range of problems and possibilities of which the reporter should be aware.

Lighting Lighting is a critical factor in the shooting of film, and the reporter should leave it almost entirely to the cameraman. In particular he should never insist that the cameraman shoot too great a contrast in light values. For example, it is difficult and often impossible to shoot an interview in an office with large windows looking out on a view behind the interviewee. The outside light is so much brighter than the inside light at our command that even if the interviewee is brightly lighted, the background will still wash out. If the background exposure is correct, the interviewee will be too dark and his features completely shadowed.

Nor should there be too great a contrast in the light values of shots which will be edited in juxtaposition, such as master shot and reverses. The editing of an interview shot on the stage of an outdoor theater was severely limited because of such a contrast. In the master shot the interviewee was seen against the background of the rows of seats. In the reverse the reporter was seen against the Stygian black background of the unlighted stage. On film alone the reverses were usable, but not on television; the abrupt transition would have required an instantaneous and impossible adjustment in the video shading. The interview had to be used without the reverses, thus limiting the editor's selection from the film.

Most interior shots require special lighting because the camera, seeing everything within the frame equally, cannot adjust to too much contrast. It has only one exposure setting at a time. The human eye, roving the scene selectively, adjusts its exposure setting automatically (within its limits) to compensate for changing light values, but the camera cannot do this. For example, to light only the foreground of a long shot down a building corridor is not enough; lights should also be placed at intervals the full length of the corridor, otherwise it will look not like a long corridor but like a black limbo.

Today's widely used fluorescent lighting, so helpful to the human eye, looks bilious to color film. It imparts a muddy green cast to everything; people may even look ill. In a large, fluorescent-lighted room the cameraman can throw his film lights on a reasonably close subject to give it a normal hue, but the news film crew seldom has enough lights to light a large room properly. If a wide shot is necessary, the reporter must resign himself to the bilious background.

Where there is so little light as to make filming seem impossible, the cameraman should be consulted before hope is abandoned. Effective and visually dramatic night street scenes can be shot with available light with today's color film. Also, the film can be pushed approximately two stops in processing; that is, underexposure can be corrected chemically to that extent. However, the laboratory must be told precisely how much to push the processing, and it will take more time than normal processing.

Fast and slow motion   Film that is shot at a speed faster or slower than the normal 24 frames per second is seldom used in news, where the obvious time distortion detracts from credibility. However, under special circumstances the technique can be used to produce interesting effects. The slow motion shot is used most often in sports coverage, where it permits a leisurely and detailed study of an important play or action. Because nearly all sound cameras run at a constant speed, fast or slow motion film must be shot with an adjustable camera, usually a silent camera, and no sound recording is possible.

Slow motion produces a floating, dreamlike effect. Fast motion is jerky and the effect tends to the comic. Only if these effects are desired and do not distort the meaning should either be used, and then only if the viewer is given to understand what is being done and why. Playing games with him is acceptable only if he understands the game.

Inserts   The insert shot is useful for calling attention to a specific item, or for showing details which are not clear on a wider (usually master) shot. It implies the use of double-chain projection.

If during an interview the interviewee refers to a chart, a close shot of the chart may be needed to convey its meaning. All the reporter needs to do at the moment is make a mental note on the need for an insert. After the interview is ended, a close shot of the chart is taken with the silent camera; if the interviewee held up the chart momentarily during the master shot, he may be asked to hold it in approximately the same position for the insert shot.

Scale Because of the limitations of the camera eye, the scale of a filmed object must be explained visually. A shot of a wall twenty feet high, with no scale of reference in the picture, might as easily be a shot of a wall twenty inches high. But if a man walks into the frame, the viewer immediately relates the height of the wall to the height of the man. A close shot of a crack in the wall is meaningless until a hand enters the frame; if a man crawls out of the crack, the scale is obviously different.

Certain sequences may require the repeated use of a person in the frame to provide scale, or sometimes merely to add movement to an otherwise static scene. When such a sequence is shot care must be taken to avoid jump-cuts. Suppose the sequence begins with a long shot of the twenty-foot wall mentioned above. The reporter, providing scale, enters the frame and walks to the wall; now we know how big the wall is. Cut to a close shot of the crack; the reporter extends his hand into the frame, then withdraws it; now we know how big the crack is, and we are also free to cut to another shot showing the reporter without creating a jump-cut.

A series of walk-through shots is sometimes used to provide scale, and here again the limitations of the camera eye must be considered. If, say, the reporter enters the first shot at frame right and exits at frame left, he must enter the second walk-through shot in the same manner, right to left. If he enters the second shot at frame left, he seems to be coming from an impossible direction; the viewer becomes disoriented, and the film continuity is lost. The viewer tends to believe what he sees, but if what he sees does not seem to make sense, the fault lies with the reporter in his function as film director.

Camera angles Care must be taken in shooting certain camera angles and camera movements, either because the resulting shots create editing problems, or because the camera cannot obtain the same effect as the human eye.

Pan and trucking shots, for example, trap the film editor in time because they best begin and end in static position. However, such shots may be useful or necessary. To free the editor, a series of static shots covering the same subject matter should also be provided if possible; this gives the editor two ways to go.

Shots from odd angles should be used with restraint because of their curiously disturbing effect on the viewer—an effect resulting from the fact that he seldom if ever sees anything from such an angle. The "arty" approach makes him uneasy. A high-angle shot of two men talking, for example, is not a common view in life; such a scene is normally viewed from a horizontal angle. If the high-angle shot con-tributes to understanding of the story (if it is a POV shot, for example), it may be used, but an entire interview should not ordinarily be shot from such an angle. A low-angle shot may emphasize a man's height, or a woman's bodily beauty, but it is often uncomplimentary to the face. Contrarily, film of unusual architecture may well gain strength from the consistent employment of unusual angles which emphasize the lines of the structure.

Some shots are ineffective because of the dimensional limitations of the film picture. While at a glance it appears to be three-dimensional, it is actually composed of lines and colors on a two-dimensional surface. It has no depth except as the mind of the viewer interprets it to have depth out of his own related experience. To stand on the rim of the Grand Canyon and look down may be an awe-inspiring experience, but the same view on film seldom conveys the full effect; it is merely flatness, shot at no particular angle, just as in an aerial shot the rough terrain below appears smooth and flat.

However, if this same high-angle shot is taken from the roof of a New York skyscraper, looking down into the man-made canyon of a street, the effect of height is clearly conveyed. The receding perspectives of the buildings contribute to the sense of vertical distance, and the tiny cars and people in the street below give the mind a scale by which to judge.

Many otherwise ordinary shots are given a three-dimensional quality by placing an object in the foreground. This is why the distant building is so often partly framed by the wind-blown branches of a tree close to the camera. (If no tree is appropriately located, a cut branch is sometimes held into the frame near the camera.) A child's shoe lying forlorn on the street close in the foreground, while in the background attendants lift the injured child into an ambulance and police question a distraught motorist, is a poignant shot in which every element speaks to the viewer in the language of film.

Shooting transitions in the camera   Once the reporter is throughly grounded in the basic principles of film coverage, he can proceed to some of the more artistic considerations of the film director. In shooting news film, these are best exemplified by the manner in which he improves and simplifies his cinematic story concept by shooting transitions in the camera. Such transitions both speed the story tempo and simplify the work of editing.

One reporter was confronted with the problem of devising a transition between two family scenes, the first an actuality scene in the kitchen, the second an interview scene in the living room. A narrative bridge could have done the job, but the reporter conceived a better method. He had the mother walk directly into the camera at the end of the kitchen scene until her black dress filled the frame. He opened the living room scene on a close shot of the same dress, then quickly pulled back to a wider shot. The effect was of a fade-out and fade-in, except that it was visibly more than that; it was inherent in the way the film was shot. The transition was achieved with a single splice of the film, and it required no action whatsoever in the control room.

Another story concerned a young woman who spends her free time dressing as a clown and entertaining crippled children in hospitals. She was shot walking into the hospital, her clown costume draped over her arm, and as she approached the camera a large clown face on the costume filled the frame. Cut to a close shot of the woman starting to apply her clown makeup in a hospital office. Cut to close shot of her fingers reaching into the greasepaint jar. Cut to close shot of her face as she finishes applying the makeup. Cut to close shot of a wide-eyed child, zoom back and discover the clown entertaining children in a ward of the hospital.

Here we have compressed half an hour into half a minute, during which the young woman entered the hospital, changed from street clothing into clown costume, applied makeup, proceeded to the ward, and began to entertain the children. We see her first as she appears naturally (a prerequisite for establishing her identity) before we see her as the clown. All the transitions are accomplished with direct cuts, in every case using the clown face as a transition motif. Every shot, in its relation to the preceding shot, uses the discovery principle.

This kind of editing can be done only if the story is shot with this kind of editing in mind; the editing is a direct consequence of the reporter's cinematic concept. A more conventional way of shooting the same story might have resulted in the following sequence: establishing exterior shot of hospital, shot of woman walking in, shot of woman entering office and preparing to change into costume, shot of makeup box with greasepaint jars, shot of hand reaching into greasepaint jar, shot of makeup being finished, shot of clown leaving office, shot of children in ward, shot of clown entering ward, shot of children's reaction. This gets us to the same place but it takes twice as much time in both shooting and editing and it generates far less viewer involvement. It is not cinematic; it is merely sequential.

Not all stories lend themselves so readily to direct cut transitions. But the newsman works under constant time pressure, which forces him to seek the "quick and dirty" way of capturing the story on film. Fortunately, "quick and dirty" also forces him to think cinematically.

It is noteworthy that such transition techniques, which the newsman has developed out of necessity, are now emulated by theatrical film-makers and acclaimed as art. Even the scorned jump-cut is deliberately edited into commercial films where cost is no object. Film fashions, like women's hemlines, may rise and fall, but the newsman is forced to create his own fashion out of his own necessity, the muse if not the mother of invention. It is precisely in his application of cinematic imagination to the art of story-telling that the reporter makes his film transcend its function as a mere recording device and rise to the level of art.

Responsibility in the Field

By coincidence, television news is arriving at what promises to be the climactic stage of its formative period at a moment in history when its influence in the reshaping of American society is the subject of widespread debate and concern. The concern is justified, and the debate may be healthful. Television's cameras are barred from most courtrooms on the ground that they alter the very process of justice. A society undergoing wrenching social and economic change views with misgiving demonstrations conducted in certain part for the benefit of the camera and riots almost certainly intensified in violence by its presence.

In this uncertain climate responsibility for preventing the distortion of events by television rests with the field reporter more than any other man. He, and he alone, works at the source of the news as the primary proxy for the public. He, and he alone, uses this new and often frightening medium in direct contact with that same public, and can exert direct control over some of the events that will shape and crystallize the attitude of that public toward television news.

When a reporter brings along his own studio-made protest signs to enliven a televised student debate, as happened at the Claremont colleges in California, he does both his profession and the public a disservice. With ironic justice the reporter found himself and his crew picketed by angry students. But what lies beyond the anger and the irony? What will be those students' future assessment of the reliability of the nation's most important news medium?

Another television reporter had a scuffle outside a *bracero* camp "re-enacted" for his camera, then broadcast the re-enactment as the real thing. As a result the Mexican government withdrew several hundred of its nationals from the camp, and the American farmer found new cause to distrust television news. So long as stations or networks tolerate this type of "reporting," the farmer's distrust is justified.

Even the business-oriented entertainment trade paper *Variety* found reason to headline what it called a "Phony Picket Ploy by TV Newsmen."[1] The story reported that a network cameraman covering the

---

[1] *Daily Variety* (November 7, 1967), p. 9.

arrival of President and Mrs. Lyndon Johnson at a Washington dinner dance "went across the street and persuaded two young hippie women with guitars to come sit on the steps of the club's entrance to block President and Mrs. Johnson . . . The women complied, but local police got rid of them before the Johnsons' car pulled up."

The same story reported that when "Mrs. Johnson spoke at Yale not long ago, one TV network cameraman personally grouped some otherwise disorganized pickets carrying anti-Johnson signs. After arranging them in the best position, he put in a request for Mrs. Johnson to pose in front of them. She did not do so."

Not only does such deliberate distortion give, as *Variety* commented in the same story, "a new definition to 'news coverage,' " it poisons at the marrow the very lifeblood of democracy, information.

More subtly, less intentionally, and yet with equal deceit television distorts events by its tendency to favor the sensational picture over the less exciting event which gives a contrary impression. "More than newspapers," the *Variety* article continued, "TV newsmen have given saturation coverage to the pickets rather than to the event being picketed. In other words, the camera has been off what the VIP was saying inside, while it has been on the protestants outside." By such distortion television lends credence to the charge that it causes violence rather than merely reports it.

Granted, this is a monolithic view which fails to discriminate between responsible and irresponsible reporters. All are tarred with the same brush. But this fact itself should be of concern to the reporter, whatever his personal standards of integrity. Every irresponsible act by a television reporter makes his and every other reporter's work that much harder, and by that much it dilutes and contaminates the continuing flow of truth upon which the public decisions must be made.

No less evil than distortion by design is distortion by carelessness or thoughtlessness, for the result is the same. When a television news film crew was assigned to cover the picketing of a military installation in Van Nuys, California, by antiwar demonstrators, the reporter observed from a distance that the demonstrators were not picketing at all, but were lounging near the entrance gate. The reporter decided to park about a block away and wait for developments. In a short time a news crew from another station arrived on the scene without "casing" the situation; they drove straight to the installation gate, and the minute they appeared the pickets began marching up and down, obviously for the benefit of the camera. The first crew meanwhile quietly drove away without offering the "demonstrators" the free publicity which was plainly their sole aim. If a demonstration is conducted for no purpose other than to attract television news coverage, it is not news; if it is filmed at all, and if the film is used, it should be accompanied by a clear explanation of the apparent purpose of the demonstrators.

After the first night of the Watts riots in 1965, local officials held a public meeting in the riot area to try to prevent further trouble. During the proceedings a teen-age boy seized the rostrum and shouted inflammatory remarks which were a clear incitement to more rioting. This boy represented no one but himself, and under the tense circumstances the broadcasting of his remarks could have had no effect but to inflame a situation that was already dangerously out of control. Nevertheless, some television stations did broadcast the boy's remarks; reporters for others refused even to film them. Never was the division between the responsible and the irresponsible more clearly drawn.

Reporters covering urban riots have learned that the use of lights when shooting at night tends to draw a crowd and incite the rioters to greater destruction. Where this is likely, or even a mere possibility, shooting should be limited to filming with available light. In some circumstances the very presence of the camera has the same effect; if so, the responsible action is for reporter and crew to leave the area. Many crews covering riots prefer to use unmarked cars to avoid notice, even though the danger is that they may be fired on by police who do not recognize them as newsmen. Grave questions have been raised about continuous live coverage of riots, such as was provided from a helicopter during large portions of the disturbances in Watts; the helicopter itself, hovering over the heads of the rioters, can be viewed as a form of incitement, and so can the pictures it is transmitting—pictures which anyone in the riot area can watch on his television screen.

An inflammatory speech, a demagogic harangue, can be more violent than violence in the streets. Its effect cannot be measured, but there is an effect. There is also a question about whether such speeches should be reported, and, if so, how. Critics of television news have accused it of raising men such as Stokely Carmichael and H. Rap Brown to prominence simply by covering their activities, or by giving those activities more prominence than they deserve. One question the reporter must ask himself is: how many people do such speakers represent, what is their constituency?

However, they cannot be ignored simply because they represent a small minority; minorities, no less than majorities, are entitled to be heard from in a democracy. Nor can they be ignored simply because what they say is inflammatory—not when they address themselves to serious social problems. Riots cannot be ignored simply because covering them may incite a few people to further violence; the public at large needs to know what is happening. The real problem is not *whether* to cover such stories, but *how*. And here the reporter is confronted with a continuing dichotomy, a conflict between the public's need for information and its need for order; society cannot survive without both.

There are no easy answers, and in some cases there are no satisfactory answers. Some members of the public are certain to be angered by certain types of coverage; others are equally certain to be angered if that same coverage is not provided. The reporter, then, cannot be swayed by the prospect of such anger, no matter what its source; he has a job to do, and his aim is not popularity. His commitment is to the continuing flow of information. His responsibility is to see that the information is as balanced as he can make it. Every story presents a different problem, and requires a different decision. A few simple rules may at least help guide him to those decisions.

He does not set up or contrive a situation to dramatize conflict; he takes the situation as it is, and if it does not lend itself to film portrayal, he accepts its lack of cinematic values.

He attempts to determine whether the participants in an event are performing solely for the benefit of the camera, recognizing that an event does not make news just because it makes good action film. Most demonstrations, of course, have publicity as one aim; that alone does not mean that they are not newsworthy. But the reporter must determine what other aims are involved, how sincere the participants are, how significant their demonstration is, and what the other side of the story is.

He attempts to determine a speaker's constituency, and to let the public know the size and significance of that constituency. He does not broadcast film of inflammatory remarks simply because such film contains the elements of drama, conflict, and emotion, which make exciting film. If the speaker who makes such remarks has no constituency, the reporter gives him no broadcast platform. If the speaker's position has validity, regardless of his manner, the reporter tries to inform the public of that validity.

If the reporter's actions and presence in a tense situation are themselves inflammatory, he leaves the scene, recognizing that second-hand coverage is preferable to any actuality film which may contribute to public disorder.

These are at least some of the major elements of such reportorial concepts as responsibility and balance. Not until television reporters demonstrate complete responsibility will the public begin to consider in its proper perspective the charge that television causes violence. Where the reporter acts responsibly, the accusation actually derives from television's greater emotional impact. It is far more frightening to see and hear a riot from its midst than to read about it in a newspaper. But certainly no one giving the matter a second thought would contend that civil rights demonstrations, urban riots, and the violence accompanying anti-war marches would not have occurred if television did not exist.

What is happening is that television is changing society at the same time that many other forces are reshaping it. The specific effects of television are likely to be as far-reaching as were the effects of the invention of printing on the oral society of Gutenberg's world. But society did not abolish printing because printing changed the status quo; it learned to live with printing, and to make printing serve its purposes. It will also have to learn to live with television, with all of television's faults and all of its virtues.

During this transition period reportorial irresponsibility aggravates the danger of further restrictions such as the courts have already placed on television coverage of trial proceedings—restrictions growing in part out of irresponsible actions by reporters and in part out of judicial ignorance of the television medium. Comparably unreasonable restrictions were placed on early automobiles, but the automobile survived and the restrictions ultimately went the way of the horse. The accident of existence in a time of change puts an extra burden on the television reporter, who is establishing patterns and traditions which may endure for generations. Television news tomorrow will be what he makes it today.

Summary

Filming television news is a team operation in which logistics and deadlines are more important than in other media. The reporter determines the concept of the story; this includes the use of single- or double-chain projection, the filming of actuality or the staging of actuality, and whether narration is to be done (1) on film (a) over actuality or (b) separate track, or (2) in studio (a) over film or (b) standup, or (3) a combination of these.

Narration considerations include lip-flap, overlapping of takes, and subordination of narration to the more cinematic considerations of the story.

Interview techniques involve sound pickup, picture editing, selection of setting for cinematic value, the rules regarding reverse shots, advance homework, and the devil's advocate style of questioning.

Sound considerations include the explanation of obtrusive natural sound, the matching of sound backgrounds, and the anticipation of unusual sound pickup problems.

Picture problems of some concern to the reporter include lighting, the use of distortion techniques, insert shots, explanation of scale, and unusual camera angles. On a more advanced level, the reporter should seek and use opportunities to shoot transitions in the camera.

The original responsibility for credibility and the prevention of news distortion rests with the reporter, who must evaluate the significance of the event he is covering, the intent of the participants, their constituency, the effect of his own presence and actions on the scene, and the public's need for information about the event.

Suggested Assignments

1. Accompany a reporter and film crew on a story, and report on the following: (a) teamwork among crew members, (b) logistic problems, (c) the reporter's advance concept of the story, and how well it was executed, (d) use of actuality or staged events, (e) use of film narration, as to both type and structure.

2. Name the considerations which might lead a reporter to use each of the following types of narration: (a) film narration over actuality, (b) separate track film narration, and (c) voice-over in studio.

3. Cite examples of the use of imagination in the choice of interview settings, as observed on a television news show.

4. Name a suitable setting for an interview on each of the following subjects: (a) air pollution, (b) real estate company bankruptcy, (c) construction of a high-rise building, (d) a teachers' strike, and (e) a narcotics-peddling charge involving a teen-age discotheque.

5. Describe the difference between a real and a false reverse.

6. Name five prominent persons in your community who would make good film interviews; explain what you would ask each person, and why; and for each question list a prepared follow-up question.

7. Explain the advantages of the devil's advocate technique of questioning.

8. Explain how you would handle the sound problems of a story involving the shooting of actuality in a boiler factory and an interview with the factory manager.

9. State how you would explain the scale of the following filmed objects in a purely visual manner: (a) a basketball player 7 feet 5 inches tall, (b) a microbe, (c) Grand Coulee Dam, (d) a 100-story building, and (e) a beauty queen measuring 42–24–36.

10. Shoot a silent film story on a subject with interesting visual possibilities, with the principal aim of shooting transitions in the camera.

11. Write an analysis of examples of reportorial irresponsibility observed in television news, including your suggestions for a more responsible type of coverage in each case.

12. Give your estimate of the social and political significance of television's reportorial responsibility as demonstrated by its general coverage (local and network) of one of the following: (a) student demonstrations, (b) the war in Vietnam, (c) the growth of urban ghettos, (d) the problem of racial equality, or (e) air pollution.

Chapter 12

The Video Reporter

The reporter who works "live" or on video tape (they are essentially the same thing as far as he is concerned) is of a different breed than the reporter who works on film. The best reporters do both equally well, but such reporters are rare; many are unable to make the transition from one job to the other successfully, so different are the requirements.

The film reporter, as we have seen, is essentially a news producer; his product is the film of the story that he covers. His on-camera performance, while important, is less so than his reportorial ability and his knowledge of film shooting and editing.

The Paramountcy of Performance

But for the live reporter, in studio or on a remote, performance is paramount; all else is secondary. This performance is likely to be successful only if it is based on broad knowledge and experience in news, but it is only through his performance that he is able to convey that knowledge and experience. He must "carry" the show while he is on, no matter what disasters occur. He must perform with ease and surety under all circumstances that are conceivable and some that are not. There are no retakes (unless he is on VTR, and not always then); his errors are broadcast for all to see, and he cannot let this disturb him or upset his performance. He can never "lose his cool."

Nearly all of the production decisions which the film reporter must make on his own are made for the live reporter by his producer, director, or writer. He may share in the planning, he may write his own material, but when the camera tally light goes on and he gets his cue from the stage manager, he is strictly a performer. The cuts or dissolves from one camera to another, the rolling of film, the use of slides, key shots, supers and stills, the decisions as to what kind of shot to take—all these are determined by the script and the director. The reporter merely follows directions.

But his performance, which looks so casual to the viewing public, is an artful contrivance rather like the old trick of patting one's head while rubbing one's stomach. At the same time that he is reading the script, for example, he must maintain eye contact with the camera, watch the television monitor, watch the camera tally lights, watch the stage manager for cues, anticipate second by second any problems that his reading of the script may cause for the director, time his reading of lead-ins and bridges in his mind to avoid upcuts, anticipate what he plans to do if the film breaks or other disasters occur, remember to keep his facial and body movements minimized because the camera exaggerates them, and meanwhile try to inject the properly meaningful inflection into his vocal delivery while concealing from the audience all else that he is doing. The easier it looks, the more artful it is.

Th actor as newsman   The performance required of the live reporter is similar in most respects to the performance required of an actor, but actors seldom make effective newsmen. They may be accustomed to all of the mechanical aspects of the job listed above, but they seldom know enough about news. This ignorance is betrayed by their delivery; they stress the wrong words and put the accent in the wrong places. An experienced television newsman can usually detect whether the reporter's primary background is that of a professional announcer, an actor, or a newsman; the public cannot so analyze the reporter's performance, but its reaction to his delivery is shaped by subconscious factors which depend on the reporter's background knowledge of his profession. (Before we proceed, we hasten to admit that if actors make poor newsmen, it is equally true that newsmen make poor actors; in a world which demands specialized talents, each has his own proper place and aspires to the other's role in peril of his reputation.)

The professional announcer tends to be overly portentous and pontifical, and he is more concerned with the timbre of his voice than with what he says; this may be fine for announcing or commercials, but it is bad for news. The actor is more casual and conversational in style than the announcer, even to underplaying, but he tends to stress the wrong words because he does not understand the full significance of what he is saying. He is accustomed to receiving direction on the meaning of the script. But the newsman is self-directed in this sense. He also tends to speak more colloquially than the actor (script allowing), because he is accustomed only to playing himself and not a variety of characters, and there are more likely to be residual traces of regional origin in his voice. But the newsman's outstanding characteristic is an understanding of what he says.

The psychological x-ray Television has a psychological x-ray quality which enables the viewer to read the performer's character, especially in the presentation of news. Part of this x-ray quality is undoubtedly due to the newsman's ability to convey understanding through proper inflection. In commercials this is not really very important; the viewer knows he is receiving a sales pitch and that the information, such as it is, is biased. But when the viewer watches the news he expects to be informed without bias, and the significance of the various parts of the information varies greatly. The viewer knows this and he reacts to the proper delivery, whether or not he bothers to analyze it.

Another factor, probably of equal importance, is the typical close or medium close shot of the newsman's face, framed in the television receiver. It is a most extraordinarily intimate view of another person's face. Almost the only other situation in which one person sees the face of another so apparently close, with the freedom to examine it in detail, is when making love. This is again the world-within-the-frame, beyond which nothing exists, and thus the viewer's attention is concentrated on the smallest changes of expression; he can even react subconsciously to the involuntary dilation or contraction of the pupil of the newsman's eye, which has emotional significance. Each such change is grossly magnified in its effect on the viewer's emotions. If the reporter's expression corresponds with the meaning of the words, a unity of sound and action is created which deepens the emotional impact of the meaning, thereby conveying an impression of authority and sincerity.

No matter how skilled, the performer simply cannot convey this impression if he does not know what he is talking about. The intimacy of the medium betrays the actor for the same reason that it reveals the newsman; the actor does not know enough, but the newsman's knowledge communicates itself if he has learned the mechanics of performance. This is how the newsman is self-directed and why his performance is paramount.

There is, unfortunately, no way to learn the mechanics of performance except by performing, any more than one can learn to play golf by reading a book about golf. However, certain aspects of performance can be practiced and studied by the reporter while he gains experience.

Voice

Vocal personality   Voice is the instrument through which the newsman communicates his knowledge, and his vocal personality is therefore extremely important. A high-pitched nasal whine will cost him his job (if he ever gets it in the first place). He cannot stutter or stammer, hem and haw, or punctuate his speech with hesitant "uhs." He need not have the "pear-shaped" tone once considered so desirable in radio, but his tone and delivery must be clear and sharp. His purpose is not to impress people with his voice, but to make himself understood.

Voice lessons are highly advisable for anyone wishing to perform. A good voice coach will sharpen and clarify the basic sounds of speech, teach the reporter how to breathe properly from the diaphragm (few people do), and correct bad habits of pronunciation. Proper breathing alone deepens the voice and by reducing strain on the vocal cords prevents the performer from tiring. The performer who speaks from the diaphragm rather than from the throat can speak all day and never strain his voice.

How much voice coaching the reporter needs, only he can decide. He does not need as much as the actor, certainly not as much as the singer. Half a dozen sessions may be enough if he does the recommended exercises on his own time. It is probably a mistake to continue voice lessons so long that all trace of regional speech is removed; some regionalisms are part of almost every man's speech, to the extent that they are part of his personality. And the reporter should not try to suppress or change his vocal personality, only to polish it. He need only learn how to speak for himself most effectively.

Conversational delivery   The style of television news delivery is conversational, casual, and cool, in keeping with the style of good television news writing. The hard sell, the pontifical tone, the overly dramatic are all old-fashioned; they became so because they simply are not effective in the television medium. The literary style comes across snobbish and affected. Slang is highly acceptable, but the excessive use of slang is as affected as the literary style and it has the additional disadvantage of being imprecise. Clarity is essential, for the reporter has only one chance to make each point.

Conversational does not mean soft. While the delivery of a television newsman *sounds* like ordinary conversation, it is actually more forceful. More physical effort is exerted. The trick is to project the voice, at the same time preserving the conversational tone.

The reporter should remember that he is speaking to each viewer individually, usually in the privacy of the viewer's living room. The reporter is a visitor in the home, and he should speak in the same natural manner that he would if he were actually visiting in the home, sitting only a few feet from the viewer. The tone and manner of such conversation is quite different from the tone and manner of, say, a person giving a speech to a large group; the vocal personality of the public speaker is strained and forced in comparison to the personality of the private conversationalist.

Practice with a tape recorder is highly recommended. The reporter should read anything and everything aloud; the harder it is to read, the better the practice. Only by listening to the playback can he hear himself as others hear him. Newspaper stories are excellent for practice because so many of them are badly written; if the reporter can deliver a badly written story well, he will find the well-written story an easy conquest.

Eye Contact

Next to vocal delivery, eye contact is the most difficult of the live reporter's purely mechanical problems. By eye contact we refer to the ability to look directly into the center of the camera lens and hold this gaze while delivering long portions of script. Good eye contact is rarer than good vocal delivery.

TelePrompTer and cue cards Most newsmen use "crutches" such as TelePrompTer or cue cards to help maintain good eye contact. Cue cards are large cards or sheets of paper on which are written either the complete script or cue words of the script. The card is held near the camera, and the reporter may read directly from it rather than from the script, or he may glance at it occasionally to refresh his memory. For obvious reasons these are often called "idiot cards."

In news broadcasting the cue card has been almost completely replaced by the TelePrompTer, which is usually called simply the "prompter." This is a machine holding a long roll of paper about the size of ordinary paper toweling. The script is typed on this paper by a special typewriter using very large letters, about an inch high. The letters can be read from a considerable distance, and if necessary they can be enlarged by placing a plastic magnifying sheet in the front of the prompter. The prompter operator unrolls the script by remote control, keeping pace with the reporter's delivery. If the prompter is placed as close to the camera as possible, the reporter appears to the uncritical eye to be looking at the camera as he reads the prompter. Another type of prompter projects the unrolling script onto a slanted glass plate directly in front of the lens; the reporter sees the script, but the camera, looking through the glass plate in the opposite direction, sees only the reporter. This type of prompter comes very close to giving the impression that the reporter is looking directly at the camera.

Cue cards or prompters are not objectionable when the performer is working before a studio audience, as in delivering a speech or as in most variety entertainment shows. The performer appears to "play to" the studio audience while he is actually reading the prompter, which is out of the camera's frame line.

However, television news is strictly presentational. That is, the reporter addresses the television audience (the camera) directly, not the studio audience. Usually there is no studio audience for a news show. And for this purpose the prompter has so many disadvantages that it is only surprising that more reporters do not try harder to avoid using this crutch.

There is the problem of keeping the place in the script while reading the prompter; this is necessary in case the prompter jams or breaks down, or the operator carelessly fails to keep pace with the reporter.

There is the problem of losing eye contact during those portions of the script which are not on prompter; for example, late-breaking news is seldom on prompter. And the habitual prompter reader becomes so used to his crutch that he cannot maintain eye contact without it.

There is the problem of one more possible source of error, in the copying of the script onto the prompter paper.

But most important is the audience reaction. Only a professional may be able to tell when the reporter is using prompter, but even among those viewers who do not realize it or analyze it, the reaction differs from the reaction to the same reporter delivering the same material without prompter. Even where the prompter script is projected onto the glass plate in front of the camera, the reporter never really looks directly into the lens; instead his eyes move back and forth across the lens. The reporter who maintains good eye contact without prompter looks directly into the center of the lens, which means he looks directly into the eyes of the viewer at home. This direct gaze is subconsciously interpreted, rightly or wrongly, as evidence of honesty and truthfulness; any failure to meet the eye squarely is subconsciously interpreted, rightly or wrongly, as evidence of evasiveness or shiftiness. There is no avoiding this subconscious interpretation and its effect on the viewer's attitude toward the reporter. Thus the reporter who maintains good eye contact without prompter becomes more trustworthy, more believable, and more authoritative to the audience.

Maintenance of eye contact is mainly a matter of training the mind to absorb whole sentences or paragraphs at a glance and to remember them long enough to deliver them. No one expects the reporter to remember all the details of everything that happened on a particular day; no one minds seeing him look down at his script occasionally. It is better for him to continue looking down long enough to absorb a paragraph or so, then to look up and hold the camera's gaze for as long as he can, than it is to keep bobbing up and down between script and camera every other word.

An exception is the reading of quotations. Here it lends verisimilitude for the reporter to look down at the script during most of the quotation, glancing up only briefly now and then. The contrast between this deliberately bad eye contact, which conveys the impression of reading, and his normally good eye contact which conveys the impression of talking about something he knows well enough to report with very little reference to script or notes, makes his delivery all the more impressive.

Reaction to film and commercials Deliberate movement is the rule for leading into film, VTR, or commercials, and for coming out of them as well. Eye contact should neither be broken off too abruptly nor resumed too rapidly.

On completion of the narrative lead-in to a sound film story, for example, the best movement is a slow, deliberate turn of the head and the gaze to the television monitor; this cues the audience to the fact that the reporter, too, is going to watch this film. If on making such a turn he sees himself rather than the film on the monitor, he should not turn his gaze back to the camera unless cued to; he waits calmly for the film to appear. Even a wait of a second or two may seem like an hour, but events at this point are out of his control; he must assume that the film is going to appear unless he is given some indication to the contrary. Any fast or jerky movement, or glancing back and forth between monitor and camera, gives the impression of panic and makes the audience feel that something has gone wrong. Similarly, coming out of film, it is best for the reporter to be discovered looking at the monitor, then to turn deliberately to the camera and pick up his narration.

Coming out of the show's opening, or out of commercials, it is best to be discovered looking down at the script. The reporter should not appear to watch the commercials in any case. If on coming out of a commercial he is discovered looking at the camera, even a slight delay while waiting for his cue to begin narration appears awkward.

And in closing the show, the reporter should try to maintain solid eye contact for his final paragraph or so, then look down when finished without waiting for the camera tally light to go off. To stand there staring at the camera with nothing more to say is awkward, and sometimes the director does not immediately cut to the closing film or slide.

Personal Appearance

Personal appearance is always important for the reporter; it is perhaps most important for the anchorman, because he is on camera more than anyone else. Simple good taste is the rule.

Clothing Generally the newsman looks best in a dark, conservative suit, although certain specialists, such as sports reporters, can wear more flamboyant clothing than others. All clothing worn on the air should be of good quality and tailoring. Expensive clothing is the cheapest in the long run because it wears better as well as looks better. Men's "high fashions" which quickly go out of style and must be discarded after only a little use will of course require a greater outlay for clothing; worse, they call attention to themselves and distract the viewer from the news.

Checked and striped materials tend to "strobe" on the video screen; with every movement of the performer his clothing seems to come alive with movement. Therefore, plain colors and subdued patterns are best.

Everyone is probably familiar with television's "blue shirt syndrome." Actually, any color shirt will do. Even a rough-textured white shirt may be satisfactory on a color broadcast, although as a general rule white should be avoided for black and white broadcasts. The worst shirt for the air man is a heavily starched smooth white broadcloth. The problem is to avoid wearing anything that "flares" under the studio lights because it provides too great a contrast in light reflection as compared with the surrounding materials. If the reporter has any doubts about the suitability of new clothing, he should ask the director to look at him on the video system before broadcast and give an opinion.

And just in case of accidental damage to his clothing, the reporter is wise to keep an extra suit and shirt handy so that if necessary he can make a quick change before air.

Grooming It should hardly be necessary to mention that good grooming is essential for the live reporter. A good barber is advisable, and the hair should not be cut too short. Actors wear extremely long hair for the simple reason that it looks normal on screen. A newsman with too short a haircut may look almost as if he had been scalped. Women reporters we shall leave to their own devices and those of the beauty salons.

While the newsman is not expected to be an object of great beauty, age does take its toll, mostly on the hairline. The objection to bald heads may be unfair, but the reporter must expect to live with it. The only real problem with a bald head is that the backlighting may flare off the head into the camera. As Jerry Dunphy of KNXT once commented, "If all the toupee wearers in news broadcasting ever appeared together *au naturel*, it would be the greatest topless show in history."

Makeup Some makeup is essential for the live reporter, although in the author's opinion much too much is made of it. If the station has its own makeup artists, the reporter need not bother himself with details of makeup. If he does his own, all that is really needed is a light layer of powder, preferably of a shade slightly darker than his skin—a suntan shade. A few reporters, such as those with very sallow complexions, may have a real makeup problem; they are advised to consult a professional makeup artist.

The only reason for makeup in most cases is to reduce the light reflection caused by natural skin oils; without makeup the reporter may look "sweaty" on camera. It is often enough simply to wash the face immediately before air.

Working with the Stage Manager

Of all the people in the studio, the stage manager is the most important to the performer. The audience never sees the stage manager, but his efficiency and ability are critical to the success of any television news show.

The stage manager maintains order and quiet on stage, and makes sure that the performer is supplied with all his needs (pencils, adequate overhead lighting to read the script, properly placed television monitor, a glass of water). The stage manager makes sure that stills and props are where they belong. He receives the news script copies destined for studio use and makes sure that the proper air men get them. Using his own script copy, and sometimes aided by an assistant director (AD) in the control room, he times the script so that the show can end at the precise second it is supposed to end. He conveys the orders of the director, with whom he has intercom connections, to anyone in studio not so connected.

During broadcast the stage manager is the air man's only communication link with the control room. All of the performer's cues come from the stage manager. The air man never starts speaking until the stage manager cues him, and when the stage manager signals him to get off the air, he gets off. If emergencies arise, it is the stage manager who by whisper, gesture, or cue card lets the air man know what is expected of him. If the stage manager cues him to keep stretching a story forever, he stretches it forever. When bulletins are rushed to the studio in mid-show, it is the stage manager who, unseen by the audience, slips them under the eye of the air man.

Whatever cues the air man gets from the stage manager, he obeys them with implicit faith. Only the stage manager knows what is going on in the control room when one of the video cameras starts to fail, or when the film breaks in telecine. The performer may not know why he is cued to do something, but he does it without question.

Without an efficient stage manager, the proceedings in studio can quickly turn into a shambles. The wise performer appreciates a good stage manager and does not hesitate to let his appreciation show. The performer is, after all, the one who looks good as a result of the stage manager's incredible behind-the-scenes performance.

Keeping the Cool

The live performer's most important asset is an ability to ride with the punches. When the film breaks, the stage manager falls dead of a heart attack, the director loses his place in the script, and the back of the studio goes up in flames, the reporter calmly goes on reporting until he gets an end cue. If he runs out of script, he repeats from the top. He ad libs what he can remember. He grabs a newspaper and reads it. He keeps the show going by whatever means, and this is where he really earns his pay.

He can make life easier for himself by following a few simple rules. One is to insist on having 2 or 3 minutes of pad copy on hand *before* air time. In many shops the writers forget to provide pad copy, either through carelessness or through ignorance of its importance. Pad copy enables the air man to save many a show from disaster, and to do it so smoothly that the audience is never aware of trouble.

The reporter also always assumes that the worst will happen, because it does often enough to warrant the assumption. For example, he never uses profanity or obscenity near a dead mike; if he does, the mike is certain to be live. He never picks his nose over the film; the TD is certain to hit the wrong button and let the audience see him.

He does his homework daily by keeping up to the minute on the news, especially by reading extensively on all the continuing news stories of the moment. With this knowledge he can ad lib for hours on any of dozens of subjects.

But, above all, the live reporter cannot panic. Panic is contagious. It communicates itself to the viewers, and they agonize for the performer. But they do not enjoy this empathic response, and they are likely to tune in someone else if it happens often. The author recalls an election night special which illustrated the contagion of panic, even within the studio. The reporter on the air was reading results and commenting on various races, working only from slips of paper bearing candidates' last names and snap tally vote totals. Coming to one such slip, he could not recall the first name of either candidate, or what office they were competing for. He paused and studied the slip. And instantly there was tension in the studio, as distinct as an electric shock. Some ninety people working behind the scenes all stopped what they were doing within perhaps 3 seconds; they were motionless, staring at the air man. He looked up, grasped the situation, and laughed. Just as quickly the tension was gone, and everyone went back to work.

The air man's reaction was reassuring; he had not "frozen," which was what everyone feared. And when he saw their fear, the humor of the situation struck him so forcibly that his reaction was laughter. Of course, no one in panic can laugh. Interestingly enough, the instant he laughed the missing information came to his mind, indicating perhaps that he had been slightly tense without realizing it. The whole incident from beginning to end lasted no more than perhaps 5 seconds.

What that incident illustrates is that mistakes are irretrievable only if the reporter loses his cool, which means losing his command of himself. In a somewhat extreme form it illustrates why the most successful television performers are those with a casual, relaxed attitude. Such an attitude must, however, be genuine; it cannot be counterfeited. The relaxed attitude is possible only if the reporter is fully prepared for his job, familiar with all the mechanics of performance, and thoroughly knowledgeable about his subject. The inexperienced performer is almost never relaxed, and his tension communicates itself to his audience and makes them uncomfortable. It is another example of the psychological x-ray.

When mistakes do occur, it is best to ignore them because commenting on them only calls attention to them. But sometimes things go so badly, or so many things go wrong, that the viewer is entitled to some kind of explanation. Such was the case on a West Coast morning network news show on which almost everything conceivable went wrong. The wrong film came up repeatedly, script pages were both missing and misplaced, the slides were not in the proper order, and finally a strip of film actually appeared running upside down and backwards. There was no concealing the fact that the show, for that morning, was a total disaster.

Out of the backward-running film the camera came back to the air man, his head cradled in his arms on his desk. After a long moment he looked up with a wry smile and observed that some mornings there was just no point in getting out of bed. In return for such good-natured honesty, the audience will forgive many an error.

Summary

For the video reporter performance is paramount. Effective performance is based on knowledge of news plus knowledge of the mechanics of performance; the latter involves vocal personality, conversational delivery, eye contact, and personal appearance.

The video performer must have complete faith in the efficiency of his stage manager.

The video performer can never panic. This requires genuine calm and confidence; simulation can never deceive the audience. Such confidence is based on a solid news background and assurance in the mechanics of performance.

Suggested Assignments

1. Using audio tape recordings of a public speaker, a commercial announcer, and a newsman, define in detail the differences in their styles of delivery.

2. Explain the relationship between the air man's professional background and the psychological x-ray quality of the television picture.

3. Write a news story and report it to the film or video camera, taking care to use proper inflection and to maintain good eye contact.

4. Tape record your own delivery of a newspaper story. Rewrite the story in television style and record this version. Compare the two in effectiveness.

5. Explain the disadvantages of dependence on cue cards or TelePrompTer, and state under what circumstances their use is helpful.

6. Analyze the styles of lead-in to commercials used by two or more television newsmen.

7. After viewing a television news show in the studio, report on the activities of the stage manager, especially in his relationship to the air man.

8. From your own observation list examples of television newsmen who handled emergency situations either very coolly or very badly.

9. Script a 1-minute standup report, record it on video tape, and subject it to class critique.

Chapter 13

The Investigative Reporter

Investigative reporting is the greatest gap in television news. Most of the best investigative reporting is seen in the form of documentaries or news specials, and there is little enough of it there. In the daily television news medium there are comparatively few investigative reporters, and fewer still who deserve the name.

Ideally, investigative reporting should be a function of the entire newsroom, from news director on down. It makes little sense to leave this vital function of responsible news gathering to a single specialist, as is commonly the case in those television news shops which bother to engage in *any* investigative reporting. But in most shops routine reporting and production duties leave the newsman little time to delve deeply into promising stories of substance which require extensive legwork and investigation, with the result that the burden of investigative reporting, if it is taken up at all, is taken up by one man. Therefore it is this rather unhappy situation with which we must be concerned, and to which we shall offer some alternatives.

The term "investigative reporting" itself is widely misconstrued, perhaps because it is a redundancy. All reporters are investigators. But the investigative reporter, as the term is applied in television, is a special kind of reporter who engages in a very personal kind of journalism. He is a specialist, but in a broader sense and covering a broader field than the more familiar television specialists such as the political editor, the sports reporter, or the weatherman.

Topics for Investigation

Some so-called investigative reporters specialize in exposés, but that definition, while accurate as far as it goes, does not go far enough. Certainly the exposé can be a valuable contribution to public information, as in the case of exposés produced by the CBS Fact Finding Unit headed by Jay L. McMullen—exposés revealing corruption in the Boston police department and the casual wholesale traffic in barbiturates and amphetamine ("pep") pills. The first of these, *Biography of a Bookie Joint*, was a special program; the second consisted of news inserts carried by a total of twenty-one different CBS television and radio broadcasts over a 3-day period. Both resulted in official action by appropriate governmental bodies, thus demonstrating that the need for exposure existed and also indicating rather clearly that it was the airing of the exposés that prodded officialdom into acting.

But the exposé is only one phase of the work of the true investigative reporter. There are hundreds of other meaningful but neglected subjects worth reporting, subjects which do not necessarily involve crime or wrongdoing. The variety of topics may be illustrated by a partial list of subjects covered by a single investigative reporter during a single month: a Young Republican controversy over civil liberties, urban renewal, a grand jury investigation of a home construction scandal, civil defense inadequacies, dangerous new drugs, scandals in prepaid medical service, the relationship between smoking and lung cancer, plans of a new school administration, the grounding of certain types of air carriers, racial discrimination in housing, the John Birch Society, issues in a senatorial campaign, operations of an air reserve unit, and a controversy between the American Civil Liberties Union and an association of policemen and firemen.

Most of these stories were exclusive, at least in part. All were "reports in depth," as depth goes in television. Some led to legislative, judicial, or public administrative actions. Nearly all were uncovered by the investigative reporter through his own widespread contacts rather than in the routine flow of news across the desk of the assignment editor.

In general, these reports exhibited two common characteristics: the public interest was involved, and the subjects were being ignored or overlooked by other news media.

The Public Interest Criterion

From this we may conclude that the specialty of the investigative reporter, if it can be encompassed by a single term, is social problems.

He is constantly prodding and needling his viewers, informing or reminding them of matters suppressed, overlooked or neglected. He is, more than the ordinary journalist, a vital part of the democratic system of checks and balances. He is the conscience of the community.

On the most fundamental level the investigative reporter is a *creator* of news. He takes the position taken by one of television's finest newsmen, Edward R. Murrow: what he reports is news because *he* says it is news. In his approach to his topics, although not necessarily in his style, he resembles the magazine reporter or, better, the news documentary producer. He deals with contemporary crises, especially those hidden from public view, and by bringing them to public attention he performs a service for his community, whether that community is the neighborhood or the nation. His motivating principle is that no crisis can be dealt with until it is recognized.

This implies that the investigative reporter must "lead" events rather than follow them. He does not wait until the crisis explodes into action to report it. He searches it out before the explosion, so that if and when the explosion occurs it comes to the public not as a surprise but as the climax of trends long developing and recognized.

News stories which conform to this principle are without exception stories concerning situations still unresolved, still in the state of tension created by opposing forces. It is often this characteristic of tension which distinguishes the investigative reporter's work from other news, and it is also this characteristic which is most often misunderstood. The investigative reporter does not do "situationers," or stories which merely sum up the existing state of affairs with regard to a particular subject; he is not a mere collator of facts. For example, if unheeded scientific investigation indicates that a certain new drug has dangerous side effects unsuspected by the public and by a large part of the medical profession, the fact is worth an investigative report. But if federal agencies have already acted to warn the public and the medical profession, the situation is no longer in tension; therefore the investigative reporter turns his attention elsewhere, leaving this particular story to those reporters who do situationers.

Viewed from another angle, the topics of the investigative reporter almost always involve a conflict between the public interest and the interests of a private group or individual. In the case of the drug mentioned above, the conflict is between the public interest and the interest of the drug's manufacturer. If the investigative reporter has found evidence of malfeasance by the mayor of his city, the conflict is between the public interest and the mayor's personal interests. In no case can there be any doubt as to which side of such a conflict the reporter supports; he is always on the side of the public. This does not mean that it is his business to prosecute or persecute, but it is his business to bring all possible facts to light and thus to encourage the proper action by the proper authorities. In this sense the investigative reporter is the exact opposite of "objective."

Most news concerns events of the past, however recent. And here again the investigative report differs from other news; it looks to the future, at least by implication. Because it concerns matters in tension, its airing is likely to affect the way in which the tension is dissolved; that can happen only in the future. The reporter's concern for the future is what impels him to make his report.

Was the hidden genesis of the black nationalist movement a newsworthy matter of public interest? If it was, few reporters apparently thought so before the movement burst explosively onto the national scene. The same kind of import attached to the treatment of migratory farm workers when Edward R. Murrow exposed their condition in the CBS Reports documentary *Harvest of Shame,* and equally to a score more of social, political, cultural, or economic topics documented by television news.

But all too seldom does the *daily* television news show enter this arena of invisible issues crying for journalistic exposure. The issues are there, all around us in every era, but only the investigative reporter seeks them out. He always swims upstream; that way is harder, but his income, both monetary and psychic, is greater. His is no job for the novice, the careless, or the weak of heart. One mistake can cost him his job, and that is the proper price. With every report worthy of his title he toes the line between news and editorial commentary, and he comes away bearing the dust of commentary on his shoes. His report *is* a comment on an existing situation.

Attacking the Consensus

The further implications of this type of creative, investigative reporting are complex and extremely controversial. It is possible that the Constitutional function of the free press, which now includes television, is involved. Jay L. McMullen hinted at this in commenting on *Biography of a Bookie Joint:*

It was said by some that this program blackened the name of Boston by hanging that city's "dirty linen on a national clothesline." I think it would be interesting to debate two of the issues that were raised:

First, should the exposure of crime and corruption be left *solely* to regularly constituted law enforcement agencies? Some in Boston contended that it should, that such exposure should *not* be a function of any news medium.

Second, is it proper to display matters of local embarrassment before the entire nation—even though the purpose of such exposure may be an illumination of a pervasive national problem as exemplified by a specific local situation? . . .

We expected that the objectivity and authenticity of *Bookie Joint* would be challenged. It was. After the broadcast representatives of the Boston Police Department stated that they did not investigate the evidence that the program presented because they doubted the objectivity of CBS (not just CBS News)—and they contended that this particular program was an outright fraud.

I doubt that the authenticity of any broadcast has been subjected to a greater degree of scrutiny. The Governor's Council, the District Attorney, the Grand Jury, the Treasury Department, the Department of Justice—all investigated our evidence and used it as a basis for official action.[1]

The reaction described by McMullen is typical of the reactions the investigative reporter must expect when he digs beneath the surface and proves that things are not what they seem to be. The investigative reporter's work in fact proves the myth of objectivity. He takes what superficially resembles an editorial position; he seems to be "for" or "against" something by the act of reporting that it exists. And there is truth in this semblance. The facts of the situation are facts, but the newsman's decision to report those facts takes him out of the realm of objectivity and into the realm of value judgments about society and his profession. He really *is* taking what amounts to an editorial position, not by expressing opinion, but by revealing selected facts and letting them speak for themselves.

And because television's method of conveying information is not well understood, and its impact is so great, the investigative reporter's work is likely to arouse anger among those whose real or conceived interests are under attack. Their response is to counterattack the credibility of the reporter rather than to examine the facts and their meaning. Don McClellan of WSB-TV in Atlanta put it this way:

An investigative reporter is never the most popular man in town. After uncovering some chicanery by governing officials in a nearby county, we sent a cameraman to cover a meeting of those officials. They refused to transact business in the presence of the cameraman, finally adjourned the meeting. However, that group never had a chance in the next election. In fact, they didn't even run, after good government groups were formed with the avowed purpose of beating them if they did.[2]

If the investigative reporter finds himself unpopular, he can take solace in the thought that his work is vital to the functioning of

---

[1] Jay L. McMullen, "Investigative Reporting Comes High," *Television Newsfilm: Content* (New York: Time, Inc., 1965), pp. 1–2.

[2] Don McClellan, "Investigations Are Service to Public," *Television Newsfilm: Content* (New York: Time, Inc., 1965), p. 7.

democracy. Free government cannot exist without freedom of the newsman to report not only the pleasant but also the unpleasant. His work is not objective, at least not in the conventional meaning of the word as used in journalism. He does not strive for "balance" in any quantitative sense. If his presentation leans precipitously toward one side of the issue, it is because in his professional judgment that is the side which needs exposure. The other side is often the consensus, which has no need for exposure and perhaps has need of puncture. But when the reporter pricks the consensus he inevitably generates controversy. The pin of truth is painful, not least to the holders of the consensus. They resent it, naturally, and in their resentment they demonstrate that the audience is sometimes more "slanted" than the news.

Support by Management

Too often the investigative reporter works under a set of conditions peculiar to television, conditions which degrade his work into a series of contrived reports on subjects either too trivial to consume air time or already so thoroughly worked over that he contributes little if any new or worthwhile information.

One of these conditions is the expense of *thorough* investigative reporting. There is seldom adequate reference material to rely on, for the reason that the investigative reporter is himself developing source information. This may take days, weeks, or even months of tedious legwork. Sometimes the search ends fruitlessly and the story has to be discarded. But all this time salaries and expenses go on.

Biography of a Bookie Joint is a case in point. It was two years in the making. Jay L. McMullen spent a year and a half preparing another investigative documentary *The Business of Heroin*. The enormous cost of such painstaking work was plainly stated by the former president of CBS News, Fred W. Friendly: "He (McMullen) was a tremendous asset to *CBS Reports*, but we could afford only one of him."[3]

Management is seldom capable of comprehending why so much work and expense produce so little result. If a handful of men can produce a half-hour news show daily, why can't an equal number of men produce a half-hour of investigative reporting every day? Management would much prefer to spend its money on new equipment or other tangibles whose value its accountants can certify; in the view of the front office, the value of genuine investigative reporting is highly

---

[3] Fred W. Friendly, *Due to Circumstances beyond Our Control* (New York: Random House, Inc., Vintage Books Edition, 1968), p. 137.

questionable. Therefore management is seldom willing to give the investigative reporter the support he needs.

A second adverse condition is also monetary in nature. A top-notch investigative reporter usually can command a fairly high salary, because he is better than an ordinary reporter. And television talent salaries are scaled in an inexact but fairly direct ratio to the amount of time the talent spends on the air. Thus management tends to expect the investigative reporter to appear on the air frequently if not daily in order to get its money's worth out of him. The reporter may easily tend to agree to these terms because there is more money in it for him.

But he is hard put to come up with a meaningful report, say, 5 days a week the year round. There simply isn't that much that is both discoverable on a daily basis and also worth reporting. And so, again, the daily investigative report descends to the level of the contrived, the trivial, or the repetitious.

The difficulty stems largely from the diversity of topics. No man can be a specialist in everything, yet that is approximately what is expected of the investigative reporter. And the television reporter's time available for research and investigation is quite limited in comparison with the time his newspaper counterpart can spend checking out stories. Investigative reporting requires at least a 10-hour day if it is to be done well, and about half of that time, on the average, is spent in production (travel, shooting and editing film, scripting, and air appearance) rather than in gathering information.

All too often a story requires more legwork than the investigative reporter can afford to give it. Many such stories are consequently abandoned by television, only to be broken later by newspapers with their greater reportorial depth.

This kind of loss could be avoided if management would provide the investigative reporter with the support he needs. A legman, or at least a researcher, can be an invaluable aid, but is almost never provided.

Even better would be the establishment of a permanent investigative unit or team to research and develop major stories. The basic unit might consist of a legman, or perhaps a legman plus a researcher. When the team developed the facts to the point where production can begin, it could be augmented by a reporter, camera crew, producer, and anyone else needed.

This type of operation would free the reporter for other duties until his specialized services are needed. In the meantime he would continue to be a "generalist." When he joined the team for its film and air work, he would be backed up by the team's research, knowledge, and planning. More effective use would be made of his time and the crew's time, both of which are expensive, and this in turn would permit more of a documentary style in production, less of the "quick and dirty" approach. Further, the members of the investigative team, who do not appear on the air, would be better able to engage in investigative work which requires a degree of secrecy; the air man, whose face is well known to the public, would be seriously hampered in such work by his conspicuousness.

While the networks have begun to establish investigative teams in recent years, it is curious that permanent investigative units have not been based in Washington, D.C. The Washington-based unit could perform much the same function for television that is performed for newspapers mainly by a few syndicated columnists, who try to fill the investigative reporting gap in that important news center.

Backed by the enormous power and prestige of a network, the television investigative unit could perform a continuing and useful public service by acting as a governmental watchdog. It could force entrée into reluctant bureaucracies and pry out facts which their managers traditionally conceal. It could literally force the swollen, anonymous federal bureaucracy to be more responsive to the public needs, a task which even conscientious cabinet officers find difficult or impossible under present conditions. The only possible rein on a large bureaucracy in a continental nation is the press. The high cost of the federal government, for example, is probably in some part a consequence of the investigative reporting gap in Washington. The television network which first attempts to fill this gap in a responsible manner and on a continuing basis is certain to gain in public esteem.

In all areas of news, as television grows into maturity it must recognize its responsibility for doing more investigative reporting. It must become the major source as well as the dominant conveyor of news that is in the public interest. If management, local or network, hesitates to support the investigative reporter because he frequently seems to attack management's standards of value—the standards of the Establishment—greater wisdom would decree that management understand that the Establishment is not immutable, that change is the heart of the American process, and that part of the business of the investigative reporter is to report on and help promote needed change.

Lacking such wisdom, management should at least understand that responsible, imaginative, investigative reporting gives television news a dimension to which the public responds gratefully and which the news can achieve in no other way. If management lets the chips fall where they may, they will fall to management's account.

Like all men, the investigative reporter is best measured by his enemies; the newsman who makes no enemies does little to justify his profession. In a news medium which many persons suspect was emasculated at birth, the investigative reporter carries on the tradition of conscientious personal journalism. It is an honorable tradition, and may his tribe increase.

Summary

Investigative reporting, the greatest gap in television news, should be a shop function but is customarily assigned to an individual, who is consequently both overworked and inadequate.

Topics include not merely the conventional exposé, but any kind of social problem. Characteristics of the investigative report are the creation of news, the leading (as opposed to the following) of events, the view to the future, and the attack on the consensus by disclosure of fact.

Management seldom understands the value of the investigative reporter and consequently gives him inadequate support. Shops with adequate resources should establish permanent investigative teams, and networks should base such teams in Washington, D.C., to cover the federal government.

Suggested Assignments

1. Discuss the quantity and style of investigative reporting, if any, done by one or more television stations in your viewing area.

2. Draw up a list of subjects in your community which appear to be in need of investigative reporting. Explain why.

3. Produce your own investigative report on one of the subjects listed in Question 2, in one of the following forms (depending on available equipment): (a) written paper, (b) film report, (c) audio tape report.

4. Detail an example of investigative reporting by local or network television which "led" the event rather than followed it, and summarize its effects.

5. Explain the relationship between investigative reporting and editorializing, using examples from local television in your comparison.

6. Explain why an investigative report constitutes commentary even though it contains nothing but facts.

7. Discuss the dangers of irresponsibility on the part of the investigative reporter.

8. Interview a local television investigative reporter on his relationship with station management, and write a report on same.

Part Four

Television
News
Production

Chapter 14

The Assignment Editor

News which is produced in television's visual manner must first be covered in that manner, and the man responsible for determining that coverage is the assignment editor. He performs a function comparable to the combined functions of the newspaper's city and photo editors; he decides which stories shall be covered, and which film crews and reporters shall cover them. In many shops he is also responsible for the maintenance of such equipment as film cameras and the automobiles used by reporters and crews.

The assignment editor's position in the newsroom hierarchy is determined in part by the size of the news operation. In a small shop the news director usually performs the chores of the assignment editor. In a network organization, on the other end of the scale, the assignment editor's functions may be divided among several people, each with specific areas of coverage for which he is responsible. To understand the function of the assignment editor in the most important aspect of his job, obtaining news coverage, it is most useful to consider the individual working for a local station and responsible for all types of coverage.

Selectivity

While the assignment editor's selection of news to be covered is based on generally applicable news values plus those news values particularly applicable to television, he must be far more selective than the newspaper editor in his selections. He has fewer reporters and crews than the newspaper has reporters and photographers, and the shows for which he gathers news can use far less of it than the newspaper.

The statement that television news is all "page one news" is an exaggeration. Some years ago an imaginative critic had every word of a network news broadcast set in *New York Times*-style type and column width; the whole show filled *less than half* of the front page of the *Times*. Television's rigid time limitations force it to take only the cream of the news; the skimmed milk is left to other media. Television news "in depth" is, like the Platte River, a mile wide and an inch deep. Or, as Walter Cronkite has observed, those who get most of their information from television news are ill informed.

Those who want more depth of information will have to read magazines, books, and newspapers. They will anyway. Television and the other media are in the broadest sense complementary rather than competitive (a proposition to which the salesmen for all media will undoubtedly take exception), just as the intercontinental ballistic missile is complementary to the infantryman's rifle. The advent of one does not displace the other; it merely alters its relative importance in the total scheme. It is the total scheme which the assignment editor must keep in mind.

In that scheme, the newspaper reader turns to television to see something he has read about, and the television viewer picks up his newspaper to get a more detailed report than he saw on television. It is futile for either medium to try to fulfill the other's function. The assignment editor who is not reconciled to the limitations of his medium will live out his career in frustration.

But if television news is, with some exaggeration, all page one news, what *is* page one news? It is perhaps easier to define what it is not, what stories the assignment editor does not cover.

The first criterion is, as always, significance. This criterion excludes many stories which the newspaper editor, with his larger staff and many pages to fill, covers without a second thought: tree plantings, ribbon cuttings, minor beauty contests, branch bank openings—all or most of those events created for the primary purpose of eliciting publicity favorable to the creator. Such stories are oriented toward the promotion of special interests, on the general theory that what's good for the Chamber of Commerce is good news. There is nothing wrong with the premise except that television air time is so precious that television cannot afford to be interested in "good" news of this type; it is interested in news that is significant and, if possible, visually entertaining as well.

It is not that promotional events are always without significance.

But their significance is likely to be inversely related to the size of the community served by the television station. The opening of a new factory employing fifty people is a major news event in a small town; it passes with no more than neighborhood notice in a large city. On the other hand, the opening of that same factory in an urban ghetto where jobs are scarce may be significant in the hope it offers as a step toward solving the problems of the ghetto; its immediate significance in the economy of the city may be very small, but its symbolic and social significance may be enormous. The assignment editor must estimate the significance of any promotional event to his audience before deciding whether to cover the story.

For comparable reasons events of primary interest to the station management should be viewed by the assignment editor with dispassion. Everyone has seen television coverage of awards ceremonies in which only those awards won by the station broadcasting the report are mentioned; this is not news, it is promotional publicity. If the station manager is honored by the city council for community service, the factors to be considered are the nature of the service, its importance to the community at large, and whether the honor is helpful to anything but the management's pride. (The city council may simply be trying to curry favor with an important news medium, or it may have been pressured into conferring the honor.) A good rule is to cover such an event only if it would equally be covered were the honor going to the manager of an opposition station.

The station manager may, it is true, be pleased by such coverage, because his business is to promote good will in the community. His pleasure may make the assignment editor feel more secure in his job. But it is the duty of the newsman to try to persuade management that in the long run promotional publicity masquerading as news creates a credibility gap to the detriment of the station. Management should expect to get its satisfaction elsewhere.

Business news, to which entire sections of newspapers are devoted, has only a minor place in television news. The audience is too general and the subject too narrow in interest (which is why the newspaper segregates business news in a section of its own, to which the general reading audience need not repair). The viewer cannot skip the business section of the show as he can the business section of the newspaper; his choice is to watch or opt out.

Where business news is covered by television it is because the story transcends purely business interests. The controversy over saving California's dwindling redwood forests was a business story that received national television coverage, not because of the comparative handful of viewers who were concerned about the fate of the lumber interests involved, but because millions of Americans wanted their children to have an opportunity to see and enjoy the redwoods. The public interest of posterity was at stake. Similarly, a strike against the automobile or steel industry is a business story, but because of the size and economic importance of these major industries all Americans are concerned, and television reports the news of such strikes.

Society news, to which many newspapers devote special sections, is with the rarest of exceptions so trivial and meaningless that no television time should be wasted on it.

The selectivity of the assignment editor is clearly in evidence at the weekly news conferences of the mayor of Los Angeles, currently a colorful and controversial personality (Sam Yorty) whose comments consistently make news. The mayor usually begins by making announcements on various matters; most newspaper reporters take notes, but the cameras seldom roll. Next the mayor submits to questions; everyone takes notes, and all of the cameras are in action. Finally there are official presentations (a scroll to this good citizen, official greetings to that distinguished visitor); there is much note and picture taking, all of it by newspaper men. The television reporters and crews by this time have already moved on to more important stories. This oft-repeated incident clearly demonstrates one of the differences between newspaper news and television news.

Visual Values

Because the motion picture of actuality is television's most natural and most effective way of telling a story, the assignment editor is always on the lookout for events which promise actuality footage: rescue crews trying to save the victims of a coal mine disaster, rioters in action, helicopter pilots airlifting power poles to remote locations, soldiers in battle, policemen flushing a criminal suspect out of hiding, wrecking crews demolishing a building—all kinds of people engaged in all kinds of action.

A story which is worth only a paragraph or two in print may have much greater value for television simply because of its visual interest, a quality entirely apart from its significance. A colorful parade is typical of this type of news, low in significance but high in visual interest. Many sports events provide opportunities to present the television audience with the visual excitement of competition which is hard to convey in cold print. Some stories, such as the story of the redwoods mentioned earlier, give the assignment editor a chance to supply the show producer with film which is moving simply for its pure visual beauty; it is doubtful that anyone who has ever seen a redwood tree has failed to be moved by its sheer magnificence. Few words can communicate the weary frustration of motorists caught in a massive traffic jam as well as film of the becalmed cars and their drivers.

The Creative Approach

The danger of this emphasis on visual coverage is that it may create a tendency to ignore the significant in favor of the purely visual. This concern must always be uppermost in the assignment editor's mind. But the significant story does not necessarily lack visual qualities, although sometimes they must be sought out. Here the assignment editor can function more creatively than almost anyone in the news shop, by conceiving and suggesting ways in which the story can best be captured on film.

Does the story concern protests of a local parents' group over excessive violence in television or motion picture entertainment? Then perhaps clips of violent action can be obtained from a theater, or from the station's own library of filmed or taped shows, for inclusion in the news report along with the filmed comments of the parents. No other news medium can so successfully illustrate this type of story.

Is a neighborhood organization objecting to plans for a new highway cutting through the neighborhood and destroying its neighborhood values? Then, in addition to filmed interviews with the organization's spokesmen, film and graphics can be used to show the proposed highway route, the homes it will destroy, and the manner in which it will divide the community.

Has a city official spoken out in a public hearing on the need for a stoplight at a dangerous intersection? Then it is not enough to cover his comments at the hearing. Properly shot film can show traffic racing through the intersection, and pedestrians crossing in peril of life and limb.

Has a businessmen's group been successful in finding jobs for the hard-core unemployed? Then television can best tell the story by filming some of the new employees at work, and by interviewing them and their employers on their feelings regarding the program, its successes, and its failures.

Even a trite and oft-told story can be made fresh and visually interesting by a creative approach. This is a perennial problem for television stations in Los Angeles every New Year's Day, when evening news coverage of Pasadena's annual Rose Parade is considered a "must," but most viewers have watched the live coverage of the parade the same morning. KNXT solved the problem one year by assigning reporter Ruth Ashton to film the entire day of the drum majorette who led the parade, from pre-dawn breakfast to tired feet at the end of the march. The viewers saw the traditional coverage of crowds, floats, bands, and marchers from a new perspective.

By an imaginative approach to the problems of show continuity, the assignment editor can also make a creative contribution to the success of the news operation. For example, if he has assigned two reporters to two different but closely related stories, he can instruct one to close his film narration with a lead-in to the other. In production the two stories can then be edited as one continuous sequence.

Few stories are not susceptible to visual improvement by the assignment editor, who has the best over-all view of the news flow of anyone in the shop. All he needs to do is to approach his task with creative imagination.

Speed of Reaction

Like any news editor, the assignment editor must be capable of reacting rapidly to fast-breaking news developments. Spot news stories, in particular, may become nonexistent for film purposes within minutes, and if a crew is not dispatched to the scene immediately there may be nothing for them to shoot; the fire will already be out, or the cave-in victim rescued and in the hospital.

To keep up to the minute on spot news the assignment editor must keep a constant watch on incoming wire service reports. Radio monitors tuned to fire and police emergency frequencies may alert him to news stories long before they are reported on the wires.

The assignment editor should keep his lines of communication to reporters and crews open at all times. Most stations equip their crew vehicles with radio telephones; despite delays caused by overcrowding of the air waves, this is usually the fastest way to contact a crew in the field. In any case, the reporter should be instructed always to leave with the assignment editor a telephone number where he can be reached while on a story. Reporters and crews should also be required to telephone the assignment desk before leaving the location of a story, especially if they have been out of contact for some time.

When air deadlines approach, the time spent getting film from location to the station becomes critical. Reporters and crews, encumbered by equipment and traveling in heavily loaded vehicles, seldom can move rapidly. Therefore a messenger sent to meet the crew on location and rush the film to the station may mean the difference between getting the story on the air and failing to make the show. The fastest messenger is usually the professional motorcycle courier.

Most important of all is the assignment editor's ability to make a rapid evaluation of alternative news stories and assign a crew to the better story without delay. This often involves pulling a reporter and crew off a story before they have finished shooting. Such decisions can be made only by an experienced newsman, thoroughly familiar with television news values and unafraid to act on the basis of his snap judgments.

What may happen when the assignment editor is unable to act rapidly was illustrated by the case of a story involving approximately 4 hours of round-trip travel time plus a number of camera setups requiring perhaps 2 hours of shooting time. In this case the assignment editor was trapped in a committee system of making decisions; the committee took 2½ hours to make up its collective mind to cover the story after the assignment editor recommended coverage. By the time the film was shot the hour was so late that it became necessary to charter a plane to fly the film to the station, at an extra and unnecessary cost of one hundred dollars. Obviously, speed of reaction is closely related to cost of operation and to the logistics of television news coverage.

Logistics

To understand the logistics of film coverage the assignment editor should have had one or more years' experience in the field, working with camera crews. No other experience is adequate preparation. Unfortunately, there is a tendency to promote writers to the position of assignment editor; while the writer may have excellent news judgment, his ignorance of the problems encountered in the field is a serious handicap.

In addition to those logistical considerations discussed in connection with speed of reaction (communications and travel time), the assignment editor needs to be able to make a rough judgment as to how long it will take to shoot any given story. He also needs to be able to anticipate any special equipment the crew may need in the field.

Special equipment   There are many items of equipment which the news film crew may not normally carry, but which it will need under special circumstances. If such needs are not anticipated before the crew leaves the station, shooting may have to be delayed until the equipment can be sent to the crew, or the resulting film will be disappointing in quality.

For example, the filming of a large dynamite blast may require a telephoto lens of exceptionally long focal length; if the lens is not available, the cameraman either fails to get a close enough shot of the blast or endangers his life getting the shot. For lack of a wireless microphone, distant sound pickups may be impossible; as a result, the crew must spend additional time shooting film to cover the need, and the film editor must struggle desperately to make a good story out of poor footage. If a large interior setting is to be filmed, the crew may need extra lights; if they don't have those lights, the audience will never see the setting the crew was sent out to film.

Anticipation of such needs requires that the assignment editor check out the shooting conditions in advance, then consult with the crew on their needs. This is fairly standard procedure in the filming of documentaries, but in the daily news operation the crew is often left to discover its special needs in the field. An advance telephone call by the assignment editor (or, on his orders, by the reporter assigned to the story) can save the crew much trouble and improve the quality of the film. Not the least of the benefits, it might be added, is the appreciation the crews will show for the assignment editor's consideration of their problems.

Shooting time   The exact time required to shoot a story cannot be predicted, but experience in the field gives the assignment editor a rough gauge for calculating. A simple interview with one subject may be shot in half an hour or less, whereas a complex visual story involving many camera setups may take all day. The time required for each camera setup is a function of the lighting problems involved and of the travel distance between setups. Thus, interiors take more time than exteriors, and widely separated setups take more time than setups in the same immediate area.

Even the time needed for a simple interview can vary enormously. The subject may be late arriving, unexpected noise nearby may cause frequent interruptions in shooting, a microphone cable may have to be repaired on the spot, fuses or circuit-breakers may go out if the lights overload a circuit—any of a thousand unanticipated troubles can delay shooting.

Therefore the assignment editor's time allotment should always be generous; it is better to shoot a few stories well than to rush the crews and, as a result, shoot many stories badly. On the average, one film crew can be expected to cover two to four stories per day; but there are many days when the averages do not apply.

Amount of Coverage

If crews and reporters are available, the assignment editor is tempted to cover every story he possibly can. The temptation should be resisted

—at least until he has considered how many stories his station's shows can use. Even a 1-hour show can seldom use more than twelve to fifteen film and VTR stories, especially if they are allowed adequate length. If, say, twenty film stories are shot, it is certain that several of them will not be used.

If possible, the assignment editor should give the show producers some luxury of choice. But considering the cost of crew time and film, he is wiser to restrict his coverage to the best stories, and to allow more time for shooting them. This improves quality and cuts costs at the same stroke.

To avoid overshooting, the assignment editor must work in close cooperation with the show producers, trying to obtain the film they want or need. If a producer indicates that he does not want a particular story, the assignment editor should abandon it unless he is so convinced of its value that he feels the producer will use it once he sees the film. If repeatedly the assignment editor proves wrong about this, he should be guided by the producer's judgment; his own judgment may be better, but it avails the station nothing if the producer will not use the film.

Foresight

One of the most creative aspects of the assignment editor's job is his use of foresight to improve the over-all quality of the news product. There are many ways in which he can demonstrate foresight.

For example, if a legislative hearing is scheduled for 2 days hence and he plans to cover it, foresight dictates that in advance of the hearing he obtain film covering the predictable subject matter of the hearing—film which often cannot be obtained at the last moment, and which will greatly enhance the visual qualities of the story. If the hearing is to concern regulation of night clubs, film of night club activities, shot in advance, can then be used in connection with film of the hearing itself.

A list of potential film feature stories with somewhat lasting or "evergreen" qualities should also be maintained by the assignment editor. On slow news days crews can be assigned to shoot these stories, which can be held for release whenever the show producers need them. Several such HFR (hold for release) stories are always available for immediate use in a well-run news shop.

Similarly, if there is a scarcity of news on a particular day, a reporter may be better occupied renewing contacts than in covering stories of dubious value simply to shoot more film. "Busyness" is not the measure of a shop's efficiency, and a few hours of a reporter's time invested in research or the renewal of his news contacts may pay dividends in the form of several good stories in the days ahead.

Renewal of his own contacts by the assignment editor is equally a matter of foresight. Although he is necessarily chained to his desk for most of his working day, he can maintain a large number of contacts by frequent telephone calls and, when possible, personal visits. His contacts can also be maintained and extended by deliberate association with news sources during his hours off duty; most men who are genuinely interested in news do not find this use of part of their leisure time irksome, and it increases the assignment editor's value to the shop enormously.

Perhaps above all, the assignment editor must be willing to gamble on his foresight. He must be willing to risk losing an ordinary story to win a better one. He must never be afraid to commit his last reporter and crew to a potentially great story that may turn out to be a dud.

Both negative and positive aspects of this gambling instinct were demonstrated several years ago when two airliners collided over the Grand Canyon in one of the nation's worst air tragedies. The first information to reach newsrooms on the story was merely that two planes were overdue and unreported. As time passed and it became apparent that both planes had gone down somewhere, the potential dimensions of the story grew. Further investigation disclosed that the two aircraft had departed Los Angeles only a few minutes apart, and that their scheduled flight paths crossed over the Grand Canyon. This, coupled with the fact that pilots often circled over the canyon to give their passengers a better view, indicated a strong possibility of a midair collision.

More than one television assignment editor wanted to rush a crew to the Grand Canyon, gambling on the chance that the crash had occurred and wreckage would soon be found. In at least one case, that of a network, the suggestion was vetoed. But another network, NBC, rushed cameraman Dexter Alley to the scene, and he obtained the first films of the wrecked planes shortly after they were found.

The assignment editor's educated hunches don't always pay off as well as that one. But the operating principle is always the same. The assignment editor will be forgiven for stories on which he tried and missed; he is never likely to be forgiven for the major stories he lacked the courage to try to cover.

Summary

Selectivity in story coverage is required of the television news assignment editor to a much greater degree than is required of his counterparts in other media. His selectivity is based primarily on significance and secondarily on visual values.

By seeking explanatory visual angles and new perspectives, he functions most creatively.

By rapid decision and due consideration for logistics, he functions most effectively.

By foresight he contributes enormously to the visual values of future stories.

By demonstrating the courage of his convictions, he may achieve greatness—or at least keep his job.

Suggested Assignments

1. From a newspaper select *all* of the stories you would choose to assign for television coverage for a half-hour show. Explain your reason for each selection.

2. In the same case, explain why you would omit coverage of any stories given prominent play in the newspaper.

3. Interview an assignment editor and report on his view of the important factors in his work.

4. Discuss the ways in which the assignment editor can function creatively to improve the quality of news coverage.

5. List the logistic factors which should be considered in assigning stories.

6. Discuss the nature and application of foresight on the part of the assignment editor.

Chapter 15

The Producer: In Principle

In the beginning and the end, there is the producer . . .

Someone has to put the show together. Someone has to decide what news goes into it, who is to report it, and how. Someone has to be the boss.

In television news the boss of each show is the show's producer. In different shops he may have different titles. In a small shop he may be the news director. In a large shop he is usually titled producer. In the early days of television news he was usually called the writer, but gradually came the realization that in selecting, writing, and editing the content of the show he was doing more than mere writing. He was producing.

However, he does not produce precisely as the motion picture producer does, for the television news show producer is seldom concerned with casting, financing, or selecting studios and equipment. His newsmen, his technical facilities, his time allotment—all of these are, so to speak, presented to him by the station. His problem is how to use them.

Motivation

If the message is merely the medium itself, as Marshall McLuhan contends, it does not much matter how the producer uses his men and materials. But television news is not like the underground newspapers of psychedelia, of which a news dealer once commented to the author:

"You used to read to understand. Now you have to understand it to read it." The purpose of news is to inform. And if there is more to it than McLuhan seems to suspect, the producer had better first decide what his message is.

Why is he producing the show?

The motives of the other participants are clear and unequivocal: the station airs the show to make money and justify its license, the sponsor buys into the show to sell his product, and the station employees work on the show to pay the landlord and the grocer and send the kids to college.

None of these is motivation enough for a good newsman, let alone a good producer. Why is *he* doing the show? The stock answer, of course, is to inform the public. But why bother? And with what kind of information?

Television news, or what passes for news, ranges from the measured jaundice of certain talk show hosts to the illuminating intellectuality of an Eric Sevareid. There are as many kinds of television news shows as there are kinds of newspapers. As the opening of a television entertainment show set in New York used to point out, there are eight million people in this city, and eight million stories. Which stories is the news producer going to put on his show?

Right here he must make a subjective judgment, a value judgment. Is the sensational rape story more important than the dull meeting of civic leaders grappling with the problems of the local ghetto? Shall he use film of a gory turnpike accident in preference to VTR of President de Gaulle's remarks about a free Quebec? Is the rather routine news of the war in Vietnam bigger news than the sharp drop in the stock market? The producer must decide. He *cannot evade* decision.

The Myth of Objectivity

It is not the purpose of this book to discuss basic news values except as they may differ from the traditional norm when applied to television. But the producer must understand the relationship between *his* news values and the fate of his show. His value judgments determine both style and content. And he must understand that they *are* value judgments. If he is obsessed with the journalistic myth of objective news, he perforce makes those judgments blindly.

There is no such thing as objective news, except in the sense that news concentrates on external reality, on facts. Objective news cannot exist for the simple reason that one man's objectivity is another man's passion. The newspaper's hay market report, a table of prices, is not really objective news. The prices may be factual, but the only reason they are in the newspaper is that someone cares about the price of hay;

that is his passion, and the newspaper caters to it. The only reason anything is in the paper is because someone cares, someone is interested. But *everyone* is not interested. Only someone. The use or nonuse of every single story in every news broadcast, the time allotted to the story, the placement of the story within the broadcast, the style of its presentation, the personality assigned to it—every one of these things must be decided deliberately, and every decision involves a qualitative value judgment. That is what journalism is all about.

But if there is no such thing as objectivity, there is honesty. There is impartiality. There is balance. There is responsibility. There is professionalism in the choice of values. There is, to sum it all up, a producer. He chooses the value standards of the show; it reflects his beliefs about his profession and the world at large. Catering to his audience, as the newspaper caters to the reader interested in hay prices, is neither objective nor objectionable. The question is: to whose interests shall he cater?

A network news producer in New York once laid it down to his staff as law that any mass rapid transit story should top the show. "What are they talking about on the subway?" he asked. "That's news."

And that is what we suppose could be called the subway standard of news values.

An anti-labor newspaper editor in Chicago was long famous for favoring what he called "goon" stories—stories of labor violence. Each year someone in his office would surreptitiously make up a list of the "Ten Best Stories of the Year" as supposedly selected by this editor; the list always consisted of ten "goon" stories.

That's the "goon" standard of news values.

Everyone has seen newspapers and television shows that concentrate on stories of crime, overblown exposés, and celebrity gossip.

That is yellow journalism, still another standard.

Educational television stations, for lack of money or imagination or both, too often present news shows consisting largely of long standup stories, detailed reports on esoteric events, and complicated discussions of an abstruse philosophical nature.

That might be called the intellectual standard of values.

The Mass Audience
and Democracy

To establish a suitable standard for himself, the producer must consider the essential nature of television, its dialectic. It is, first of all, a mass medium, for better or for worse, and this means that television news should be addressed to the mass audience—to the public at large, and not to any special segment of that public. This concept, so obvious it is a cliché, both presents limitations and offers opportunities, but immediately it begins to shape the producer's system of values. His is not a job for a dilettante, and he has no business catering to an audience whose tastes are in any sense specialized, whether intellectual, economic, ethnic, morbid, depraved, snobbish, or simply trivial.

The producer's business is everyone's business.

Secondly, the commodity he purveys is knowledge. And knowledge, as men wiser than we have pointed out, is power. Since the consumer of the knowledge the producer purveys is the public, we are talking about public knowledge. And public knowledge is public power.

The producer must therefore be the prime defender of the public's right to know, in full confidence that the public in its ultimate wisdom will make proper use of that knowledge. If it should not, that may be his concern, but it is not his *business;* it is another matter entirely, in relation to which he functions not as a producer but as a member of that very same public. (It should be added that the "public's right to know" does not, of course, imply any defense of invasion of privacy except where private actions involve the public interest.)

To insure the public's right to know, the producer must cultivate relentless hatred for all censorship, including his own. He must be willing to fight government, business, special interests, his own employer, and his own instinct of self-preservation. He must be as ready to take on the Establishment as the Disestablishmentarians. He must be willing to bite the hand that feeds him, for its own good. All this is of course true for all newsmen; the producer should merely be the best of them all, because he more than any other man is responsible for what the public knows, and what it does not know.

The business of the producer in a democratic society is in fact the survival of that society. If it can survive, it will survive first of all because the public has determined that it shall survive. That determination is based on the public's conclusions on thousands of matters of which it has knowledge. Only an informed public can make a wise decision. It is no accident that the very first controls imposed by all authoritarian systems are controls of the most rigid kind on news; no such system dares let its people know what is happening, because the free flow of knowledge inevitably destroys all authoritarian and ideological systems. It is also no accident that the first amendment to the Constitution of the United States guarantees against such controls; the framers of the government intended it to be nonideological and nonauthoritarian, and they well knew how best to keep it that way. Man is incapable of designing for eternity, but he is capable of governing himself if he knows enough. If the public's decisions are not wise, the reasons—assuming it is adequately informed—lie elsewhere, outside the scope of this discussion.

This, then, is the meaning of the public's interest in a democratic society. If the producer bases his system of values on that interest, he will know what to include in his show and what to exclude, what emphasis to give and how to give it. He works for the public.

Relations with Management

Unfortunately, the producer we have now defined is a contradiction in terms. He may have the authority to function as suggested, but if he uses that authority he may lose it—and his job as well. His weakness lies in his relationship to management.

The producer of a television news show is a staff producer; that is, he is an employee of the station or network which airs his show. He is in the same category as the janitor, whose ideas he may occasionally steal, the only difference (from the station's point of view) being that he is slightly higher in the pecking order.

The great motion picture producers, the great theatrical producers, are not staff producers. Alfred Hitchcock works on no one's staff; he works for Alfred Hitchcock, and his pictures have not acquired distinction because he allowed anyone else to tell him what pictures to make or how to make them. Greatness and staff status do not seem to go together.

The staff producer's problem is that someone he cannot afford to offend is always disagreeing with him. Talent, for example, is a determinedly and persistently insubordinate breed, single-minded in advancing what it conceives to be its own interests, both willing and able to gamble for far higher odds than the producer. Being under contract rather than employed, as a rule, talent has already bought insecurity as a way of life and gambling as a way of improving its lot. The producer must also take well-meant advice and/or orders from the news director and the station manager, sometimes even from the sales manager and the promotion director. Their functions are better understood by management, which consequently values them more and pays them more than the producer.

Still, the producer must somehow prevail.

The Committee System

These psychological and sometimes not so subtle pressures lead many producers to drift into the committee system of making decisions. Northcote Parkinson to the contrary, this system may work well enough in more predictable businesses such as automobile manufacture, where the premium is on imitation rather than imagination.

But in television news the committee system leads surely, however slowly, to disaster. Television is really a blue-sky business, no matter what efforts management makes to alter this fact, and a committee cannot function in a blue-sky business because a committee never gambles. The committee always plays it safe. Granted, the committee will seldom if ever produce a terribly bad show. Neither will it ever produce a memorable show. It will do all the routine things routinely well. But it will do none of the things of which great shows are made. The committee is doomed to mediocrity.

This is because the committee—*any* committee functioning as an executive—is purely and simply a device for passing the buck. For some participants it also appears to serve as group therapy, but its real function is to so disperse executive responsibility that no individual member of the committee can be blamed for anything. Who ever heard of a committee being fired?

The weakness of the committee is particularly evident in its reaction to news. News is the most perishable of commodities, and the news producer must react to events instantaneously, instinctively, automatically. If he must pause and debate what action to take, he is not a producer, just a committeeman. The author has known news committees to take weeks, months, even years to make a simple decision: do the story, or forget it. This is the way some of the best stories are lost to an alert, fast-reacting opposition.

The committee system also leads to fiscal waste. The decision to cover a story is delayed so long that "catching up" with the lost time becomes inordinately expensive. Planes must be chartered to fly in the film on time, crews work overtime to shoot it, editors work overtime to cut it, video transmission lines must be rented, all needlessly. In the largest shops such waste can run to many thousands of dollars a year.

Above and beyond this direct waste and the loss of stories is the psychological impact of committeeism. The executive indecision which characterizes the committee, and the mediocrity of its decisions, offend and demoralize the news organization's most creative, most valuable members—the people it cannot do without in the long run. Creative people are always hard to integrate into a corporate operation; they are more or less nonconformist, aggressive, inner-directed, and decisive. Their philosophy was perfectly expressed by comedian Danny Thomas: "If I die, let it be suicide, not murder." Executive indecision is a form of murder; it makes the functions of the shop's creative people uncertain, dilutes their effectiveness, and annoys and frustrates them. Most of them will accept a decisive news management if its decisions are not consistently bad or mediocre; all they really want is to know what the rules of the operation are, and then to be let alone to do their jobs within that framework.

But if the decision-making process is allowed to deteriorate into committeeism, the result, after a period of time, will be the debilitation of the news show. A feeling of dissatisfaction, a vague unease, will spread through the shop like a plague. Newsmen will give up trying to "sell" their ideas because their proposals are seldom acted on, or the action comes too late. The operation will settle into a rut—a disastrous occurrence in any business where constant change and innovation are the only certainties.

The underlying reason is that the newsman, like any other human being, wants to feel that he is needed and that he is making a useful, creative contribution. He requires repeated assurance of this; it is the psychological thumb he sucks. He and his ideas must be used, or corrosion sets in. But the committee asks him only not to rock the boat; eventually he does not care if it sinks.

The author is well aware that this argument runs counter to many of the so-called "modern management" theories. But the application of those theories to television news is highly questionable. In comparison to many businesses, television news requires greater creativity, less reliance on tradition, a more skeptical stance (more cynicism, if you wish), and a deeper philosophical understanding of the substructure of society. One cannot look at events through glasses of rose or any other color and see them for what they are.

But these questioning, skeptical attitudes are not customarily regarded with great favor by television management, no matter how much lip service is paid to them. And the producer of the news show finds himself squarely in the middle. As a staff member, an executive, he must be management oriented and pro-Establishment. But as a newsman he must be willing to oppose management and criticize the Establishment. He must have the courage to put his job on the line.

Most newsmen understand this dichotomy, if in some cases vaguely, because they all share it to a degree. Certainly it is an uncomfortable situation for the producer. He is seldom so well paid that he can afford to quit on a moment's notice; on the other hand, there will be days when he can continue on the job only at the expense of his conscience. It is easy to understand why he may take refuge in any self-protective device, such as the committee, which diffuses his authority and allows him to escape decision.

Unhappily, he cannot thus escape judgment. Whether he uses it, abuses it, or ignores it, the responsibility for the show is his. And the show mirrors more than the world; it also reflects the producer's soul.

Summary

The producer must understand both his own motivation and the essential nature and meaning of television news, because both determine the nature of the show he produces.

He must understand that his decisions are based on value judgments, which are largely subjective, that he works for a mass medium, and that its function of news dissemination is critical to the survival of democracy.

As a staff employee, the producer should avoid dependence on the executive committee system, which leads to fiscal waste, staff demoralization, and production mediocrity.

Suggested Assignments

1. Explain the social importance of the television news producer's motivation.

2. State and explain your view of the proposition that objectivity in news is unattainable. If in your opinion it is, define the acceptable alternatives.

3. Define your own standard of news values.

4. Explain your view of the function of television news in its relation to the mass audience.

5. Interview a television news producer on his standards of value, and report whether in your opinion they are adequate.

6. Examine and report on the use of committees to perform executive functions in a television news operation; if the committee system is not used, report why.

7. Study and report on the effectiveness of a committee charged with executive responsibility in any area of human activity.

Chapter 16

The Producer: In Practice

Just as the newspaper has a makeup or format, so the television news show has a structure which determines the placement of stories in the show and the relationship of all of its elements. It also has (or should have) a calculated pace, style, and particular personality of its own, all of which contribute to the total impression it makes on the viewer.

The makeup of the show is far more critical than the makeup of the newspaper. The paper to some extent can lead the reader from story to story by page placement, headline styling, and artful composition; but the reader himself determines which stories he reads, and in what order. (The author's wife reads the bridge column first, no matter what is on page one.) In contrast, the television viewer can see the news *only* in the order predetermined by the producer. If the continuity is boring or displeasing, the viewer's sole option is to opt out. The producer's job is to make sure the viewer does not pick up that option.

Since the abandonment of the segmented show, the structure bears no resemblance to that of the newspaper, with its specialized sections on sports, business, entertainment, society, and comics, each in the same place every day. Nor does the structure resemble that of the press wire service story, which can be trimmed from the bottom with little loss; nothing in television is like that. The show has a beginning, middle, and end, each with its own special requirements and characteristics.

The Top of the Show

The rule of "first things first" has as much application in television as in other media. The lead story should *always* be the *most significant* story in the day's news.

But there are many days when it is difficult to select one story as most significant; there are more likely to be two or even more stories of roughly comparable significance. In determining which story is to top the show, the producer is forced to rely on those values which are distinctively applicable to television.

The lead story is not necessarily the same story that the newspaper banners (with, all too often, a 120-point line which promises more than the 9-point type delivers). The banner line is designed for newsstand sale, to catch the eye of the passer-by. But television news is not "sold" this way. All the viewers the show is likely to attract are already tuned in at the top of the show; the lead story cannot add to their number because it has no means of catching the attention of those who are not tuned in. Aside from promotion and advertising—matters beyond the scope of this work—building an audience is a matter of building the show's reputation for interest and quality day after day over a long period of time.

All other things being equal, which they seldom are, the most significant film or VTR story is a better top of the show than the equally good nonvisual story. The film story is uniquely television's; the producer is therefore anxious to let the viewer *see* the news, as opposed to merely hearing or reading about it, and his instinctive preference for the film story cannot be questioned.

But it is only too easy to overstress film's importance. A boring or trivial story is not made earth-shaking by superior film coverage; it is still boring or trivial. The tendency to use action footage must be countered with restraint; exciting action film sometimes magnifies an event in the mind of the producer, but its importance must be judged without such magnification—which is to say, without regard for its purely cinematic qualities. The same restraint must be exercised with regard to film of powerful emotional quality; what is important is who cares and why, not the mere generation of emotion without regard for significance.

But where the values of action, emotion, and significance occur together, the film story deserves the top spot in the show. It combines all of the elements worthy of the producer's first consideration.

The Ending

In some ways the ending is the most important part of the show, simply because the news broadcast *is* a show. There is wisdom in the old show business adage, "Always leave 'em laughing." In television news the producer is limited by what he can cull from the day's grist; rather than a laugh, it is likely to be a chuckle, a wry twist of irony, or a memorable deed to rise in the mind when the rest of the show is long forgotten.

What is needed here is not as obvious as what is needed at the top. The choice of material is difficult, the handling of it even more so. Many shows whose producers apparently are unable to cope with the problem have no particular style of ending, and unless a stylized closing can be achieved consistently with good taste, this is perhaps best. An ending that is coy or cute, or that offends by reaching too far for humor, is worse than one which is merely boring. Some significance is a desirable ingredient, but it is not necessary.

A brief, upbeat feature story is a good closing, and if it is a film feature, all the better. An important item of news just received of course may take precedence at the last minute, but such items cannot be counted on; we are concerned with the ending which can be planned well in advance. Unless it is unavoidable, the show should never close with tragedy or unpleasantness; the bad taste will linger, and the audience will stray.

No matter what style of closing is planned, it should be *backtimed*. That is, the closing story or section is prepared well in advance (often it is the first part of the show to be written), precisely timed, and if possible rehearsed. Just ahead of the closing is a pad section consisting of several short items, any or all of which can be dropped to adjust for time. When there is just enough time left for the closing section, the air man "dumps out" of the pad and begins the prepared closing. Thus he is able to end the show unhurriedly, with polish and style, and precisely on time. The viewers may not recall what he says, but they will long remember the way he leaves them.

The Middle Section

What comes first or last in a news show may be reasonably obvious, but what comes fifth, or twenty-fifth, is not so easy to determine. The show is not simply a collection of news stories thrown together in random manner. The necessity of putting the most important news at the top of the show does not mean that it is structured on a scale of descending values. The last impression the viewer should get is that each successive story is less important, less newsworthy, and less interesting than the story that preceded it. The name of the problem here is continuity.

Audience psychology The psychology of the audience is the key to continuity. In the dear dead days when Hollywood film factories ground out B movies like so many sausages, there was a rule of thumb by which scripts were written. And if some of them seemed to have been scribbled by writers who were all thumbs, this may explain why. The rule was to bring the members of the audience to the edge of their seats every 10 minutes, then let them relax.

How well this purely mechanical means of achieving Aristotle's catharsis works depends on the artfulness with which it is used and the sophistication of the audience. The most artful producers never underestimate the audience; its collective perception is overwhelming. But the method has direct application to the longer television news show, which demands changes of pace and which contains no automatic, built-in means of supplying them. The continuity of television news is as artificial as that of the B movie.

However, the problem is the reverse of that of the B movie; it is not to stimulate the audience into interest, it is to give the audience a moment of relaxation. The news, like a pep pill, is overstimulating, excessively exciting. But no viewer can remain in a constant state of excitement for 30 to 60 minutes. After 10 or 15 minutes of war, riot and revolution, he needs psychological if not physiological relief. There may still be important news to come (the governor's news conference, a scandal at city hall, a society murder), but the viewer needs a "chuckle break," or at least a chance to calm down a bit. He needs some *good* news: his taxes are going to be reduced, the latest space probe was a success, the lost children were found safe. He needs an upbeat story.

Wave structure The body of the show might appropriately be viewed as an example of wave action, with peaks and valleys of interest succeeding one another. The climax is at or near the top (like the climax of the individual story), but there are many lesser climaxes.

The secondary climax may be more than half-way through the show; certainly one or more strong stories should be held for the latter portion of the show. Seldom, however, is the secondary climax (the second highest wave) the second-best "hard" news story; common sense will dictate higher placement for that story. More often the secondary climax is an exposé, or an exclusive report in depth, or a story which lifts the entire show to a new plateau because of its dimensions of insight and perspective. It is almost never a feature story; substance and significance are its hallmarks.

In general, as the show progresses, its hard news element diminishes, while its philosophical and feature content increases. But this rule cannot be applied arbitrarily without consideration of the effect of content on audience psychology. A show is not a tossed salad. It may contain stories of war, fashions, riot, circus clowns, plague, weather, a funeral, political humor, and tragedy on the highway; but in that order there is no continuity, only confusion. The audience cannot be expected to jump back and forth too abruptly, or too often, between moods of tragedy and comedy, importance and trivia. One or two such transitions may be made in an hour, especially where a shock effect is desired, but it should be remembered that the effect *is* shock. Repeated shock induces mental fatigue; the mind wanders, and the hand reaches for the channel selector switch.

Packaging   To avoid transition-induced shock caused by wide variations in content, it is desirable to "package" related items: international news in one package, domestic politics in another, urban problems all together. Within each package variations in mood can be achieved without inducing shock simply because the items within the package are related in subject. For example, a controversial political story which stirs heated emotions might well be followed by a thoughtful article on another aspect of politics, and this by a humorous political incident of the day; the change of mood is gradual, not abrupt.

It is also advisable to turn each package over to a single writer and let him, in effect, produce his own package. When the same writer handles the same subjects each day, his expertise helps to reduce redundancies and the package acquires a day-to-day continuity of style, thought, and material.

One of the most frequent violations of the packaging rule occurs when a sports story tops the news, as for example during baseball's World Series. In such a case the sports reporter may give the news of the series high in the show, then return later to report the run-of-the-locker-room sports news.

The sports package, it might be mentioned, is usually placed late in the show on the theory that sports fans will wait through anything to get their favorite news, but that a large percentage of the general audience tunes out the moment that sports comes on. By this theory, carried to its obvious conclusion, the general news show should not contain a sports package. This is the theory followed by the main network news shows, which report only major events in sports. For local shows, however, the theory probably does not hold; interest in sports is highly localized, depending on the presence of hometown teams or stars in the station's broadcast area.

The packaging rule is frequently broken to accommodate stories which reach the studio too late to be included in what would normally be considered their proper place in the show. These may be bulletin items hot off the wire service teletype, or film stories on which editing is not completed until, perhaps, the show is already on the air. The bulletin, since it usually consists of standup copy only, is easily inserted at the first convenient place; if it is of major importance, the stage manager may be instructed to hand it to the air man even in the middle of another story. The late film story may have to be placed on a separate film reel and projected on a separate film chain; its use therefore may depend on the facilities available.

Other changes of pace   Aside from packaging, the producer has at his disposal several other means of making the gradual changes of pace and mood demanded by audience psychology.

One is the change of talent. To switch from the anchorman to the political reporter creates a change of pace purely by change of personality, regardless of content. The film report from a correspondent in the field is a change of pace from the air man in studio, again regardless of content.

Variations in the style of presentation also affect the mood of the audience. A filmed interview, consisting mostly of "talking head" shots, is a change of pace from a film action story. Or, after a long, involved story of any type, a series of short items picks up the pace and also gives the viewer the impression that he is getting a lot of news. If such short items concern personalities in the news, and the standup copy is covered by a series of stills of the people involved, this too creates a change of pace.

Other transition considerations   Where transitions must be made between dissimilar stories not part of a single package, the producer must consider the demands made on the air man and whether those demands are compatible with audience psychology.

The problem here simply emphasizes the importance of packaging and the need to avoid shock transitions. For example, in moving from one story to another of roughly similar vein (as from a murder story to a story on police activities), the air man usually effects the transition simply by pausing for a second or so. There is no need for the producer or writer to worry about the transition because the continuity flows naturally.

But if the two stories are of vastly different character (say, a hilarious film story followed by a story of death and destruction caused by tornadoes), the abrupt change of mood demands an impossible readjustment on the part of the air man—a readjustment which emphasizes the failure of the producer to consider continuity. The performer must react with a smile to the film, then within a second or two suppress the smile, then adopt a somber mien and tone appropriate to the story of the tragedy. If he achieves this lightning transition successfully, he will get credit from the viewer only for insincerity. But the credit should go to the producer; obviously, these two stories should not be directly juxtaposed. A story of neutral emotional character, neither funny nor tragic, should be placed between these two stories as a buffer to allow both performer and audience time to readjust.

Transitions between stories which are contrasting in content but not in mood may be achieved by scripting the lead of the second story with a casual reference to the first; it is up to the producer, who assigns the stories their places in the show, to suggest such a transition to the writer. A sports report immediately following the weather news might begin: "The weather may have been bad in Cleveland today, but the sun was shining on the Indians in Chicago where they beat the White Sox. . . ." Nonsensical as it may seem on close examination, this type of transition, which might be termed the "reference transition," helps to suggest the conversational flow so desirable in television delivery. However, there must be *some* connection, some reference which is common to both stories, even if relatively unimportant. The danger lies in reaching so far for a connection that the transition becomes strained and calls attention to itself; this, too, destroys continuity.

Reference has already been made to the resemblance—in style, although not in content—between the television news show and the variety entertainment show. This resemblance is clearest in the need for continuity at transition points. Variety shows employ aptly named "continuity writers" whose business it is to script appropriate transitions between acts. While the news organization seldom can afford a writer to script nothing but continuity, any sizable shop usually has at least one writer who is demonstrably more apt at continuity than the others, and the producer should assign transitions as part of that writer's work. Curiously, some writers never seem to grasp the problem of the transition. One widely known and otherwise highly capable television news writer—let's call him Smith because that is not his real name—is so famous for his inapt transitions that newsmen in his locality have come to call all such breaks in continuity "Smith yaks."

Blocking out the Show

Continuity has its most obvious natural limitations in the available news, in the technical considerations (the time required to recue film or tape, the number of film chains and other facilities available), and in the necessity for inserting commercial spots.

In blocking out the show, one common approach is to locate the commercial spots approximately equidistant from one another in time, then drop the news stories into the time slots between commercials. While this is perhaps the easiest procedure, it has the unfortunate effect of letting the mechanical problem of commercial insertion dominate the structure of the show. The time slots are all of approximately the same length, and the tendency of the producer is to order the news stories tailored to fit these time slots regardless of the requirements of the stories themselves.

A better approach is to block out the show solely with regard for news and production values. First to be determined is the order in which the major visuals (film, VTR, graphics) will be used. Standup copy is used to fill in around the visuals to provide the necessary time for recues, refocusing of video cameras, and the like. Once the structure is thus determined, commercials are dropped into the show where they least interfere with continuity. It is better to have commercials only a minute apart, or to double-spot them, than to squeeze a 6-minute news story into a 4-minute time slot.

A package may stretch over one or more commercials, but it is not good practice to break a single story with a commercial in the middle unless the story is so long that this cannot be avoided. Nor is it good practice to stretch a package beyond a commercial break, then start another package. The commercial provides a clearly defined break between packages; it is the one built-in transition device in the news show.

Commercial Lead-ins

The style of the transition from news to commercial spot is determined by the producer unless, as sometimes happens, it is set by higher management. There are four basic types of commercial lead-ins:

1. At the end of a news segment the commercial comes up immediately on a direct cut. This transition, which is almost a nontransition, fails to set the body of the news apart from commercial content and sometimes misleads the viewer, especially if the content of the com-

mercial is somewhat related to the content of the preceding news story.

2. The picture fades to black between news and commercial. This is always an effective transition, but hyperthyroid producers dislike the fadeout's effect, which is of a momentary pause in the show. The author does not consider that objection valid, believing that the viewer is not as impatient as the producer. The fadeout also gives the director some leeway in rolling the commercial film or VTR, and thus makes for a clean transition.

3. A title slide identifying the show precedes the commercial. This has the same advantages as the fadeout transition. In addition, it serves to remind the viewer which news show he is watching; such reminders are of doubtful value, but they are highly regarded by sales-oriented management.

4. The newsman in studio (or, occasionally, on film) delivers a vocal lead-in, and the commercial follows on a direct cut. This type of transition, like the first one mentioned, requires an accurate roll cue; if the air man hesitates or stumbles in his delivery, the commercial may be upcut.

The effectiveness of the vocal lead-in depends mainly on its style. Some producers live in constant fear that the audience will change channels during commercials, and for this reason they "tease" the viewer with a "promo": "Coming up next, the governor shoots his wife!"

The tease lead-in reflects a subconscious feeling of inadequacy on the part of the producer, as well as a subconsciously disparaging view of the audience. In the first place, the producer feels that he has not produced a show interesting enough to hold the viewer through the commercial; in this, of course, he may be right. In the second place, he fears that the viewer may tune out on the assumption that the show is over; this same view of the audience as a collection of eight-year-old mentalities leads the entertainment show producer to hit the viewer over the head with the obvious and thus deny him the pleasure of involvement and discovery.

In fact, the tease lead-in is offensive to the more discerning viewer, who does not appreciate being "talked down to." Nor is the audience so collectively stupid as to think the show is over; the viewer has seen commercial interruptions before, and he is quite capable of recognizing another one without explanation. Further, the tease lead-in may *cause* him to lose interest if it refers to a story he does not care about; he is less likely to tune out if he does not know what is coming than if he does. The news by its very nature is a mystery; he watches to find out what happened.

Also, in a 1-hour show a succession of tease lead-ins to commercials may occupy a total of 1 or 2 minutes—time better devoted to news. Therefore, the best vocal lead-in is a simple statement: "More news in a moment," or, "Back in a minute, after this."

The worst vocal lead-in is one which allows the newsman to promo the commercial: "More news after this message for Blotto, the paper towel that soaks up ten times its own weight!" The more professional news operations flatly forbid any such degradation of the newsman into commercial pitchman.

With the qualifications already discussed, the type of lead-in used is largely a matter of personal preference. The author happens to prefer the fadeout and, secondarily, the title slide; both are fast, simple, effective, and less likely to be awkward than either the direct cut or the vocal lead-in. The fadeout in particular is best after a story with a strongly emotional ending; it allows the viewer a brief moment to muse over the story without distraction.

The Set

The fundamental requirements for the stage setting of a news show are simple, but they require careful thought and planning. Normally the producer will be involved in this planning, although some of the final decisions are likely to be made at a higher executive level.

The air man must have a desk or podium at which to work; its surface must be large enough to accommodate both the used and the unused portions of his script. He must have a television monitor, so located that he can glance at it with minimum movement of his head and body. He must have adequate reading light (against the glare of the studio lights), and he must be able to see the cameras without having to search for them in the relative darkness of the unlighted portions of the studio. The stage manager must be close to the air man, so positioned that the air man can see him but the audience cannot. The setting should function with minimum movement of the video cameras; still boards, for example, should be positioned so that a simple panning movement enables a camera to take either a shot of a still or a shot of a performer.

Office set The news set which actually or purportedly is in a news-room has the advantage of placing the performer in a "working" situation recognizable to the audience. At this writing such a set, which is actually a working office as well, is used very effectively by the *CBS*

Evening News. Anchorman Walter Cronkite is seated at a desk, his co-workers are busy nearby, and behind him is an FP screen. One camera takes a wide angle profile shot from the side of the desk, sometimes showing some of the co-workers in the background. A second camera shoots from in front of the desk, taking either a close shot of Cronkite face-on or, when graphics are displayed on the FP screen, pulling back to a wider angle to include the screen. Other graphics are shot by a third camera which, because of space limitations, is in another studio. Cronkite's monitor is conveniently hidden in the desk in front of him.

Occasionally the show opens with Cronkite standing at a large wall map or graphic display which he uses to illustrate certain specifics of a story. This shot is taken with the side-angle camera. When the story is finished, Cronkite steps to his desk and sits down; this movement is sometimes covered by the main title supered, sometimes by a commercial spot.

Thus, in minimum space and with minimum effort, a large variety of camera angles and visual possibilities can be achieved.

Tacit stage set   Another widely used type of set is one in which no attempt is made to conceal the fact that the setting is a stage or studio. The performers may be seated at desks, or they may stand at podiums, but they are plainly in a place designed solely for the broadcasting of the news show. Two walls of the set are ordinarily visible; the other two do not exist. In multi-performer shows a wide shot may be used showing all the desks or podiums.

This type of set, while it functions as well as any other, has a "stagey" look which calls attention to the set itself and by so doing distracts the viewer and detracts from the credibility of the news. Sometimes this disadvantage is emphasized directorially by a closing wide shot, with credits over, in which the air men, having finished their work and with nothing to do but pose for the cameras, stand uncertainly at their respective podiums or group together awkwardly (being poor actors) and pretend to discuss the day's events while waiting for the stage manager's "clear on stage" cue. Any shot in which the subject has no function is a bad shot, and this is a perfect example.

Limbo set   In the limbo set the viewer never sees the relationship of the various podiums (and newsmen) to one another or to the set itself. All he sees is the newsman, part of the podium at which he stands, and a backdrop or flat behind him. The limbo set may sometimes create a certain disorientation in the viewer, a vague uneasiness about the relative positions of the air men, but this does not seem to be a significant disadvantage. The set's great advantage is that it does not call attention to itself.

Physical limitations of studio space and technical facilities play a considerable part in the choice of sets. No general rule can be laid down, except that many otherwise unforeseen problems can be avoided by consulting a professional set designer; he should have a knowledge of design, color, lighting, and many other considerations which are beyond any newsman's competence.

Credits The style of opening and closing titles and credits should be closely related to the style of the set. The live studio shot, with title and credit supers, is common but has the disadvantage, already mentioned, of the shot with no function. Many producers prefer to open and close with prepared films or slides. One good rule is to keep both opening and closing as short as possible.

Style and the Hour

The hour of broadcast is a prime factor in determining the style and character of a news show. The show that is highly successful in the morning may be disastrous at dinner time, for the simple reason that the audience is not the same in composition, in mood, in interests, or in the time it can give to the news.

Morning The morning news show requires fast pacing, with lots of hard news packaged in short items. Film and VTR should be cut to the bone; reports in depth and lengthy commentaries are deadly.

The morning audience is for the most part an audience either on the go or getting ready to go; it wants the top of the overnight news, and it wants it quick and uncluttered. For much of the fast-breaking morning news no film is available, but film is less important in the morning. More and more people are using small, portable, transistorized television sets at the breakfast table; mostly they listen, as to radio, and they must be cued vocally to look when interesting film is coming up.

In the United States, the farther west one goes the more morning news there is. Most news happens in the morning, at whatever local time. The sun has seldom reached zenith when courts rule, congress acts, presidents proclaim and kings decree. At 8 A.M. in New York most of the news is still last night's news. But at 8 A.M. on the West Coast it is late morning in the Eastern United States, late afternoon in Western Europe, and tomorrow in the Far East, and an avalanche of fresh news is pouring in from all parts of the world. Much of tomorrow morning's newspaper front page is already on the wires and on the air when Westerners eat breakfast.

The networks recognize this by updating most of their morning news reports for the Western audience; the show that was news 3 hours earlier in New York is no longer news. (In contrast, so little happens between dinner hour in the East and dinner hour in the West that the network evening news shows are customarily taped at the time they are broadcast in the East; the tapes are replayed at the comparable local time in the West. This procedure, not incidentally, saves the networks hundreds of thousands of dollars yearly in line charges.)

But whatever the time zone of the morning news show, the character of its audience is approximately the same everywhere. To meet the needs of this audience, the morning show should be more flexibly structured than the evening show, mainly so that late news items can be inserted fresh off the wires without wrecking the show's planned structure. Frequently such fresh items are follow-stories on the previous day's news; in such cases they serve well as standup lead-ins to film or VTR of the earlier developments. This means, for example, that rollthrus between film stories are seldom advisable; a recue permits insertion of a fresh item in its most appropriate place at the last second.

Similarly, the morning air man must be flexible, able to adapt quickly to changing developments. He must be able to ad lib his way smoothly through badly written wire copy which he has never seen before. He must be able to rearrange his script at a moment's notice; for example, he must be able to read fresh copy long enough for telecine to roll through a film story which the control room has just decided to drop from the show.

Sometimes the morning show can be structured in anticipation of predictable news. The author was writer-producer-anchorman of a West Coast morning network show during the presidency of John F. Kennedy, whose scheduled news conferences invariably resulted in wire service bulletins beginning about 5 minutes before the show aired. It required no great foresight to anticipate the major subjects on which the President was likely to comment, and to schedule the first film or two on related subjects; the film then followed naturally out of the bulletin news made by the President, and by the time the film was run there was usually more detail fresh off the wires to be added. Thus the show acquired a "hot off the press" quality without losing its advantage as a visual medium. The same principle can be applied to many stories on a morning news show.

Because of its need for fast pacing, the morning news show does not stretch comfortably into a format even as long as half an hour. Few viewers can sit and watch that long; they miss either the top of the show or the last half of the news. For the longer show this problem is sometimes solved with the so-called "news wheel," in which the same basic news is repeated one or more times, each repeat being updated with fresh developments. The assumption of audience turnover upon which the news wheel concept is based, while valid in the morning, is highly questionable at any other hour of the day.

The morning news show can never hope for as big an audience as the evening show, but if properly produced with regard for its particular audience it can compete strongly with *any* type of daytime show, including the most popular entertainment shows. In addition, it is one of the most stimulating and challenging of all news shows to write, to produce, or to handle on the air.

Midday The midday news show partakes of some of the qualities of both morning and evening shows. The news is still breaking, although not as rapidly as a few hours earlier. More details are available on stories which were little more than bulletin leads at breakfast time. More film or VTR is also likely to be available. But not as much detail, not as many visuals, are available as will be at dinner time. However, if the show leans either way structurally, it leans more toward the patterns of the evening show.

The primary consideration, again, is the nature and mood of the audience. The midday audience consists largely of women and children (although the manager of one station in a city of half a million population reports that 40 per cent of his midday audience consists of men). At noon these viewers have settled into their day's routine; they are no longer in the midst of the morning rush, they have more time, and they are willing to give the news more attention.

The news can therefore be presented at a more leisurely pace than in the early morning. Reports in depth are viewed with interest, and the feature content of the show can be much greater. Features appealing especially to women and children are desirable, although they should not be overdone to the detriment of the hard news coverage. With these variations, then, the midday show bears a close resemblance to the evening show.

Late afternoon The late afternoon news show leans more to tabloid journalism than any other type of show, again because of its audience. One highly successful late afternoon show aired for several years in one of the nation's largest cities was an outstanding example of the television tabloid style, low in significance but high in entertainment value. It was a television caricature of a typical tabloid evening news-paper, concentrating on crime, sensationalism, exposés, and entertain-ment gossip; it even employed a Hollywood reporter whose commentary sounded like an updated rewrite of an old Louella Parsons column of the 1930s, with nothing changed but the names of the celebrities.

Technically the show was sloppy—some observers suspected it was deliberately sloppy—to the extent of using unedited film of what can only be described as non-news nonstories accompanied by flip comments that almost made a virtue out of this vice. On occasion the show made excellent and imaginative use of visuals. In its coverage of celebrity funerals, for example, it eschewed the traditional voice-over identification of prominent persons attending the funeral; instead, there was *no* voice-over, only funeral music over a typical funeral film clip, ending with a superslide identifying the deceased and the years of birth and death. The result was simple, nonredundant, and effective; it was pure tabloid translated into television terms.

This show's excellent ratings demonstrated that it was aimed with great accuracy at the late afternoon audience. It is, if you wish, a lowbrow audience: the factory or construction worker whose laboring day ends at 4:00 or 4:30, the elderly stay-at-home whose day never ends and who wants to escape from soap opera into reality, the teen-ager home from school, the tired suburban housewife taking a beer break before she prepares dinner. Almost entirely missing from this audience are the business, professional, and academic people whose working hours extend much later into the day. The audience wants entertainment as much as it wants information, and the tabloid late afternoon show satisfies that demand.

Early evening The general thrust of this book is in the direction of the early evening news show of the type presented by most stations in the 6:00 to 7:30 P.M. time period. Many of these shows, local or network, are among the finest programming offered by television. They give weight and time to news of significance where the public interest is involved, they make much use of packaged film reports from newsmen in the field, they handle features with skill and taste, their intellectual content is relatively high for television, and their technical polish is often brilliant.

The audience of the early evening news show is the mass audience representative of all the interests of all the people, a few intellectuals excepted. It is the audience for which television was invented, intentionally or not. The entire family is likely to be gathered around the television receiver at this hour, although some surveys indicate that even the highest rated of early evening news shows attract relatively few viewers in the age bracket from late teens to middle twenties. This may presage trouble for such shows in years to come; more likely it indicates that the personal concerns particular to that age group do not coincide with the broader interests of the rest of us, both younger and older. In other words, the late teens and early twenties group will grow out of the habit of not watching (or will be forced into watching by such economic factors as the cost of baby-sitters).

This audience is relaxed at the end of the day's work, ready and willing to sit for an hour or more and get acquainted with the rest of the world and the great events being played out on the stage of mankind. It has both time and inclination to watch lengthy reports as long as they are informative. It seeks the meaning of events which concern its own destiny, and therefore it appreciates analysis which puts the news in perspective. No less than any other audience it appreciates being entertained, but it wants at least a nugget of information in its barrel of news, or it would be watching something other than the news.

On both the East and West coasts the early evening news shows are the prestige shows; the Middle West differs somewhat, for reasons to which we will come in a moment. The main network news shows also appear in the early evening hours. Against such competition, the producer of the early evening news show needs to present as complete and professional a news package as he can within his means.

Late evening   The late evening (10 P.M. or later) news show superficially resembles the early evening show, but too close a resemblance can work to its disadvantage because of the difference in audience characteristics.

The closest resemblance is probably found in the Midwest, where because of network prime time the local news shows with the highest ratings often appear at 10 P.M. rather than in the early evening. Network prime time consists of the hours from 7:30 to 11 P.M. in New York; during those hours the networks preempt the air of their owned and affiliated stations for the main network entertainment programming. Thus a local late evening news show cannot begin in the Eastern time zone until 11 P.M. except at independent stations. The network shows are taped and replayed on the West Coast in the same local time period ending at 11 P.M.; therefore the Western program pattern is identical to the pattern in the East. But in the Midwest the network entertainment shows are broadcast on the Eastern schedule, which means that local news shows of O&Os and affiliates must end by 6:30 P.M. and can begin again at 10 P.M. in the Central time zone. This forces the main local news shows into the late evening category, but still early enough to catch a large audience; after 11 P.M. the audience potential drops off rapidly.

The later the hour, the more the audience differs from the early evening audience. By some surveys it consists largely (about 80 per cent) of different people, but these surveys apply to areas where the early evening news is dominant. The late evening viewer is more relaxed, more receptive, more sophisticated than any other viewer; the audience includes many professionals, civic leaders, and business executives, who work long hours and cannot watch the earlier news programs. In particular, the late evening audience includes very few small children.

At the late hour these viewers are tiring; they want information but they do not want to work very hard to get it. They are not attuned to the rapid-fire pace of the morning. The mood of the show should be casual and relaxed—as relaxed as the news content permits. The professional polish of the show should be high; the writers and editors have had sufficient time to rewrite and recut and improve the stories which perhaps had to be rushed into the early evening show. Because children are not in the audience the news can be racier, the language more frank, controversial topics such as sex more permissible. The show can even edge into the area of entertainment, provided the content is related to news; a poet might be interviewed and asked to read some of his work which has generated a cultural controversy, or members of an *avant garde* musical group might be asked to play and discuss their music (union rules allowing their performance).

The producer of the late evening news show, in short, can allow himself a broader range of subject matter, and a wider variety of styles of presentation, than the producer of any other news show in television. He has the best of all audiences if he desires to demonstrate his creativity.

Summary

The producer must give separate consideration to the three basic parts of the news show: top, middle, and end. The top should be the most significant news story of the day, a visual story if other values are equal. The ending should be upbeat if possible and backtimed under almost all circumstances.

The middle section should be planned as a wave structure with succeeding peaks and valleys of tension, to accord with principles of audience psychology; the secondary climax is placed fairly late in the show. Changes in mood should not be made too abruptly unless shock reaction is desired.

Elements of the show which are related in content should be packaged. Continuity throughout should be planned with audience reaction in mind.

In blocking out the show the first considerations are news and production values; commercial insertion is secondary. Commercial lead-ins should be styled to reduce the potential of error in the control room and to avoid shock or confusion in the audience. Sets should be designed for simplicity of function and with the aim of attracting attention to the news, not to the set.

To some extent style and content must be adapted to the differing character of the audience at different hours of the broadcast day.

Suggested Assignments

1. Explain why the structure of a television news show is more critical than the makeup of a newspaper.

2. Analyze a television news show in terms of its definable structure: top of the show, middle, and ending.

3. Explain why the wave form of continuity is essential to a television news show.

4. From observation of a television news show or shows, give examples of the apparent use of backtiming.

5. Select the story which in your opinion is the secondary climax of a television news show; if it seems to be misplaced, explain why you think so.

6. Cite examples of packaging and of failure to package in a television news show.

7. Using stories from a local newspaper in assigned order, script standup transitions into each story; where no transitions are needed, explain why.

8. Report on the styles of commercial lead-ins used by two or more television news shows; discuss which style is the most effective.

9. Visit a local television news show during broadcast and report, with diagrams, the details of its stage setting.

10. Monitor available television news shows in the morning, midday, late afternoon, early evening, and late evening time periods, and estimate how well each is tailored to its audience; compare your estimate with the actual audience ratings of the various shows.

11. Analyze the effectiveness of a "news wheel" format for an early evening news show.

Class Team Assignment

Produce a television news show under the supervision of a designated student producer. This assignment requires full video facilities; a minimum of 3 class sessions plus extracurricular time should be allotted for its completion. The work might be divided as follows:

a. Shooting of film or VTR by students on topics of their choice, subject to producer's approval.

b. Classroom viewing and discussion of film and VTR (including any film or VTR obtainable from local stations).

c. Editing of film and VTR by student teams. (The teams should be as small as available equipment allows, each team being assigned one story.)

d. Scripting of the show by teams assigned packages.

e. Preparation of graphics.

f. Video taping of the show. (Students should perform all possible functions, including those of control room; all students should be given an opportunity to do air work.)

g. Viewing and discussion of the show VTR.

Chapter 17

The
Panel
Show

The television panel show is nothing more than a collective interview, a news conference conducted within a rather rigidly structured format and in front of video cameras. Most panel shows have a definite time limit, the half-hour length being the most common; however, a few are open-end (that is, they continue until panelists and guest run out of things to say). Usually the panel show is video taped in advance of broadcast, often at a time most convenient for the guest. The video tape is not edited in the case of most shows, with the result that the show has the character of a live interview.

Because the guest is often a person of some prominence whose opinions and statements are worthy of note, panel shows frequently create news. One of the favorite broadcast periods for the panel show is the "Sunday ghetto" of the air, and since Sundays are "slow news days" the Monday morning newspapers frequently carry reports on the statements made on such shows. This is especially likely to occur if one of the panelists is a newspaper man; his paper almost invariably uses the story, which seems to indicate a certain prejudice, or at least a predisposition, in the selection of news.

For station and network managements the panel shows have two advantages: (1) they constitute a public service in the view of the FCC, and (2) they are cheap to produce. They utilize on-duty technical personnel who must be paid anyway, the fees credited to newsmen are often at the minimum level, and the guest ordinarily receives no payment whatsoever except the publicity he derives from appearing on the air. The panel show is, in fact, probably the cheapest of all television shows to produce, whether news or entertainment. That is why almost every station, however limited its resources, can manage to broadcast at least one half-hour panel show on a regular weekly schedule.

Format and Stage Setting

While the panel show occasionally features more than one guest, the multiguest show is a relatively rare phenomenon. There are usually two to four panelists. At least one and sometimes all are drawn from the ranks of the station's or network's news staff; others are hired from other news media on a one-time-only basis. One of the panelists, a staff man, customarily appears on the show regularly and functions as moderator.

The term "moderator" as used here is often stretched a little. Some moderators take part in the questioning of the guest; others merely act as monitors to open and close the show, channel the questioning, and lead into commercial breaks. The other panelists have no duties other than to come to the studio well informed and to ask pertinent questions.

Stage settings vary as little as the formats. The guest and panelists may sit around a table, or at facing desks; the important thing is that the cameras be able to get face-on shots of everyone involved.

Brief descriptions of three of the network panel shows indicate the rather minor differences among them:

ABC: *Issues and Answers*, half-hour. Participants: one guest, two ABC newsmen. Setting: three chairs around a coffee table. Format: moderator opens with a statement of three or four basic issues on which the guest is to be questioned; moderator takes part in questioning; panelists appear to try to alternate questions.

CBS: *Face the Nation*, half-hour. Participants: one guest, three newsmen, usually two CBS newsmen and a newspaper reporter. Setting: four chairs around a coffee table. Format: show opens on close shot of guest, identified by superslide, with moderator asking a question calling for a fairly brief answer; moderator takes part in remainder of questioning, which appears to be mostly unstructured.

NBC: *Meet the Press*, half-hour. Participants: guest, moderator, four panelists. One of the panelists, Lawrence E. Spivak, is a regular; the others are NBC and newspaper reporters. Setting: guest and moderator at a desk, facing panelists at another desk. Format: moderator introduces guest, cues panelists to ask questions in turn, takes no part in questioning himself; panelists apparently pursue subjects of their own choice and are allowed follow-up questions.

Each of these shows varies in some detail or other from time to time, but the variations are not significant. However, despite the limited latitude offered by the panel show, there are certain procedures which help to insure that any panel show will be informative.

Planning the Show

Once the guest has agreed to appear on the show, producing the show is primarily a matter of gathering and organizing research material relating to the guest, his interests, and his activities. The research should not be left to the individual panelists (although most will probably do their own research as well); the producer usually has a reason for wanting a specific guest, and that reason can be justified only if he supplies the panelists with research which enables them to pursue the lines of questioning which the producer originally had in mind.

After the panelists have had an opportunity to go over the research, a meeting of panelists and producer is advisable to plan the questioning. At such a meeting the potentially most fruitful areas for exploration can be discussed and decided on, the general order in which each of the areas of discussion is to be approached can be determined, and follow-up questions can be planned. It is extremely important for the panelists to take part in such strategy decisions. No matter how well a producer has organized the research and blocked out possible lines of questioning, it is the panelists who must execute the strategy and it will be more effective if they act in coordination. Further, if the panelists happen to differ with the producer's concept, they will almost certainly go their own separate ways once the show begins. Sometimes they will anyway, but that cannot be helped; they are brought into the show because of their knowledge and expertise, not to act as monkeys on the producer's string.

Depending on how rigidly the show is structured, it may be advisable to assign specific areas of questioning to specific panelists, according to their own inclinations and interests. While each area thus becomes one man's primary responsibility, this does not mean that the other panelists should sit by in silence if the lead panelist fails to ask a pertinent question in his area or fails to follow up a promising opening. This type of prestructuring works best if there are only two panelists; it is difficult to coordinate three or more in the same manner.

In an unstructured show (that is, a show in which any panelist is free to ask any question he pleases any time he can get it in), a system of planned signals is advisable so that a panelist who is particularly eager to put in a question can let the others know. The signals must of course be unobtrusive, since the cameras may be on any or all of the participants at any given moment. The simplest signal is for the panelist who wishes to ask the next question merely to lean forward in his chair, a natural attitude for an eager conversationalist. Conversely, if he is willing to let the other panelists take over for the moment, he relaxes and leans back. Whatever the signals, they should be explained to any panelist new to the show.

After the show begins, the producer is not necessarily finished with directing strategy. In the Olympian remoteness of the control room, he is a far better judge of the show's pace, content, and texture than the panelists who are in the midst of the fray in studio; also, they have no opportunity to consult on strategy except during commercial breaks (which do not always occur during the question-and-answer period of a panel show), and even during breaks any consultation tends to be inhibited by the presence of the guest. If the discussion bogs down in one area and the panelists are still pursuing the subject fruitlessly, the producer can have the stage manager hold up a "change subject" cue card. If an obvious follow-up question has not been asked, or if time is getting short and a major subject area remains unexplored, he can have the stage manager slip a note to that effect to the moderator or one of the panelists. The producer's work is never finished until the show is finished.

The Panelist

For the panelist all of the standard techniques of the interview (see Chapter 11, The Film Reporter) are applicable, except that the panelist need not concern himself with any of the details of production. He should prepare his homework beforehand and come to the studio armed with specific questions and issues which he hopes to discuss. Half a dozen basic questions are enough for a half-hour show; there is seldom time to cover any more when each panelist gets only a few minutes for his own questioning. And he should, of course, be prepared with follow-up questions.

Listening to the guest is always important. When a question elicits a completely unexpected answer, the panelist must be able to make an instant evaluation of whether the new line of inquiry thus suggested is worth following; such answers often produce the most news. Everyone has seen newsmen who do not listen to an interviewee and doggedly ask questions he has just answered; nothing makes the newsman appear more incompetent.

The short question is always the best question. A long question almost invariably gets a short answer, the short question gets the long answer. Some newspaper men, unaccustomed to the television interviewing technique, tend to ask long, involved, multiple-part questions during which the audience (and sometimes the guest) loses the trend of thought. Often the guest answers only the first part of the question. It is always preferable to split a two-part question into two questions, using the second part as a follow-up (if, in the light of the first answer, it is still appropriate). The short question is much more important in the panel show or live interview than in the film interview, in which the questions and answers can be edited.

The best question of all, especially as a follow-up, is the one word "Why?" It *demands* an answer, usually in some detail.

When the guest refuses to answer or answers evasively despite persistent questioning, it is best to drop the subject. His refusal or evasion is apparent to the audience, and pushing the matter too far makes it appear that the panelist is badgering him. As was mentioned earlier, on television the nonanswer sticks out like a sore thumb.

The Moderator

The moderator's job is to keep the show moving, to get into commercial breaks cleanly, and to get off the air on time.

Commercial breaks The best way to get into a commercial break is to have the stage manager hold up a commercial cue card at the appropriate time (ordered by the director), and to forewarn the other panelists to ask no more questions once the cue is up. This returns control of the show to the moderator, who may then either deliver the commercial lead-in when the guest finishes answering the last question asked, or pursue the subject with a follow-up question if the situation seems to require it. The exact position of the commercial in the show is not important, but it should not be delayed overlong.

For many panel shows the commercial lead-ins are scripted in advance to provide the director with a precise roll cue for commercial film or VTR. If the lead-in is not scripted, the moderator ad libs it and the director must try to sense when to roll his commercial film or tape. In either case the lead-in should be brief: "We'll continue our questioning of Dr. Jones in just a moment."

Tagging the show   The moderator's last task on a panel show is to get it off the air on time, and hopefully without confusion. It is helpful to have the stage manager show time cue cards at 1-minute intervals during the last 5 minutes of the Q and A portion of the show; during the final minute the cards should indicate 30 and 15 seconds remaining. When the "End" card is up, the moderator must close the show immediately even if he has to cut the guest off in mid-sentence. However, he has a few seconds of allowable error, for which the director can make adjustment over the show's closing credits. As in the commercial lead-in, after the 1-minute cue goes up the other panelists should ask no more questions; the moderator must control the show at this point.

It is best to let the guest complete an answer before closing, rather than to open up another question and then be forced to cut him off in mid-answer. The timing here is not critical; it is better to close the show 15 seconds early than to end on a note of incompletion. The moderator can best judge how to handle this problem on the basis of the guest's performance during the show; the longer his answers, the more careful the moderator must be about asking another question during the final minute. Some guests, especially professional performers and many politicians, can time their answers if given some indication of the time remaining, but most cannot.

In particular, the questioning in the last minute or two should not open up a complex new subject on which the guest cannot possibly be expected to express his opinions in the short time remaining. In anticipation that a subject may be closed out with perhaps a minute of Q and A time remaining, the moderator should be prepared with one or two "tag" questions which the guest can be expected to answer briefly, especially if the tag question is coupled with a warning that the remaining time is brief.

Keeping the show moving   Part of the moderator's job is to keep the show moving as to both pace and content. If the other panelists pause or seem at a loss to continue, he must always be ready with an appropriate follow-up or a new subject area. Even a 1-second pause makes a good moderator nervous; but he should not be so nervous that he steps on a follow-up question by another panelist.

When esoteric references are made, it is the moderator's job to make them clear for the audience. Scientific terms and alphabetical or acronymic names of governmental agencies are not always familiar to all viewers; when they crop up in the conversation, the moderator should inject a brief explanation. This can be done most discreetly in the form of a question (even if the moderator knows the answer): "N-A-M—that's the National Association of Manufacturers, isn't it?"

The moderator should also be quick to sense when a line of questioning is exhausted and the subject should be changed. The producer may be backstopping him in this, but he can act more quickly than the producer and thus steer the show to cover most if not all of the desired topics.

In the rather unusual circumstance that a panelist becomes argumentative or abusive, it is the moderator's job to take whatever action necessary to demonstrate that such an approach does not represent the attitude of the show or the station. Persistent repetition of a question which has already been answered, or which the guest has stated he will not answer, calls for the moderator to step into the dialogue and point out that the answer has been given or will not be given. The best way to cut off such a dialogue is to make the point and quickly shift the subject: "I believe Mr. Smith has already answered that question, but there's another subject we'd like to get his views on."

In the extremely rare event that a panelist persists in abusive questioning despite the moderator's efforts, an open rebuke to the panelist is in order. An apology should be made to the guest if damaging and unsupported accusations are made or implied. This duty, while distasteful, helps to clear the station of offense and to preserve the reputation of both show and station for impartiality and responsibility. (And of course the offending panelist should not be invited to participate in the show again.) The moderator can never forget that he is the show's host; in this professional home the guest deserves the same consideration and courtesy that he would be given in a private home.

There are a number of so-called guest shows, usually having one person functioning as moderator and questioner, on which the guests are regularly insulted, their opinions belittled, and their arguments blithely ignored or treated in derogatory fashion. In the author's opinion such shows have nothing to do with news and no responsible newsman would be caught dead in such a format.

Summary

The panel show, one of the cheapest of all shows to produce, is a controlled collective interview or news conference, usually conducted within a preset time. The format, with minor variations, involves a guest and two to four newsmen.

Preparations include research followed by a meeting of panelists and producer to select the most promising lines of questioning. Areas of questioning may or may not be assigned primarily to specific panelists.

In most shows an unobtrusive system of signals is advisable so that panelists can indicate when they wish to speak. To some extent the producer can guide the questioning from the control room.

Panelists should do their homework, ask short questions, listen to the guest's answers, and be prepared with follow-up questions. The devil's advocate approach is the most effective, as in any interview. The high visibility of the nonanswer in television should be recognized.

The moderator must keep the show moving, get into commercial breaks cleanly, and close the show gracefully and on time. He should inject explanations of unclear references. He should change the subject when a line of questioning seems to be exhausted. He should cut off argumentative or abusive questioning, or any other action which places the show or the station in an improper light. He is prepared with tag questions requiring brief answers. In brief, he edits the show as it airs.

Suggested Assignments

1. Observe a local television panel show and report on the following: (a) stage setting, (b) number and type of participants, (c) format, (d) capability of the moderator, and (e) progression in terms of subject areas covered.

2. Explain what function, if any, the devil's advocate approach to interviewing plays in the panel show.

3. Define the general differences between a news conference and a panel show.

4. Prepare three possible tag questions to be asked a specific panel show guest.

5. Research a guest for a hypothetical half-hour panel show and block out a line of questioning to be followed.

Class Team Assignment

Using assigned students as guest, panelists, and producer, conduct a panel interview in the classroom (video taping it if possible), and critique the show in terms of the following: (a) questions asked, (b) topics covered, (c) effectiveness of the moderator, and (d) effectiveness of the producer.

Chapter 18

The
News
Special

The news special, whether it is produced live or on film, presents problems of an entirely different nature than those of the regularly scheduled news show. The differences are most striking in the live special, which is put together even as it airs, and in which the viewer actually witnesses much of the news gathering and evaluation process in progress, rather than merely seeing the end product of that process.

This means that the newsmen involved must be able to make instant evaluations of rapidly changing situations, and to translate those evaluations into instant action. There is no time for second guessing; the live special, therefore, quickly exposes the amateur and the irresponsible.

With the film special the newsman has a little more leeway for mistakes, but not much more. The production problems are very much like those of the daily news show, except that there are more of them and usually there is little if any more time. The format, while similar to that of a documentary, is deceptive; a better name would be "instant documentary," meaning a production which is usually conceived and executed in haste, yet is expected to have the production polish and depth of content of a show which the producer and staff have labored over with loving care for many weeks or months. So, again, the same instant evaluations and decisions must be made.

In general, the live special is most likely to be the product of a network or one of the more affluent stations (with, of course, the usual exceptions to any such rule). Many smaller stations lack the mobile equipment, the personnel, and the money to produce live specials.

However, almost any station can produce a film special with a little extra effort. Therefore we shall give some consideration to both types.

The Live Special

The most common form of the live special involves the origination of all or part of the show from a remote unit in the field. The remote unit may be simply a unit with a single video camera, transmitting its signals to the station by microwave or coaxial cable; or it may be a vast complex of equipment such as the networks use to cover the national political conventions, the most elaborate type of remote special coverage yet used by television.

Convention coverage Some idea of the magnitude of the networks' convention coverage is indicated by the fact that at the 1968 Republican National Convention in Miami Beach, Florida, there were more network employees on hand than convention delegates.

CBS, for example, used approximately 800 employees at Miami Beach, published a special 33-page convention telephone directory to help them keep in touch with one another, and issued a 90-page manual solely to describe the CBS technical systems, which had taken 30 days to set up and had been many months in the planning. The CBS facilities amounted to a complete duplication of a major network operation: newsroom, suites of executive offices, broadcasting studios, film processing laboratory, graphic arts department, operations and engineering rooms, warehouses, film editing rooms, video tape operations and storage, telecine, and control rooms, plus eight remote units. Most of these facilities were housed in a huge fleet of vans and trailers parked inside and outside the convention hall; when the convention ended these vehicles were unplugged from their thousands of electrical connections, driven or hauled to Chicago, and plugged in there for coverage of the Democratic National Convention. (The NBC facilities for convention coverage were similar, those of ABC less elaborate.)

The video-audio system was organized in roughly concentric perimeters, each with its own control room and all feeding into CBS convention central control. Each control room and each remote unit had its own producer and director, plus other personnel depending on the complexity of the operations it controlled; central control, for example, was manned by 18 persons. The following were the main organizational units:

The basic convention coverage of public activities, such as speeches from the platform and the casting of ballots from the floor, was handled by *pool control.* This service, organized by the networks, was available at all times to them and to any other subscribers, such as individual stations or station groups.

Central control, in addition to controlling all the subordinate units and selecting whatever it wished to air from the pool, was in direct control of the anchor booth (Walter Cronkite, in a studio high above the convention floor) and the analysis studio (Eric Sevareid and Roger Mudd, in a studio in a trailer outside the hall).

Floor control was responsible for all CBS material originating from the convention floor, such as interviews with delegates by CBS correspondents.

Perimeter control was responsible for all CBS material originating from the convention hall perimeter—corridors, entrances, adjacent streets.

Remote control was responsible for all CBS material originating in Miami Beach outside the immediate area of the convention hall (that is, beyond perimeter control). This included:

1. Three hotel units, at the Fontainebleau (convention headquarters hotel), the Plaza Hilton (Richard Nixon headquarters), and the Americana (Nelson Rockefeller headquarters). These were extremely complex units in themselves. The unit at the Fontainebleau, for example, controlled nine video cameras through 8 miles of coaxial cable; its control room was housed in a trailer parked outside the hotel, a mobile unit "permanently" emplaced for the duration of the convention. (Such is permanence in the electronic age.)

2. Two mobile units capable of operating anywhere they could plug into coaxial cable and electric power connections. Such connections had been preinstalled at numerous points of possible action around the city (the airport, for example).

3. Three "flash" units for emergency coverage anywhere in the city. These were small, highly mobile vehicles capable of generating their own power and transmitting their video signals to remote control by microwave relay.

Such an operation, extending over several days and plainly costing millions of dollars, is of interest to the average newsman only as a kind of extravagant curiosity. As a result of the 1968 conventions, its effectiveness also came under question—a question which will be discussed in Chapter 20. But the setting up of any remote unit, however small, involves certain basic technical considerations of which the newsman who may have to make the decision should be aware.

The remote unit Remote units, however simple or elaborate, may be divided into two categories: those which operate completely independently, like roving television stations, and which carry their own VTR facilities; and those which are connected with and controlled by a master control room in the station.

Where microwave or coaxial cable connections to the station are impossible, the former is the only answer. But its usefulness as a producer of VTRs is somewhat questionable, because of the necessity to ship its VTRs to the station for airing. The same thing can be done more effectively, with better control, and (most importantly) cheaper with film. The only real advantage of the remote unit is the immediacy of its live transmission. Within a few years, when very lightweight and highly mobile video equipment comparable to present film equipment will almost certainly be available, this will no longer be a valid argument, but at this writing it makes no sense to spend more money to do the same thing that film can do better and cheaper.

Therefore, unless coaxial cable or microwave connections can be established between the remote unit and the station, the remote unit is not advisable. Where such connections can be made, the live special is worth considering if the story warrants that type of coverage. Not only can the product of the remote unit be broadcast live, but it can also be taped on the station's VTR facilities for quick replay if something else of more importance is going on at the moment. Thus, one of the primary considerations is the availability of the live connections if a live special is contemplated.

And here the newsman must consult the station engineers. It may take several hours to set up the remote unit and connect it to the station; 3 to 4 hours is probably average. Only the station engineers and the telephone system, which usually provides the connections whether cable or microwave is involved, know the answer. Obviously, there is no point in dispatching a remote unit if the story is likely to be over before the unit can get into action.

Even if the remote unit is capable of transmitting directly by microwave, the engineer must be consulted. He must determine whether adequate power is available at the desired location (if the unit does not have its own generator). He must also determine whether natural or man-made obstacles, such as hills or buildings, will interfere with transmission of the signal, and whether, if such is the case, it is possible to set up a relay transmitter between remote unit and station. The newsman has no competence in any of these matters.

The producer If the live remote is decided upon, its effectiveness becomes the responsibility of the producer, who is (or should be) a newsman.

Both the producer of the special and his subordinate producer in charge of the remote unit must be constantly on the alert for developments which affect the total story. Each must advise the other, immediately, of any information which might change either's plans; otherwise, neither can make an accurate judgment on what to cover and what to ignore. Both must try to plan their coverage in advance as much as possible, and both must be prepared to change their plans on a moment's notice. Even plans for such changes should be made.

The producer of a one-camera remote covering a lively meeting of a city council has to make the same quick decisions required of the producer of a network's convention coverage; the only difference is that he does not have to juggle quite so many possibilities. If pickets create an unexpected disturbance outside the city hall, he moves his camera to a window and tries to get a shot of the disturbance. If for technical reasons he misses an important exchange during the council session, he tries to line up the participants for interviews before the camera. He replays video tape recordings of important activities which some in his audience may have missed, which need repetition to be understood, or which simply are so overwhelmingly significant that they need to be rerun, perhaps more than once. He uses whatever facilities he has with whatever ingenuity he has. He always prepares, to the extent that he can, for every possible contingency, fully aware of what happens to the best-laid plans and always ready to change those plans instantaneously if circumstances require it. And he has plans for that, too.

The live-special reporter   For the reporter the live special demands the fullest possible knowledge of the subject and its background, and the ability to extemporize and interpret, for hours at a time if necessary, often while lacking possession of the latest facts. His homework must be done before he goes on the assignment.

Viewers of television news specials have probably noticed that the air men wear ear plugs, or ear phones (usually called "cans"), or sometimes exotic devices with antennae sprouting from their heads. Whatever their design, these have two purposes: (1) to carry "program," or whatever is going on the air, so that the reporter can keep up to date on events occurring outside his immediate area; and (2) to convey information and cues from the control room. For example, the reporter may be instructed to cut short an interview in progress because of something more important which is occurring elsewhere; he receives this instruction by earphone on a "program interrupt" even as he is conducting the interview, and immediately it becomes his job to cut short the interview with as much grace as possible and, perhaps, to ad lib a lead-in to the other activity of which he has just heard.

This really requires two heads, but at this writing no reporter so equipped has been found. Having only one head, the reporter must train his mind to sort out the various types of information he is hearing, discard whatever does not concern him, and store what may be useful in separate mental compartments from which it is instantly retrievable when wanted. The only thing the author can guarantee is that 2 hours or more of this will give the reporter a headache.

It is particularly important that the reporter have the ability to move around, to get away from the camera and microphone to gather information. If he must remain near the camera, he needs a legman to gather information. The author, reporting from a California candidate's headquarters on an election night special, was required by an overly cautious network remote unit producer to remain for 2 hours directly in front of the camera, ready to report on an instant's notice if the producer in New York so desired; meanwhile it was impossible for the reporter to cover what was happening at the headquarters, and his knowledge slowly became completely outdated.

The reporter's problems in obtaining interviewees also should be respected by the producer. The reason for the live special is that something is going on, and that very fact sometimes makes it difficult to persuade a busy participant to drop what he is doing and come before the camera for an interview. Too often the producer delays taking the interview for 20 or 30 minutes because of some other activity being aired; the other activity may be more important at the moment, but the delay is an imposition on the participant, and it is usually unnecessary. The interview can be taped immediately, and used half an hour later when appropriate.

The reporter who is primarily accustomed to working on film needs to make an adjustment in his habitual procedures when working live video. The camera does not start and stop like a film camera, and this means the reporter must assume that he is "always on." When beginning an interview, for example, he faces the camera to introduce the interviewee, then turns toward the interviewee (that is, with his back to the camera) to ask questions. The line of questioning should be quickly planned in his mind; he should have a specific objective in seeking the interview, and unless the interview leads into a completely unexpected and fruitful area of information, he should stick to his plan. Redundant, rambling, and irrelevant questions are not going to be edited out; they are going on the air, so the interview must be "edited" by the reporter as it proceeds. When his objective is attained or obviously cannot be attained, the reporter should close the interview, usually thanking the interviewee (a small pleasantry which is customarily edited out of the film interview) before turning back to the camera with a concluding statement. At this point he should be able to summarize the content of the interview in a sentence or two if that seems necessary, even while on program interrupt he is getting instructions on his lead-out ("Throw it back to George in the studio") or other information which he must simultaneously include in his closing statement.

In narration the reporter seldom has the benefit of any writing except such "writing" as he can do in his mind while narrating. He may have made a note or two on some new development of which he has learned off camera, or a brief note may be handed him on camera; but whatever information he picks up, and however he picks it up, he must be able instantly to sort it out mentally, arrange what he wants to say, and say it—hopefully as well as if a writer had toiled over the story for an hour. It is especially in live narration of this type that the importance of the reporter's background knowledge becomes apparent; he must know what the story is about, who the various participants are and the relationship of each to the main issues, and the significance of new developments as they occur.

Example: The Robert F. Kennedy assassination It is impossible to anticipate all of the problems of the live special, but a few examples from the television coverage of the Robert F. Kennedy assassination may illustrate the need for instant reaction.

All three networks were covering the 1968 California primary election results, controlling the coverage, in each case, from New York. At the time of the shooting in the Ambassador Hotel in Los Angeles (approximately 3:14 A.M. in New York), CBS network had gone off the air, having long since declared Kennedy the winner of the state's Democratic presidential primary. NBC was still covering with in-studio discussion in New York. ABC was closing its special with closing theme music over a slide.

At 3:15 A.M. (New York time) ABC's field producer at the Ambassador, Paul Altmeyer, telephoned the control room in New York to report, "There have been shots, there have been shots. . . ." The control room instantly decided to hold the closing theme and slide, while ABC reporters at the Ambassador confirmed that the shooting involved Senator Kennedy. At 3:17 the election special anchorman in New York, Howard K. Smith, came back on the air to report the shooting. This was the fastest of the network responses.

NBC, although still on the air, delayed its first report of the shooting until 3:36 A.M. CBS was in the worst position because its New York cameras were down (it takes some 20 minutes to bring a video camera into operation), but it managed to get back on the air with a report from Correspondent Terry Drinkwater at the Ambassador at 3:38 A.M. The CBS cameras at the hotel had remained in operation for local coverage by KNXT, the CBS-owned station in Los Angeles, where the hour was earlier because of the time zone difference and where there was high local interest in the still undecided senatorial primary contest between the incumbent Republican senator, Thomas Kuchel, and his opponent, Dr. Max Rafferty.

The fact that the local O&Os were still covering was perhaps the only factor that made network coverage at all possible that night. But within half an hour after the shooting all three networks were covering the shooting story, with stations coming on the line all across the nation as they were able to.

The Los Angeles stations were, of course, the quickest to respond to the shooting, because they were already operating special coverage. At the moment of the shooting a KNXT legman at the Ambassador, Gordon Hughes, was on the telephone with the station's election special producer, Mike Kizziah. Hughes told Kizziah, "Something is happening here." He didn't know what it was, but from his description—sudden screams, crying, hysteria, confusion—it was obviously something extraordinary. Kizziah ordered Hughes to hold the line (don't break the communications link in a crisis) and send someone to find out what had happened. Within a minute or two a researcher returned to report to Hughes that there had been a shooting, and that the senator might have been involved. Immediately Kizziah ordered a direct cut from a studio discussion being aired, and at that instant the audience became aware that something was amiss.

The video picture of the hysterical crowd, which only 3 or 4 minutes earlier had been cheering Kennedy's victory statement, clearly showed that something had gone wrong. CBS Correspondent Drinkwater was seen pushing uncertainly through the crowd on the speaker's platform to the full length of his microphone cord, obviously not knowing what had happened or where. (The shooting took place in a pantry behind the platform, to which the video cameras had no access.) A film cameraman was visible pushing his way into the pantry; it was only the film cameramen who obtained shots of the scene inside.

At this point no one at the station and few at the Ambassador knew exactly what had happened. Information trickled in in bits and pieces, by intercom, by telephone, by video. There had been a shooting. There was no information on who was shot. Several people had been shot. The senator might be one of them. Others might be Steven Smith, Kennedy's campaign manager, and Jesse Unruh, speaker of the California assembly and Kennedy's California campaign manager. A woman was among the victims. Kennedy apparently *had* been shot, but how seriously was uncertain. Smith appeared and seized a podium microphone to call repeatedly for a doctor to treat the senator; obviously, then, Smith was not hurt, but to *which* senator out of several in the vicinity did he refer? A hysterical woman seized the microphone from Smith to make the same plea. Smith grabbed the microphone back to ask the crowd to clear the room. The hysteria, the weeping and screaming and aimless milling, went on and on.

All of this went on the air live, and over it the studio anchorman, Jerry Dunphy, repeated such information as he could piece together from the video and from other sources, qualifying every statement repeatedly and emphatically to avoid alarming the audience unduly. His performance, which the author observed at close hand, was highly professional. At such moments it is of unparalleled importance to stay with the story, but also to recognize that the first information received in such a situation is almost invariably inaccurate and at best incomplete. In no other situation is the responsibility of the newsman clearer, or his ability to work with restraint under extreme emotional tension and with partial or inaccurate information more important.

Meanwhile film crews and reporters scattered around the city for election coverage were pulled off their assignments and rushed toward the Ambassador. Word that Kennedy was being taken to Central Receiving Hospital diverted two KNXT crews to that location, where no video remotes were available. An attempt to fill that video gap was made by ordering one of the election remote units to the hospital. The unit, owned by KHJ-TV but rented and staffed by KNXT, had been covering Kuchel headquarters several blocks from the Ambassador and not far from the hospital. But the only coverage obtained at Central Receiving was film coverage; by the time the mobile unit could pack up its cumbersome equipment and start moving, Kennedy was being moved to Good Samaritan Hospital, so the mobile unit was redirected there. At Good Samaritan it finally managed to establish video, but for some reason the usually more reliable audio transmission failed; it reached the control unit from the microphone, but could not be fed out. An engineer solved the problem by holding a microphone near the loudspeaker in mobile control and patching that mike through to the station on a telephone line; the audio quality was bad, but bad is better than none.

All this is only a sampling of the problems encountered and surmounted by all of the television stations and networks on that tragic night, and in the 4 days of intermittent special coverage which followed.

That coverage also demonstrated the value of cooperation among stations in pooling special coverage. The NBC-owned station in Los Angeles, KNBC, authorized the use of any or all of its assassination coverage by five Los Angeles independent stations, including KCET, the local educational channel. This was a public service gesture which enabled these stations, with their lesser facilities and smaller staffs, to provide their audiences with coverage (amplified by their own staff coverage) of a scope and quality which they could not otherwise have managed. And the independents made their contribution, too. For example, KTLA, the only Los Angeles station with regular telecopter service (a helicopter carrying a television camera), fed its aerial coverage of the Kennedy funeral cortege from Good Samaritan Hospital to Los Angeles International Airport to all three networks and all of the local stations; at one time all seven VHF stations in Los Angeles were airing the KTLA feed simultaneously. Such pooling of facilities broadens enormously the possibilities of costly special coverage and contributes to a better informed public.

The live special, in summary, is the broadcasting of news in the making. The public shares in the news gathering process and participates vicariously in the event itself. And the newsman shares both his knowledge and his ignorance with the public.

The Film Special

The film news special closely resembles the regularly scheduled daily news show except that it concerns only one subject and is produced under emergency conditions. It is usually decided to preempt regular programming for a film special on the occasion of a major spot news event, such as the death of a prominent citizen or a major local disaster.

The film special may contain live studio segments interspersed with film, or it may be entirely on film. The former eliminates the need for many film transitions and is therefore easier to produce. Such film as is used may be shot entirely for the special, or it may be a potpourri of new film and old footage from the film library. Because the basic element is the film, the special usually airs after the event, not during it like the live special, but its timeliness is its most essential quality. It seldom has the lasting values of a good documentary in terms of content, nor is it likely to have the production values of a well-made documentary. It is, in short, a special kind of news story.

Unlike the live special, which tends to be open-end, the length of the film special is usually determined in advance. The end of the live special can seldom be predetermined because the event itself cannot be predetermined. But the event which the film special reports is over; and, just as for any news story, a judgment can be made as to the time needed to report it most effectively, and a time slot in the programming schedule can be preselected for broadcasting of the special.

On occasion, the subject of the film special may be a predictable or scheduled event which can be covered only on film; in such a case the haste in producing and airing the show proceeds purely from a desire to make it timely.

Although the film special lacks the immediacy of the live special, it has the advantage of being structured in the dramatic sense. Its form can be planned, and the result can be an artistic distillation of the essence of the event. All of the filmic principles of time compression and unity can be used to generate audience involvement. Therefore it is important that a *concept* of the show be formulated before production begins, because it is only by measurement against the concept that the value of any particular film footage can be judged. This concept, a view of the story as a unified whole bearing a specific meaning, is quite different from the concept of the live special, which is merely to cover whatever happens as it happens.

The author was involved, as writer-narrator, in a film special which presented most of the problems common to such productions, plus a few that were uncommon. (It is the uncommon problem which the producer needs to anticipate; every such show differs from every other, but every one presents uncommon problems.) It may be useful to trace the planning and production of that special to illustrate some of the problems which can be anticipated, and some of those which cannot.

The event   The subject of the special was a scheduled event, the last voyage of the Cunard liner *Queen Mary*, which had been purchased by the city of Long Beach, California, to be refitted as a floating hotel, convention center, and museum. Under the terms of the sale, she could never put to sea again.

Preparation   Because the show was planned weeks in advance, early preparations could be made by the producer, Mike Kizziah. He compiled reams of information on the ship's construction and history. He obtained historical film footage of her World War II service, and of her launching (with the queen for whom she was named wielding the champagne bottle).

A four-man production crew was assigned: producer, writer-narrator, cameraman, and soundman. The crew began to make technical preparations for filming on board; the big problem would be power for lights and cameras, because the ship's electrical system was not compatible with American equipment. This meant special adapter plugs and plenty of power packs. But it was desirable to travel as light as possible; we finally took about 300 pounds of equipment and film, plus our personal baggage.

It was decided to pick up the ship at Acapulco, its last port of call before Long Beach. Travel arrangements had to be made.

Concept   The producer and writer agreed on a basic concept for the show. It was to be a mood piece, a nostalgic farewell to a great lady of the seas and a vanishing era of gracious, luxurious transatlantic travel. Even as we made this decision, newspapers were filled with articles detailing passenger complaints about heat (the ship had to travel around Cape Horn, and she was not designed for the tropics), poor service, and poor ship's maintenance. But these were not typical of the ship's transatlantic career, and we decided that they had nothing to do with our concept. We were doing not a news story, but a special.

On the basis of the concept some segments of the show could be anticipated, if not in detail at least in general. These included interviews with the captain and old-timers in the crew, the farewell party in the main lounge the last night at sea (for which lighting would be difficult because of the enormous size of the lounge), and the arrival at Long Beach, where a flotilla of thousands of small craft was expected to welcome the Queen. Other known elements were the historical film footage, and a brief résumé of future plans for the ship (for which the only available visual was an artist's photo-diagram). We would have approximately 3½ days for filming on board. For the arrival sequence at Long Beach we would have news footage to be shot by other crews for the regular news programs, in addition to whatever we might shoot from on board.

It was decided to make it an all-film show, though with some voice-over narration in studio because the precise timing of all the narration could not be done until the film was cut. We would have less than 24 hours to edit the show and VTR after our arrival. Key narrative sequences would be shot on board; these would include the opening and closing of the show.

Shooting   Once aboard, the first tasks were to scout the location for the best shooting sites, and to hunt out the best potential interviewees. This alone took the better part of a full day, part of which was occupied by shooting certain action which could not be obtained later (the last raising of the anchor, the departure from Acapulco). Hampering conditions included extreme heat below decks and mild cases of the "turistas" picked up in friendly Acapulco. Also, we discovered that our special adapter plugs for lights were incorrectly made; the ship's electricians had to be manipulated into making new plugs. It was 2 days before we got the new plugs, and meanwhile all lighting was done with power packs. Because of the enormous size of the ship, it was immediately obvious that all shooting would have to be planned with care to reduce the logistical problems of moving around and making many camera setups.

All of the writing was done on board or after our return. To enhance the mood we sought, a narrative opening was shot on the bridge at twilight, with the three huge stacks floodlighted behind the narrator. A closing narration was shot at midday on the fantail, with the ship's wake streaming behind. Extra footage of this was also filmed, so framed that closing credits could be supered. Transition narration shots were filmed at various other locations, such as the observation deck and the sun deck. The captain was interviewed on the bridge, and a bittersweet nostalgic interview was filmed in the bustling Observation Bar with its head bartender, who had sailed on every voyage of the Queen and who would leave her with no memento except a postcard picture of the ship (he could not bring himself to take anything away from her).

As usual, there were a few unexpected bonuses, one of which (as it turned out) probably saved the show from disaster. This was the presence of another film crew, from station KCRA in Sacramento. We teamed with them to shoot the farewell party, the KNXT cameraman shooting from the lounge deck and the KCRA cameraman shooting from a projection booth high above; this film was shared by both stations. A day out of Long Beach a welcoming jet bombarded the ship with roses, and the last night out the ship's officers made a surprise presentation of a gold watch to the captain, whose British reserve came visibly close to breaking.

Among the disappointments was the captain's refusal to permit a helicopter to land aboard and pick up our film before the ship docked; the time gained in processing would have eased the last-minute editing pressure considerably.

But we had (we thought) all of the elements we needed to execute our concept: mood shots, action shots, interviews, opening, closing, transitions. And the arrival in Long Beach surpassed everyone's expectations. Some 5,000 boats sailed out of the harbor to welcome the Queen on a windy, bright, crystal-clear day. A Navy cruiser and half a dozen Coast Guard cutters solemnly escorted the liner through horn-tooting bedlam, while scores of planes and helicopters swooped and pirouetted overhead. Half a million people lined the shore and the docks, several bands played, and fireboats tossed dozens of streams of water into the sky, painting rainbows. The captain, interviewed again on the bridge, admitted that he had never seen or heard of such a welcome.

Editing The film shot on board totaled 5,800 feet; another 2,100 feet on the arrival had been shot by other crews. To view this much film requires about 8 hours. And by the time the film began coming out of the processor, only 16 hours remained to cut the film into a half-hour show and begin to VTR it. To complicate matters, the writer-narrator was developing laryngitis and had to be sent home to bed in the hope he could return in good enough voice to finish the narration.

Further, almost all of the mood shots and all four takes of the opening narration were unusable because of technical problems with the picture and sound. This represented about one third of the planned concept, and meant the entire show would have to be restructured. Producer Kizziah and two film editors labored through the night on that task.

Since the planned opening could not be used, Kizziah used the farewell party footage for an opening, and this actually improved the show. No one in the audience had seen it, and it set the mood of nostalgia perfectly, in addition to which it was footage of unusually colorful elegance. Another major rearrangement was the stretching of the spectacular arrival footage; although audiences had seen some of this on regular news shows, it was an essential element of the story, and it was exciting and colorful. The writer-narrator returned, in passable voice, in time to script the voice-over narration. However, so short was the time that he had to ad lib the entire 9-minute segment which included the arrival. The taping was concluded with exactly 1 minute to spare, and the show aired as scheduled the evening after the Queen's arrival in Long Beach.

This show was perhaps not typical of the film special in many respects, but there really is no typical film special. Each one presents its own special problems for which special solutions must be found, and this one illustrates that point: despite the best-laid plans, technical and logistical failures will occur, and ways must be found both to shoot and to edit "around" the difficulties that result. But most important of all is the concept; without it the film special does not deserve its name.

Summary

The live special is assembled as it airs, allowing the viewer to participate in the process of news gathering and evaluation. Frequently it involves the use of one or more remote units, the usefulness of which must be determined in advance on the basis of news values and technical communications considerations.

While coverage is planned in advance to the extent possible, the producer must be prepared to change his plans on a moment's notice and adapt to entirely new conditions. Maintenance of communications among producer, reporters, remote units, and the station is of extreme importance.

Reporters must know as much as possible of the subject matter, background information, and participants. They must be able to ad lib endlessly, and to edit their own comments as they do. They must develop the mechanical facility of delivering extempore narration while receiving information and cues on program interrupt. They must edit interviews in progress, add new information in a relevant manner to narration already under way, and reject or qualify new information which is vague or suspect.

The film special resembles the documentary except that it is usually produced under emergency conditions. Timeliness is its essential quality, and the producer's concept of the show is the gauge for the inclusion or rejection of material. Normally it concerns a single subject, and its length is preset.

All of the production techniques applicable to a single news story or to the daily news show are applicable to the film special. As with the live special, advance planning is important, but it is even more important that all involved be able to adapt plans almost instantly to unexpected circumstances. Most important of all is adherence to the concept.

Suggested Assignments

1. Define a "program interrupt" and explain how it is used.

2. Name the principal requirement for any newsman involved in any special, whether live or film.

3. Explain how the remote unit reporter edits an interview.

4. Write a critique of any recent live or film special you have observed.

5. Interview the producer of a recent news special, live or film, and report on the problems he encountered.

6. Discuss the major differences between the live special and the film special.

7. Explain the importance of concept in the film special.

8. Define the major differences between the film special and the film documentary.

Class Team Assignment

Select a subject and produce a half-hour live or film special. VTR for class critique.

Chapter 19

The
News
Director

Directing a television news operation of any size is a murderous, thankless job. The news director must battle management to keep the news free. He must maintain happiness, or at least satisfaction, in a stable of fractious talent. He must handle administrative and budgetary tasks which are not congenial to the average newsman. He must create and carry through to completion new show formats and new concepts in news coverage. He must keep the craft unions off his back with diplomacy. He is required to worry about stage sets, complex technical equipment which he does not understand, audience ratings which he does understand, and what the opposition is doing. He must maintain cordial relations with departmental heads whose cooperation he needs and who have not the slightest understanding of news. He must happily hire and sadly fire. He must attend an infinite number of trade meetings, conventions, awards dinners, and professional gatherings at which he acquires more indigestion than information. He must expect to be telephoned at home at three in the morning to settle trivial problems. He is required to provide the basic proof that his station operates in the public interest, convenience, and necessity. And for all this he is paid less than some of the people who work under him.

On entering a television news shop, anyone can identify the news director instantly. He is the man with the harried look. His job is forever at stake, and his wife is forever about to leave him. He spends as much time in his doctor's office as in his own home, and he knows his prime show's rating better than he knows the age of his eldest child. Why anyone wants the job is a mystery.

And if this seems like exaggeration, consider a few of the details.

Dichotomy

News directors are hampered by television management's almost universal failure to recognize that the job is really two jobs: news production and departmental administration. The larger the shop, the more exasperating the dichotomy. The news director who is forced to spend the largest part of his time in budget and staff meetings, negotiating with craft unions, signing papers, and attending public functions as the station's representative, cannot really direct a news operation. He needs an assistant to take charge of one task or the other, and since the news director is usually a newsman by background and preference, the assistant ideally should be a person with some knowledge of journalism and thorough training in business administration. Such a division of authority would leave the news director free to do what his title implies: direct the news.

Unfortunately, such a division of authority is impractical. The rivalry it would create between the two executives would be destructive of the best interests of the news organization, and the man who dealt with top management (in this case the business administrator) would probably very soon become top dog, in contradiction of the proposition that a news department should be run by a newsman.

Over the years newspapers have developed a pattern of executive structure which fits their needs well and functions, in most cases, very effectively. But television below the network level has yet to develop more than a rudimentary pattern of executive structure; the medium is only at this writing beginning to experience the growing pains which call attention to the need. What is required first is a definition of the *potential* executive functions in *any* news operation, large or small. With such a definition in hand, the news director could go as far as his budget allowed and the size of his operation required in delegating authority. The smaller the shop, the more the functions would be concentrated in fewer hands, but at least it would be recognized that certain executives *were* performing more than one function—a recognition that up to now seems to be lacking.

Television news can be viewed as consisting of five parts: (1) daily hard news (that is, spot news and other news of great immediacy and rapidly perishable value); (2) soft news (features and reports on current events, the value of which declines comparatively slowly with the passage of time); (3) specialist reports; (4) news specials; and (5) documentaries. Obviously, then, in the largest shops an executive could be placed in charge of each of these five categories of news.

In smaller shops where functions must overlap, the hard news is the most obvious area requiring an executive. And since the specialists often report hard news, they could be placed under the same authority. If the shop could afford two news executives, the second would then control soft news, specials, and documentaries. It can be argued that soft news should be under the jurisdiction of the hard news editor; but while the hard news editor is more in tune with daily events, the soft news editor is more likely to spot and develop a good feature story. Certainly news specials and documentaries are so similar in nature that they would normally be assigned to one jurisdiction.

In the smallest shops, the news director himself will continue to perform all of these functions, plus that of dealing with management. Economics will always dictate the size of the news department's executive structure.

However small the organization, the news director can at least consider the physical arrangement of his shop. As newspapers discovered long ago, this is far more important than it might seem to be at first glance; and this, too, is a lesson which television has yet to learn. *Physical proximity* of executives is extremely important to the effective functioning of any news organization; the larger the organization, the more important this is. The executives charged with selecting and supervising the gathering of news *must* be in close physical proximity; the more they must depend on intercom systems, memos, telephone calls, or even walking a few steps to consult with one another, the less effective the news organization will be. If, for example, the show producer and the assignment editor have to make even a minor effort to consult on a story, each will ultimately to some degree go his own way to the detriment of the other's concepts. This is only human nature. The solution is to accept people as people, and put them close together if their functions overlap or conjoin; put the assignment editor and the producer side by side at a desk, and they will automatically consult one another and coordinate their decisions without being asked or ordered to do so. Psychologists undoubtedly can explain this; the news director needs only to recognize it. The author has yet to see *any* television newsroom as well organized in the physical sense as almost *any* newspaper city room.

The Staff

Staff structure   Below the executive level the staff of the typical television news shop is still stratified along cumbersome lines which actually prevent it from operating effectively to originate news. There are "reporters" who are really reporter-writer-director-producer-performers. There are "writers" who are really producer-editor-rewrite men. Such men will always be needed, but in the explosive growth of television news other needs have been broadly overlooked.

A legman is hard to find, and the beat reporter is almost nonexistent. Yet these are the men, as newspapers discovered long ago, who develop and nurture the primary sources of original news. Their functions are fulfilled in television almost entirely by the field reporter and the assignment editor. And since the primary duties of these men keep them busy simply covering the obvious or attending to the logistics of coverage and production, the shop's development of source information is inadequate. Writers and producers, chained by duty in their plastic tower, and often lacking comprehension of the value of personal contact, tend to lean entirely on the wire services for information —even to the point of rejecting conflicting information from their own shop's staff reporters on the scene. The author has seen innumerable instances where information telephoned by field reporters was discredited in the shop on the ground that the same information had not appeared on the wires; such a destructive attitude is bred by lack of familiarity with news at the source. The inhabitants of the plastic tower subconsciously come to believe that news actually originates on the wires.

There is, of course, the occasional specialist who functions as a source reporter in his own area of specialization. But, as was pointed out earlier, the specialist is hampered by the fact that much of his time is spent not in *gathering* news but in *producing* his segment of the news show. And in any case the average shop's source contacts in many broad areas of news—local government, crime, schools, natural resources, urban affairs, community relations, science, and technology— occur only on an infrequent, haphazard basis.

The dominant news medium of our time cannot afford to let its coverage of such critical news be left to chance; or, if it can afford to do so in the economic sense, it is abdicating its responsibility to the public. The news director should assign reporters to the important news beats in his area. These reporters need not be performers or producers; they need have no particular knowledge of film or video production, but they should be newsmen. Their function should be to maintain the station's "news presence" in critical areas of news origin, to keep likely sources aware of the station's needs and desires, and of course to inform the assignment editor of possible stories. The shop should also have roving leg men with the sole function of working on stories requiring extensive investigation and development. When the work of beat men or leg men has progressed to the point where production can begin, field reporters and camera crews can be assigned to complete the story in a form suitable for airing.

With an organization thus capable of developing original news of importance, the news director should give further thought to the manner in which such news is aired. Important original stories should not be thrown away as if they were run-of-the-mill items. They offer opportunity to drop into the news show "capsule documentaries" of any length required. Such reports, original in nature, researched in depth, produced with style, filling as large a portion of the show's air time as is needed to cover the subject thoroughly, would give substance to television's pretensions to stature as a news medium.

Pay and promotion The newsman who demonstrates his value over a period of time is naturally eager for promotion and an increase in pay. But the rapidly expanding television news operation often tends to respond to this need irrationally, in a manner which debilitates its news product. One of the reasons is the arbitrary stratification of pay levels. Especially where union contracts prevail, established minimums tend to be viewed by management as maximums. A writer, for example, can earn only so much as a writer; to earn more, he must move into another, higher-paying stratum, and so he yearns for promotion to the rank of producer.

Such a system fails to take into account the all-important factor of ability. All newsmen in a given stratum are viewed as equal, and differences in competence and productivity are ignored by the accounting office. More significantly, perhaps, such a system provides a refuge for the cowardly news director; he can always tell the competent, ambitious newsman that the system does not allow a raise in pay.

The fact is that some writers are not worth the minimum scale and should be discharged as incompetent, while others are worth twice the minimum. This is true not only with regard to the quantity of their output, but also with regard to its quality. One good, fast writer is a better buy than a dozen poor, slow writers, yet all are paid the same amount.

The news director who is willing to recognize this fact can improve his shop's product and reduce operating costs at the same stroke, simply by paying fewer people what they are worth. Many writers, for example, desire only to write, but they seek promotion solely for the money; advanced to the status of producers, such men are often ineffective and less valuable to the shop despite their higher pay. Producers should be hired on the basis of their value as producers, not simply because they are such valuable writers that they deserve more money. Because of this irrational system, television news is full of people who have been promoted to their level of incompetence; most of them would have been glad to take the cash and let the title go.

The Independent Station

The news director of an independent station operates at some disadvantage in competition with network owned or affiliated stations, but the razor cuts both ways. The O&Os and many affiliates subscribe to either the network's daily microwave VTR feed or its film syndication service; for since the disappearance of the independent film syndication services, comparable coverage is not always available to the independent station. But this disadvantage is not as great as it might seem at first glance. The syndication film is aging rapidly, and the microwave feed in at least one case consists of the outs and rejects of the network news operation and is therefore inferior in quality despite its immediacy. However, the independent station may not have this type of coverage of national and international affairs.

Local orientation On the other hand, everything that goes into a network show, and everything that goes into a microwave feed or syndication film, is of national interest, whereas news is always local in orientation. In Peoria the death of a prominent local official may be bigger news than the prospective tax increase on which the microwave feed carries congressional comment; in Detroit the threat of an automobile industry strike may be bigger news than anything happening elsewhere in the world.

Here the independent station has the advantage. The news director can tailor his shows to appeal directly to the local interests of his community, just as every newspaper does. He can make a virtue of his weakness by concentrating on local matters which are within his reach and within his means, matters of immediate concern to his audience. This does more than build audience; its builds loyalty, because the viewers respect the station's concentration on *their* problems. And, lacking the national and international coverage, the independent also has more time to devote to local news; therefore, it has a better opportunity to present such news in depth and perspective. Viewers may look first to networks, O&Os, or affiliates for information on matters outside the community, but they can be induced to look first to the independent for news of their own community if the independent's news shop is geared to provide that information.

Emphasis on personality The independent station also has more freedom to exploit the important personality factor in television news.

Many stations with network connections tend, by dictum or desire, to emulate the network style of news presentation; the air men for certain O&Os and affiliates are noticeably imitative of their networks' star newsmen. But the resulting homogeneity of their air personalities leaves room for the independent to create a different image for itself and thereby to attract a different audience, or an audience which does not respond to the competing network image.

Thus, the independent station tends to lean more heavily on the personality and performance of its anchorman and its other air men. Most of the sharply stylized newsmen work for independent stations, and these men often are able to build their own loyal audiences and even to take these audiences with them if they change stations in the same community.

Unfortunately, this emphasis on personality often means an emphasis on opinion as opposed to facts. For example, a consistently conservative point of view, expressed in the personality and delivery of the newsman as well as in the selection of news and the style of production presentation, is demonstrably capable of attracting an audience of conservative viewers who unwittingly are more interested in confirmation of their beliefs than in information which challenges those beliefs. The same, of course, is true of many liberals, or of those committed to any faith—political, religious, or whatever. Such viewers are impervious to most information which contradicts their assumptions.

While the television audience is necessarily a mass audience, the local station without network connections usually makes its appeal to a specific section of that mass audience. It may be argued that particularized audiences such as those described above deserve to have their point of view represented on the air. However, such an argument evades the critical issue, which is the informational function of television news in relation to the democratic process. That function is transcendental; or, to put it another way, the purpose of television news is not merely to corroborate. When critical public issues are slanted in presentation by *improper* emphasis upon personality, with the intent of attracting a particularized audience, the result is contamination of the flow of information to the public. In the independent news operation which depends upon personality emphasis for its success, the news director's most difficult task may be to try to achieve balance and responsibility on the part of the news personality; this effort may bring him into direct conflict not only with the personality involved, but also with the station management. If the personality is highly successful in attracting a particularized audience, the news director is not likely to win any such conflict. If he loses, he then must resolve a personal conflict between the demands of management and the requirements of his professional conscience; his only responsible alternative is to quit his job.

Selection of Talent

Selection of talent is one of the news director's most important concerns, and he should insist on having the dominant voice in such decisions. The station manager and the program director, whose opinions usually weigh heavily in such matters, are seldom able to distinguish among actors, announcers, and newsmen, whereas the news director should be able to spot the difference in an instant. As television news matures, the trend is away from the actor or announcer and toward the genuine newsman, even though his delivery and presentation may seem less effective to those with only a superficial knowledge of news. Station managers and programming executives tend to favor the newsman who is handsome, who has a mellifluous voice, who smiles much of the time (especially leading into commercials), and who projects personal charm through the video tube; when judging women for air work they may favor physical beauty at the expense of professional ability.

While none of these attributes can be entirely disregarded (except, perhaps, that ever too-ready smile), they are all of secondary value in the newsman or newswoman. The air man's first requisite is the ability to convince the audience that he knows what he is talking about; this derives from his own inner conviction of his authority, which in turn is based upon his own background and experience. (All this, of course, assumes that he has mastered the mechanics of air performance.) The image of authority cannot be counterfeited to deceive the audience, but oddly enough it can easily be counterfeited well enough to deceive the station manager and the program director, probably because they are more interested in sales prospects than in distributing information. Among the decision-makers only the news director is likely to view prospective talent with a clear eye.

The image which any newsman projects is multifaceted, only one facet being authority. Most anchormen, in particular, are to some extent either sex symbols or father images. In the author's opinion, Walter Cronkite and Chet Huntley are father images; David Brinkley is a sex symbol—which is to say not that they themselves try to project such images, but only that these are the images of them which the public subconsciously forms and to which it reacts. The Huntley-Brinkley team has been a brilliant combination of both images. Whatever the projected image, the news director is best equipped to discern it.

The Talent-Format Relationship

The news director should also be aware of the subtle relationship between talent and show format. The original success of the Huntley-Brinkley team in the 1950s, usually ascribed to the pairing of Huntley's somberness with Brinkley's wry wit, was probably due as much to format as to the combination of personalities, fortunate though the latter was. Format contributed to their success in two ways:

1. NBC's news from Washington, the largest news source in the world, was reported not by a correspondent of visibly lower stature in the network hierarchy as on CBS and ABC, but by the co-star of the show. The public responded instinctively to this apparent recognition by NBC of the importance of its man in Washington. It was several years before CBS began to display the analytical talents of Eric Sevareid, based in Washington, in a manner which differed in detail but was similar in effect.

(Interestingly enough, at this writing NBC has recently moved Brinkley to New York, again relegating Washington coverage to its lower echelon talent. Whether the move affects audience ratings may be evident before long; however, with the Huntley-Brinkley team so well established in the public mind, other factors may now be of much greater importance.)

2. There was an audience carryover, or mutual feedback, between NBC's daily news coverage and its coverage of special events such as national political conventions. The reason was that Huntley-Brinkley anchored both.

It is noteworthy that CBS news ratings, which suffered for years in competition with the Huntley-Brinkley success, began to rise comparatively when both of these format considerations were corrected, the first by the use of Sevareid as Washington analyst, the second by the installation of Cronkite as anchorman for both daily news and major special events.

A similar format factor can be used to strengthen the image of the local station anchorman. He is able, as network anchormen seldom are, to go into the local field and cover news at the source. The viewer, seeing him thus as a working reporter, grants him greater authority than when he merely reads a script in studio.

Success and Overkill

During the recent period of rapid expansion in television news, the sudden financial success of some news operations has resulted in news "overkill," characterized by misuse of talent and subtle deterioration of format. While this has thus far been a problem for only the largest and most successful news shops, the promise of further television news expansion and concomitant increases in revenue justifies a word of warning. The *nouveaux riches* are the most likely to become office empire-builders.

Examination of a hypothetical 1-hour news show produced by a shop employing fifteen persons in the talent category illustrates the problem of overkill.

Approximately 11 minutes of the hour are devoted to opening, closing, and commercial breaks. This leaves only 49 minutes for news.

If the format calls for the anchorman to lead into each story covered by other reporters, and also to deliver tease lead-ins to commercials, this will take up perhaps another 2½ minutes, leaving 46½ minutes for news.

If certain specialist reports are "locked in" for nightly use, as is all too common, the time left for hard news is further reduced. Assume that the nightly specialist fare includes sports, weather, politics, an investigative report, and a human interest feature, averaging 3½ minutes each (a fair average). The hard news time is now reduced to 29 minutes.

It must be admitted, before we go further, that much of this is justifiable. The specialists, most frequently the political and investigative reporters, may be covering hard news. But our "1-hour" news show has already been reduced to less than half an hour, *most* of the hard news has not been covered, and we have thus far used only six of our fifteen air men.

The bind begins to be painful when the reports of out-of-town correspondents are also considered as "locked in" nightly segments. These people and their offices and crews are expensive, and management is apt to take the view that it is not getting its money's worth unless they are used every night. Thus Our Man in Bucks County must be on every night, no matter how little news originates in Bucks County. Add Our Man in Albany, Our Man in Washington, and Our Man in God-Knows-Where, give them each 3 minutes, and the time left for hard news is down to 17 minutes.

Again, what the correspondents report may be hard news; but also, it may not. To decide that they must be used simply because they are getting paid is not a news judgment; it is a promotional judgment.

And we still have five reporters to be heard from. If we put one in the hospital and another on vacation, and assign each of the remaining three to a hard news story running 2½ minutes, the total news time remaining is only 9½ minutes.

That 9½ minutes must accommodate all the remaining hard news of the day (which is most of it) plus the time needed for recues, refocusing, etc. It is obvious that we have only a semblance of a news show; what we really have is a self-promotion masquerading as adequate news coverage.

The way to expand, if luckily the revenue is available, is not to add more and more people to the staff without considering how badly they are needed or what use can be made of them. The way to expand is to consider what television news does *not* do, where it fails, and to move in that direction.

The Need for an Overview

Television's failure to originate news has already been pointed out. In part this failure is the result of the failure of news directors to sense the opportunities of the medium and to apply imaginative effort instead of expanding according to outmoded patterns. This means leg men, beat reporters, investigative units, capsule documentaries, analysis and interpretation of complex events, and more artistic use of the motion picture.

But most of all, it means dreams. Dreams are the beginning of all things. The American Union was first no more than a dream of a handful of revolutionaries. A trip to the moon was a dream of Jules Verne's. The name of Albert Einstein will live as long as man survives, because he dreamed of a new and greater source of energy. Dreams, seemingly gossamer and insubstantial, are really the levers with which men move the world. The man who never dreams leaves the world as he found it; he lives out his life in a web of millions of dreams woven by millions of men, never seeing the web, bequeathing nothing.

The news director should be a dreamer, and his dreams should provide the stimuli which enrich society and promote the better dreams of all men. With his shop in order, divorced to some extent from the day-to-day exigencies of the news, he can afford to dream, to muse on the great developing stories of our time and the shape of the future.

Scientists warn that pollution of air and water is altering the planetary ecology and threatening the very existence of man. Exploding cities strangle on their own wastes and are hobbled by transportation complexes which grow daily more inadequate. Overlapping governments squander the energy of the people in duplication of functions and intraurban power struggles. The rejection of one section of society by another breeds violence and anarchy. Capitalistic corporations, imbued by nature with an insatiable need for growth and stifled by contracting horizons, turn cannibalistic and devour one another to appease an irrational tax system. Plundering of natural resources is encouraged by law. The spread of medical knowledge and sanitation breeds overpopulation and threatens Malthusian tragedy. And on a planet that shrinks terrifyingly with each axial rotation, two inimical systems of society blindly follow the patterns of a once-wider world toward mutual destruction.

There are these and a thousand other things on which to dream, and in dreaming perhaps to find a new perspective and even sometimes a solution. Many articles have been published, many shows produced, on these and other entangled, interrelated problems; but not enough has been said or we would not have the problems. Not enough information about them has yet been disseminated to trigger the dreams that will provide the answers. We need an overview, and it is the imaginative news director who may help us find it.

In this age of increasing specialization, in which one man cannot even imagine what another man does, the need for an overview is paramount. The lesson has already been demonstrated, after World War I, when the newspapers of America failed to respond to the increasing complexity of society and the public's need to understand. Europe was exhausted for a full generation, Adolf Hitler was already dimly visible, China writhed in ominous anarchy, the Soviet Union was embarked on a socio-political experiment without precedent, and the United States was locked in a dream of instant wealth without work and power without responsibility.

But the great newspaper stories of the 1920s were mostly concerned with trifles: the vain effort to rescue an obscure young Kentucky cave prospector (Floyd Collins), the death of a movie actor (Rudolph Valentino), the Hall-Mills murder trial, the transatlantic flight of a stunt flyer (Charles A. Lindbergh) seeking a money prize. One of the few events of significance which received major newspaper coverage was the Tennessee trial of John Thomas Scopes on a charge of teaching the doctrine of evolution; but this event, like the others, was treated with sensationalism and ballyhoo. Not until the stock market crash of 1929 signaled the beginning of the Great Depression did the newspapers begin to demonstrate a sense of responsibility.

But if the public was not fully conscious of the failings of the media, it was at least uneasy. Beneath the superficial symptoms of the flapper and speakeasy era, powerful forces were at work changing the world; there were moments when the dream felt like a nightmare. Communism was part of the nightmare, but with the typical superficiality of the age it became a cause, not an effect. It became the bogeyman and therefore all bad, and by that judgment all discernment of what communism really was became impossible. The newspapers, superficial and provincial, did almost nothing to enlighten the public, and today we still pay the penalty for their nearly total abrogation of their responsibility to examine the world with an open mind and to report the results of that examination.

On this chaotic scene the modern weekly news magazine suddenly appeared and soared to success. *Time* and its imitators tried in some degree to do what the newspapers were failing to do: make sense of what was happening. That was all the public asked. *Time*'s success was not astounding, its failure would have been.

Today's reporting is better than the reporting of the 1920s, but today's need is even greater. And therein lies the television news director's golden opportunity. He has at his command the most effective means of reporting news ever devised, and an audience which is not merely available but eager. With insight and determination he has the power to stimulate the dreams which mankind needs, and to generate the public awareness which alone can make the greatest dreams come true. Even with his legion of troubles, if he cares about his fellow man, he can rightly consider himself among the favored of the ages.

Summary

The basic dichotomy of the television news director's job is between departmental management and administration of news production; where station resources permit, the two should be separated. In large shops, production responsibility should be divided as far as possible among the areas of hard news, specialists, soft news, news specials, and documentaries.

Physical proximity of the desks of news executives whose functions overlap, such as producer and assignment editor, contributes to improved news coverage.

More emphasis on leg men and beat reporters is needed to improve television's origination of news. With the development of more original news, capsule documentaries can be dropped into the daily news show.

Television news pay structures are irrational, tending to limit the prospects of competent news men and to retain or promote incompetence. Fewer and better newsmen, paid more, would return greater profits and prestige to the station.

Independent stations can seize the advantages offered by local orientation of news and emphasis on personality, but the latter should be approached with caution and a sense of responsibility to the community.

Selection of talent should be left primarily to the news director. The effect of the talent-format relationship on news success should be analyzed. Successful news operations should beware of overkill.

Beyond shop management, the news director's fundamental function is to inspire his staff to investigate the shape of the future, thereby offering the public an opportunity to mold that future closer to man's desires.

Suggested Assignments

1. Investigate the executive structure of a local television news operation, diagram the chain of command, and report on its effectiveness and its handicaps.

2. Compare the use of leg men and beat reporters by a local television news shop and a local newspaper.

3. Interview a television news director and report on the manner in which he divides his time between office administration and supervising news production.

4. Compare the orientation of news (local vs. national-international) demonstrated by the product of two television stations, one an independent and the other a network O&O or affiliate. Suggest any changes you would make as news director of the independent.

5. Compare the emphasis on personality in the news operations of the same two stations.

6. State your own concept of the most important functions of a television news director.

7. Assuming you were the news director of a television station in your own community, state what long-term local problems you would emphasize in news coverage, and how.

Part Five   Coda

Chapter 20

Television News and American Society

Galileo's recantation, which failed to alter the mechanics of the solar system to accord with the wishes of the Inquisition, demonstrated both the futility of ignorance and the ephemeral nature of truth. Yet man, however ignorant, must put his faith in something, no matter how ephemeral his children may discover his truths to be. It is the author's proposition that man must put his faith in television, that in fact he has no alternative as far as communication is concerned. If that proposition is correct, it is high time for all men to begin to understand television and the manner in which it affects their world.

Marshall McLuhan, the cryptic and often incoherent oracle of the electronic age, proclaims the birth of a global village in which all men are destined to relapse into an "oral" tribal culture under the pervasive influence of television. But history refutes McLuhan's notion, at least in part. We do not go home again; we never have. Nor do we ever escape its influence. Print, the medium of reflection and the repository of man's great abstractions, will remain with us and will continue to influence us even though it must coexist with the motion picture, the medium of emotion. Neither gunpowder nor nuclear bomb has yet replaced the short sword of Caesar's legionnaires, which the modern infantryman still carries in the form of the bayonet. Within a few years

---

Note: On many of the views presented in this chapter there is no conclusive evidence pro or con. The following discussion, therefore, must be taken largely as an expression of personal opinion. It is the author's hope that the airing of these views may stimulate investigation and research into the social effects of television.

your morning newspaper may be delivered by electronics instead of a truck, but you will still read it. Your television picture may come directly into your home from a satellite rather than from a local station, but you will still watch it. The difference will be, as it already is, in the *relative* importance of the news media; and television's influence is probably as great now as it ever will be. Only understanding is lacking.

This is where the television newsman comes in. It is his business to understand his medium, its effects, and how those effects are achieved. It is a totally new kind of journalism in which he engages, using new tools to convey information in a new manner which creates results far different from the results of conveying that same information via the older media.

And here the newsman is wise to heed McLuhan. If McLuhan is right in contending that the medium itself is the message, if television makes its point more by involvement of its audience in the emotions of the participants than by stating the facts, the effect on society is bound to be profound. Evidence of this is already visible in every arena of social interaction.

War

The widespread American disenchantment with the long war in Vietnam, the swelling urge for peace, almost certainly derived in part from the fact that this was the first war since the Civil War in which the American civilian participated—by means of television. His participation was vicarious, but his emotional involvement was excruciatingly painful. It was the first war fought in everyone's living room. The news films were not John Wayne war movies, and the blood on the living room screen was not catsup but life fluid draining from human beings. Death was no longer a telegram of regrets or a name in a newspaper casualty list; it was reality, and it was unbearable. The tension and weariness on the faces of the combatants, the sorrow and resignation on the faces of civilians bombed and burned out of their homes, had too great an emotional impact. Nothing could quite wipe the blood off the living room screen.

What this reaction to the world's first televised war means is not yet clear and is deserving of competent study. It may have made hawks more jingoistic just as it made doves more doveish; certainly the war became a divisive national issue. It polarized opinion, leaving the middle ground a no man's land. Such might not have been the case had not opinion been somewhat divided in the first place; television coverage of World War II, for example, might have energized the nation toward greater unity. In the case of Vietnam the television coverage seems to have helped give substance to doubts about the rationale of the war, a rationale never clearly explained by the news media. The causes and implications of the American involvement were many and complex (too many and too complex for this discussion), but to a degree the war was a symptom of American irresolution and misdirection, fostered by the long term failure of all the news media to perform responsibly and resulting in a direct threat to the survival of the human race. Thus, in the end, America was confronted with a war which had no possible satisfactory solution, which was also the way it began. A significant number of Americans, finally sensing their dilemma, and unaccustomed to wars which could not be ended in clear-cut victory or defeat, just wanted out.

As far as television was concerned, this effect appears to have been the effect of the medium itself, its immediacy and its emotional impact, and not a result of the adequacy or inadequacy of the coverage. Much of television's coverage was criticized as being in bad taste. As a generalized criticism, this was pointless. War itself is in bad taste; it symptomizes a failure of human communication, a breakdown of normal relationships and understanding, and, because of modern technology, it is a fruitless enterprise.

Television made this only too clear, not by explaining the American predicament rationally but simply by bringing the war into the living room. The viewer's resulting deduction of his own dilemma was as inexorable as Greek tragedy. It was not the television coverage that was offensive; it was the war.

True, as charged, the coverage of the war was one-sided. American camera crews and reporters could not accompany enemy troops and film their actions, and the few enemy-made films distributed in the United States were propagandistic rather than reportorial in character. The enemy side of the war was most effectively reported by indirection, as in the films of American marines cowering in their inadequate bunkers at Khe Sanh under rocket and mortar fire.

To the credit of the American network newsmen in Vietnam, they made an effort to report the enemy side of the war as far as was possible. They reported the apathy of the South Vietnamese, and they cast doubt on the credibility of the "body count" communiqués. But apathy and body counts are not good subjects for film, and the greatest effect of such reports may have been to reinforce the doubts created by the emotional involvement of film.

To the discredit of American newsmen, they did little to report the widespread corruption of South Vietnamese government and business. Doubtless the firm attitude taken by the South Vietnamese government toward such reports had something to do with this, and the leniency of

American officials in Vietnam contributed to stifling the flow of information. But the newsmen in Vietnam could have gathered the facts
and reported them after returning to this country; why so few did,
only those who were there can answer.

If any conclusive statement can be made about televised war as
demonstrated by the experience of Vietnam, it is that television proves
that General William T. Sherman was right: war *is* hell. The outrage
generated by films of American marines burning a village suspected of
harboring Viet Cong, the revulsion churned up by films of the bodies of
slain enemy soldiers being thrown into cargo nets for disposal, were
natural reactions of dismay over man's inhumanity. However dark or
distorted the mirror of war, it shocked and shamed those who looked
into it in their living rooms. We would prefer to ignore the bestial in
our nature; television will not let us ignore it.

Dr. Wilbur Schramm, director of the Institute for Communications
Research at Stanford University, has concluded: "Television is showing war as outmoded as a means of national policy . . . Now, something may get done."[1]

If television can prove Dr. Schramm's optimistic conclusion, it may
be humanity's savior in the nuclear age. Nothing else offers much
promise of survival.

Politics

The national political convention, a purely American phenomenon in
process of transition, presented television newsmen with especially
difficult problems in 1968. The Republican National Convention in
Miami Beach was for the most part a boring affair, however important
to the nation. It was a bad show. In contrast, the Democratic National
Convention in Chicago was a good show, inadequately covered because
of technical limitations imposed by a strike of communications workers—a strike which, by plan or coincidence, was settled almost as soon
as the convention ended.

The Chicago situation was a perfect demonstration of how denial of
the technical means of modern communication can hamstring television coverage. Even such simple devices as telephones often were not
available for the network newsmen, who in consequence had to do
much of their work in the informational dark. Mobile unit coverage
could not be aired live; the VTRs produced by mobile units had to be
"bicycled" to transmission centers for airing, and more often than not
they were outdated by the time they arrived and thus were never aired.

---

[1] *U.S. News & World Report* (March 4, 1968), p. 29.

One network mobile unit (4 cameras, 18 people, $13,000 per day cost) produced a miniscule total of approximately 5 minutes of VTR that ever saw air; this was a fairly typical example.

Lack of technical facilities due to simple lack of technology contributed to stifling the flow of information. Nighttime attacks on police in Grant Park, for example, could not be covered by the clumsy video cameras. (Film coverage of the same events was hamstrung by police restrictions on film crew movements.) As a result, the only immediate visual coverage of one major demonstration was that afforded by video cameras in the well lighted area in front of the headquarters hotel; what the cameras captured there was the overreaction of the police to earlier violence in the park which cameras had not been able to cover. Television news analysts, secure in their studios and able to see only what their monitors carried, were unaware of the full scope of the events on which they were required to comment.

Their perspective was further influenced by incidents on the convention floor, where newsmen were knocked down and summarily hauled off the floor under temporary arrest in full view of the cameras, and for no discernible reason except that they were trying to do their job. The near-paranoid security measures taken by police, convention officials, and convention hall guards so restricted the flow of information that newsmen could only wonder who wanted to prevent them from informing the public what was happening. The newsman is always suspicious of anyone who tries to impede the flow of information, and rightly so; such people almost without exception have something to hide.

It seems fair, however, to conclude that there was fault on both sides. The network newsmen began their convention coverage in a state of annoyance over restrictive security measures and inadequate communications which hampered them severely in their work; their resentment focused on Chicago's Mayor Richard Daley, who appeared to run the convention from his delegate seat on the floor and whose political machine was perhaps the last bastion of 19th century big city machine politics in which the police functioned in part as a recognized arm of the machine's political overlords. Proceeding from this point of view, and perhaps because of it overlooking the fact that they were proceeding on the basis of inadequate information, the newsmen found fault with Chicago.

That the public did not fully agree is attested by the reception given Mayor Daley's 1-hour documentary, broadcast in prime time in 142 cities a few weeks later, in which he defended the security measures as necessary and declared that the violent demonstrations were the work of professional agitators, including *agents provocateurs* from Hanoi and Havana.

The demonstrations which attended the Chicago convention must be viewed in the light of the determination of the demonstrators to disrupt the convention and to discredit the Daley machine by confrontations designed to produce precisely the kind of reaction which they did produce among police untrained for the politics of street confrontation. The restrictions and obstructive tactics to which newsmen were subjected on the convention floor are not so easily explained away, and at this writing no explanation satisfactory to responsible newsmen has ever been suggested.

Unfortunately, it seems likely that the news media—and after them, the public—were the big losers in Chicago, no matter where the faults of performance lay. The Chicago coverage contributed to the developing "credibility gap" concerning news in general and television news in particular, a growing lack of public confidence in the news media (among other institutions) which threatens the survival of the democratic process.

Noting that some polls indicated that 60 per cent of the American people approved Mayor Daley's version of what happened in Chicago, columnist and social critic Art Seidenbaum concluded that "the credibility gap, once connected with government, has crept into the rest of the community. In order to be at considerable odds with what media present, the public obviously has to disbelieve many of its information sources."[2]

In other words, because of the news coverage at Chicago, public confidence in television news may have peaked and begun to decline in August 1968, after two decades of steady rise. At this writing no new study has been made to determine whether this is true. But it is true that at least eight investigations of television news, five of them focusing directly on television coverage of the 1968 Democratic National Convention, are in progress or planned. The investigating bodies include the FCC, a federal grand jury, the attorney general of Illinois, the President's Commission on Crime and Violence, and four committees or subcommittees of Congress.

In the long run the conclusions to be reached by these various investigations may prove less significant than the simple fact that television news is under the scrutiny of so many accusing microscopes. The public demand which prompted the investigations appears to be sufficient evidence of public mistrust, which in itself is cause for concern.

"We seem on the way to becoming a nation of cynics," said former presidential press secretary Bill Moyers in commenting on this problem even before the Chicago convention. "While skepticism is the mark

---

[2] Art Seidenbaum, *Los Angeles Times* (October 11, 1968), Part II, p. 5.

of a healthy climate in a democracy, cynicism—widespread cynicism directed at the basic institutions of a society—can cripple a nation's will and undermine her spirit. . . . Cynicism about the press and government ultimately will infect the very core of the transaction of public affairs; it will eat at the general confidence we must be able to have in one another if a pluralistic society is to work."[3]

The newsmen sought the truth in Chicago. They did not wholly find it; they could not have been expected to find it. But unless they admit their own shortcomings and the subjectivity of their reporting, the public cannot be expected to trust them when it discovers that the picture they presented was less than the whole picture. Their irreproachability must be as perfect as that of Caesar's wife; when it is less so, as it was in Chicago, democracy itself is threatened. If the people cease to believe the news media, they close their minds to the last source of truth. And, as Moyers put it, "a journalist can lose his credibility in the fashion that many ladies lose their virtue: with the very best of intentions."[4]

The Republican convention in Miami Beach was another matter entirely. Here again television was the dominating medium of information in a show which it could not (and should not) control, and which it relentlessly exposed for the shadow-boxing game it was. Such exposure, as in Chicago, was more the natural effect of the medium itself than of conscious effort on the part of the television newsmen. In Miami Beach at least, they could not defend their inadequacies on the ground of lack of communication; they had every single electronic connection they desired.

The networks' problem in Miami Beach was not how to cover the convention, but how not to cover it. Both CBS and NBC (the third network, ABC, did not provide the kind of gavel-to-gavel coverage under discussion) spent a large part of their air time ignoring the official floor and podium proceedings; instead they repeatedly cut away to interviews with delegates on the floor, to activities in corridors and headquarters hotels, and to comment and analysis by their own newsmen. In general, this is the way to cover a convention; most of the significant action takes place outside the official arena.

But, in retrospect (granting it is easier to be a Monday-morning quarterback than to call the plays on the field), it can be seen that the television newsmen themselves frequently "made the news" in a desperate attempt to inject some drama into the otherwise dull proceedings. Richard M. Nixon had the presidential nomination "locked up"

---

[3] Bill D. Moyers, "Press or Government: Who's Telling the Truth?", *Television Quarterly*, Vol. 7 (Summer 1968), p. 20. By permission of *Television Quarterly*, The Journal of the National Academy of Television Arts and Sciences.

[4] *Ibid.*, p. 20.

long before the convention began, and foregone conclusions make poor television drama.

An outstanding example of this determination to make news was the flurry of televised floor interviews concerning a last-minute liberal revolt against Nixon's announced choice for a running mate, Governor Spiro T. Agnew of Maryland. The "revolt" lacked the support to make it meaningful (the leading liberal, New York Governor Nelson Rockefeller, was known to have denied it his support) and had not even an outside chance of success. The flurry of televised interviews grossly exaggerated the importance of the revolt, to the discredit of the newsmen.

The ABC network, which covered only major convention events live and reprised each day's developments in a 90-minute special, did extremely well in the audience ratings despite excessive emphasis on the bickering of its commentators, Gore Vidal and William F. Buckley. And the Republican convention had barely closed up shop when demands were heard for a streamlining of convention procedures to adapt them better to television's needs; one such proposal came from Vice President Hubert H. Humphrey, the leading contender for his party's nomination, and was adopted in part for the Democratic convention.

Future political conventions, it seems certain, will be greatly altered to improve the television coverage. This trend has already been criticized as "staging" the conventions for show business purposes. But what is really going to happen is the mutation of the convention form to fit the realities of the television age, which is a far different thing.

The national political convention is really a private party affair, at which the public and its proxy, television, are guests. They are invited guests, to be sure, but they are admitted on sufferance and are expected to conform to the rules established by the host. The proceedings of the convention are designed to satisfy the divergent demands and aspirations of individuals and groups within the party, and to give public recognition to relatively minor politicians in return for political favors granted or promised. Almost all seconding speeches fall in the latter category, and they are usually the dullest part of a convention. The floor demonstrations attending the nominations of candidates are designed to whip up enthusiasm and generate a bandwagon effect among uncertain and uncommitted delegates in this encapsulated party atmosphere. The convention was designed primarily for the party's benefit, and only secondarily for coverage by the print media, whose reporters can sift out the nonsense, the tedium, and the inconsequential in their written summations.

This traditional format is not adaptable to the show-business demands of gavel-to-gavel television coverage. The nonsense, the tedium, and the inconsequential are all too obvious to the electronic eye. Floor demonstrations, for example, may sound exciting on radio and may make splendid newspaper copy, but on television they are transparently staged affairs without a spark of spontaneity, especially when the viewer is treated to the sight of a program director cueing the convention band to start and stop the music to which the delegates parade.

Television has changed the private affair into a public spectacle, especially by changing the size and character of the convention audience. A generation ago only a handful of the party faithful were admitted to the convention hall as spectators. Today millions watch via television, and to these millions the vacuous, self-serving nature of much of the proceedings is only too apparent. The television audience demands meaning in its news, and there is little meaning in most of what happens at the traditional political convention. This is why television so frequently cuts away from the formal proceedings, and it is why the convention format is certain to be abbreviated to its more meaningful parts before many more of these quadrennial spectacles have come and gone.

Television also applies pressure on the parties to democratize their methods of selecting delegates. It reveals the dictatorial methods used by many states; the Georgia Republican delegation, for example, was hand-picked by two men. The only defense offered for such a procedure was that it was traditional; by the same argument we would still have slavery. To read about convention battles over such an issue brings the point home intellectually, but to see and hear the antagonists argue their causes in the heat of the convention struggle brings the same point home with the far greater impact of emotional involvement.

Television, therefore, is a democratizing force in politics. The medium *is* the message, and the message is that television has made the traditional form of the national political convention obsolete. Television demands drama that is better, more meaningful, and more honest.

Nor is this the end of television's effects on politics.

When William Jennings Bryan made his famous "cross of gold" speech at the Democratic National Convention in Chicago in 1896, the thousands of listeners in the convention hall sat in almost breathless silence to hear him; that silence was imperative if anyone was to hear him.

When Robert F. Kennedy, campaigning for the Democratic Presidential nomination in 1968, addressed a mere five hundred or so of his supporters in an airport terminal lobby in Los Angeles, so deafening and continuous was the noise of the small crowd that few could hear anything he said even though he used an electric-powered bullhorn to project his voice.

This is the phenomenon of inattention, a mark of the electronic age. The more we devise new electronic means of projecting our ideas, the less we listen and the louder we must shout. To the crowd in the airport terminal the emotional release triggered by Kennedy's presence was more important than his arguments. Kennedy fully understood this; he did not argue, he did not discuss issues, he spoke in vague and purely emotional terms of reaching toward a "better America." Kennedy was completely a man of the electronic age, a man who combined a basic concern for humanity with the ambition required to make such a concern effective in politics and with an apparently instinctive knowledge of how to use the techniques and technology of his age to get his message across to the people. He said virtually nothing, but in his style he spoke volumes, and the crowd knew what he meant.

Many critics of television, including even those who admired Kennedy, viewed this "Kennedy effect" with alarm. Attention, they said, is no longer imperative, but reaction is. And thus, the argument continues, charisma transcends character, image overrides issues, and style replaces substance.

The truth is, it has always been thus. The alarm of the critics arises from their failure to grasp the essential nature of human interaction, which television is returning to its only effective level—the person-to-person level. In personal relationships the style of a man—his clothing, his home, his wife and his manner toward her, his haircut, his idiosyncrasies, his loves and hates, his affectations and commitments—all are inseparable from the man himself. They *are* the man. And this cannot be less true because we know him not in the flesh but in the television tube.

Granted, it is possible in the television age for the candidate for high public office to present to the public a carefully tailored image, manufactured by professional merchandisers to fit the public's preconception of its need as measured by supposedly scientific selective polling. No matter, say the critics, whether the image fits the man; it must supply the demand. Positions, the argument continues, thus are adopted not on principle but on polls, slogans replace logic, sophistry succeeds debate, and the aging movie star can aspire to steer the ship of state despite inexperience in navigating even the shoals of county politics.

But the real question is whether this artificial image-making works. The basic premise has some validity. We can mistake the image for the man in a way that was impossible when the town hall was the seat of government and the debating platform stood in the county fair-grounds. The illusion of personal contact is deceptive; we do not see the gravy stains on the trousers. The valid argument that was so persuasive in print goes in one ear and out the other. We have become so inured to the more overt blandishments of a medium that contin-ually spoonfeeds us the most incredible pap about everything from deodorants to used cars that we react to all argument with inattention unless we are emotionally involved.

And we do not realize that we react so. Instead we soak up image by osmosis. If the conservative candidate promises a tax cut, we assume that he can deliver it in spite of population growth and rising techno-logical costs. If the liberal espouses another round of Rooseveltian remedies, we cheer him on without considering whether his prescrip-tion is passé. If the black militant looks and sounds angry, we assume that he is determined to destroy our society rather than merely re-arrange it somewhat more to his own benefit.

In the 1968 presidential campaign the phenomenon of heckling, on a scale and in a mood not seen for at least a century in the United States, forced the Republican presidential candidate, Richard M. Nixon, to adopt a "position paper" tactic in the final weeks of the campaign—a tactic which few newsmen seemed to understand fully, at least in the television medium, and which was nevertheless of critical importance in the campaign.

It must be remembered that the organized heckling to which all three major presidential candidates were subjected in 1968 was anar-chistic in nature. The hecklers, disenchanted with "the system" of American politics, were more interested in destroying dialogue than in creating it; they had no program of their own, they merely wished to prevent the candidates from presenting their programs to the people. To accomplish this they formed claques to shout down the candidates in their public appearances, to create such noisy disturbances that the presentation of reasoned arguments would be impossible. Although very few in numbers, they achieved their immediate aim; if anything prevented them from accomplishing their ultimate objective of de-stroying the presidential candidates' dialogue, it was television, the very instrument which they had hoped to use.

One of Nixon's closest friends and advisers, California's Lieutenant Governor Robert Finch, said that Nixon found it impossible to present his position in public speeches because of hecklers.[5] Consequently, Nixon issued a large number of position papers in the final weeks of the campaign; aside from controlled television appearances (to which

---

[5] Private conversation, reported to the author by Bill Ames, political editor of KNXT.

hecklers were not admitted), this was the only way he could state his positions on the many issues of consequence in the campaign. When hecklers were present, as Finch explained it, Nixon was forced to abandon his planned presentation to respond to the hecklers and to "keep the cheer lines coming" (that is, to keep the crowd on his side by delivering quips and slogans that would elicit cheers to drown out the heckling). He was forced to play to the television cameras, with their limited vision.

In such a situation, where both candidates and hecklers are depending on television coverage to advance their arguments, an extra burden is placed upon the television reporter. This was not the polite, structured, often witty heckling typical of English parliamentary debate, which is one of the most sophisticated and delightfully informative forms of political confrontation ever devised by man. This was heckling for the sole purpose of destruction, and both of the other candidates (Hubert H. Humphrey for the Democrats, and George Wallace for the American Independent Party) were subjected to it in greater degree than Nixon. One of the most effective responses was found by Humphrey's vice presidential running mate, Senator Edmund Muskie of Maine, who silenced hecklers on more than one notable occasion by inviting their spokesman to the platform to present his views, on condition that the hecklers, in their turn, would respect Muskie's right to speak.

For the television newsman, with his instinctive orientation toward the filmable conflict, the Nixon position papers are of great significance. This was where the candidate had an opportunity—one of his few opportunities in this campaign—to state his intentions. Position papers, like Vietnamese apathy and body counts, are not the kind of material which television tends to cover. But in this circumstance they were of great importance, and television should have paid them more attention than it did. In this particular case the newspapers did a much more creditable job than television. Only in the controlled television appearance, more often than not a paid political commercial, were the candidates able to present their arguments unmolested; television newsmen were too busy presenting the molesters to present the arguments.

Eight years earlier, the 1960 presidential contest between Nixon and John F. Kennedy provided the first test of television's effect on candidacies of national scope (assuming, as appears evident, that Adlai Stevenson was no match for Dwight Eisenhower in 1956, with or without television). The lessons of that campaign remain valid, and one of the lessons was that where the margin of victory is thin (a little more than 100,000 votes could have changed the outcome) the effect of personality projected through television can be decisive.

Kennedy's margin of victory was his "cool." Nixon worried over-much about polls and makeup; Kennedy took delight in the combat. The image which Nixon thus projected through the psychological x-ray screen of television gave enough voters enough pause to defeat him. As was remarked earlier in this work, television is the most intimate of media. And, after experiencing that intimacy, not enough voters cared enough about Nixon. It is not unreasonable for the wavering voter to opt for the man with the mark of assurance and the manner of authority; no one wants an indecisive, uncertain president. It was Nixon who sweated on camera and Kennedy who went to the White House.

In 1968 it was a different Richard M. Nixon who campaigned against Hubert H. Humphrey for the presidency—a Nixon visibly more ma-ture, more confident of himself and his ideas, quicker to laugh, seem-ingly more positive in argument, easier and more relaxed in face-to-face repartee with his critics, apparently less concerned about his dark beard (or, perhaps, with better makeup or a better barber). Almost every political reporter noted the difference, which can be confirmed by a comparison of news films made during the two campaigns. Some of Nixon's confidence in 1968 may have been inspired by the polls, which showed him leading by a substantial margin during most of the campaign. But whatever the cause, his confidence was evident, and it contributed to his victory in the election.

However, in respect to this image of confidence, the difference be-tween Nixon and Humphrey was hardly noticeable; and if there was a difference it favored Nixon, whereas in 1960 the difference was marked and it favored Kennedy. Thus it seems probable that other factors were more decisive in 1968, among them the Democratic party's bitter factionalism exacerbated by the disastrous national convention, Hum-phrey's connection with the unpopular Johnson administration, and the poverty of the Democratic campaign funds.

Where the decision hinges on the projection of personality, charac-ter, and attitude, only television makes it possible in the modern continental nation. Lesser matters—the election of a city councilman, for example—may not receive enough television coverage to affect the outcome. And when great, divisive issues are at stake, the positions taken by the candidates on those issues may dominate all other fac-tors. But the revelation of genuine character by television is *one* factor which cannot be ignored: no candidate can fully conceal his own state of emotion from the television eye, and through television the voter reacts emotionally to the emotion of the candidate. It is a valid basis for judgment. Sitting in his living room, the voter can judge the candidate not only on the basis of reports sifted through the minds and prejudices of print reporters who have made personal contact with the candidate; he can judge the candidate on the basis of his *own* personal contact, simply by flicking a switch and viewing the candidate on his screen.

The voter's judgment, influenced by television, may be as imperfect as the judgment of a blind man fingering the features of an ugly woman whose only beauty lies in the play of facial expression reflecting an inner grace, but we have as yet no evidence that this television method of arriving at political conclusions is worse than any other. It is only different. And television may be the only medium which can make a pluralistic continental democracy viable; it was invented in the nick of time.

Urban Violence

One of the characteristics of American urban society in the 1960s was increasing violence. Statistics, though an uncertain yardstick, indicated startling increases in all categories of violent crime; the flames of massive riots fanned by racial and economic discrimination flickered on television screens in every major city; and assassination became a repeated, if not accepted, tactic of political opposition.

Many of television's critics accused it of causing this violence, although no scientific study has yet established such a connection. However, in the opinion of many television writers, including David Karp and Paul Schneider, co-chairman of the committee on television violence of the Writers Guild of America, West, the charge has some definable validity. Karp and Schneider argue that television programming which depicts violence as the simple solution to every problem does breed violence by breeding confidence in violent, simplistic solutions.[6]

The same accusation has been made by Frank Mankiewicz, press secretary to the late Senator Robert F. Kennedy: "I can't recall seeing on television the victim of violence in the hospital for 3 or 4 months with no health insurance, or perhaps dead—and then taking a look at his family to see what sort of effect that might have. We don't see any of that, we don't see any of the consequences of violence, only the act itself . . . The dominant theme . . . is the resolution of conflict by a single violent or symbolically violent act . . ."[7] From Mankiewicz the accusation comes with terrible poignancy.

---

[6] David Karp and Paul Schneider, in a filmed interview with the author, *The Big News*, KNXT, August 18, 19, 20, 1968.

[7] Frank Mankiewicz, comments in *Violence on Television—Cause and Effect*, a seminar of the Hollywood Chapter, National Academy of Television Arts and Sciences, Beverly Hills, California, September 11, 1968.

The western movie is the archetype of the format: there are the good guys in the white hats and the bad guys in the black hats, and it all ends with a shootout in which the bad guys are killed. Problem solved, and fadeout. The locale may be changed to outer space in the future, to Chicago in the prohibition era, to London during World War II, or to Istanbul a thousand years ago, but the picture always ends with the bad guy getting killed, which solves the problem.

Of course, history proves that violence solves some problems, at least in part. The ancient Romans solved the problem of Carthage by destroying it, but the inhabitants of southern Italy live in poverty today because of the ravages of the Punic wars. The problem of Carthage still plagues the Romans.

Children in particular may be sensitive to the suggestion that violence solves problems, because they are receptive to any and all ideas. The whole of childhood is a search for ideas that seem to work. And if the statistics (again, those unreliable indicators) mean anything, the average child in an American television home spends as much or more time watching the "tube" as he spends in school. The Rev. John Culkin, S.J., director of the Center for Communications at Fordham University, tells the author that in his opinion today's child actually learns more from television that he learns in school, because television, even unintentionally, is a more effective teaching medium.

Father Culkin's conclusion, although shared by perhaps a majority of television critics, is disputed by many of the outstanding authorities on the subject. For example, Dr. Wilbur Schramm and his associates contend that the "most likely social effect of television is no effect."[8] And in studying the influence of television on juvenile delinquency, they conclude that "the young people who are influenced by television toward crime seem to be different from others who are not so influenced, even before they are influenced by television."[9]

In the same work, Dr. Lawrence Zelic Freedman adds, "The child's task of developing into an adult human being is psychologically far too complex to make it likely that any single stimulus pattern will predictably produce a particular behavioral response."[10]

Without disputing these conclusions, based on extensive research, the author wonders whether further, equally meticulous research might not find some support for the beliefs so widely held by the concerned and thoughtful men who write for television and those who criticize it. That little or no evidence of social effect has yet been

---

[8] Wilbur Schramm, Jack Lyle, and Edwin B. Parker, *Television in the Lives of Our Children* (Stanford, Calif.: Stanford University Press, 1961), p. 136.

[9] *Ibid.*, p. 164.

[10] *Ibid.*, p. 190.

discovered is a negative finding; it does not disprove, for example, the hypothesis of the television writers mentioned above.

That basic hypothesis is that life imitates art. There have been countless instances of the working of this mechanism in the history of the theatrical motion picture, and a few examples may make the point:

The countdown to blastoff used for military and scientific rockets was invented by Fritz Lang, a motion picture director, who in 1928 thought it made more sense than counting up (in the first science-fiction feature, *By Rocket to the Moon*). As Lang explained it, "When you count, 'One, two, three, four, five, six,' no one knows when you are finished."

White carpeting became the national rage after set decorator Cedric Gibbons, a multiple Academy Award winner, ordered a white carpet installed on a Hollywood movie set.

The men's undershirt industry almost went out of business when actor Clark Gable took off his shirt in the movie *It Happened One Night* and revealed—no undershirt.

The men's hat industry at one time made repeated pleas to Hollywood to make actors wear hats in movies; when they didn't, hat sales dropped alarmingly.

If the theatrical motion picture has had such tangible social effects, it seems unlikely that television can have none. If the author did not believe that television has social effects, and that some of the technical and psychological mechanisms by which it achieves those effects can and should be examined, he would have no purpose in writing this book, and it would be pointless for anyone to read it.

No matter whether cause and effect can at this moment be clearly discerned, it is a fact that on one television program after another, year after year, violence is depicted as the simple solution to complex problems. It is a fact that the average American spends an enormous portion of his life watching television; it has been estimated that the average American in his early twenties today has watched *more than 20,000 hours* of television. These facts cannot be without consequences. One of the consequences, it appears to the author, is the fact that many Americans today are increasingly engaging in violence (demonstrations, riots, murder, and mayhem) in the pursuit of social aims. Most of the participants in the urban and campus riots of the 1960s were too young to remember when there was no television; they had been educated by the medium, and they got its message. They were life imitating art—bad art.

This discussion, primarily of entertainment programming, may seem far afield from the problems of the television newsman, but his concern, too, is the imitation of art—his art—by life. The imperfection of his art was pointed out explicitly by the report of the National Advisory Commission on Civil Disorders, which concluded that the over-all effect of news coverage of the violent civil disorders of 1967 was "an exaggeration of both mood and event."[11] What is that but bad art, fated to inspire imitation?

The report further concluded that "the media have thus far failed to report adequately on the causes and consequences of civil disorders and the underlying problems of race relations."[12] The point was fortified by the statement, regarding television coverage in particular, that it "tended to give the impression that the riots were confrontations between Negroes and whites rather than responses by Negroes to underlying slum problems,"[13] and that "the media—especially television—also have failed to present and analyze to a sufficient extent the basic reasons for the disorders."[14]

This criticism relates directly to the author's previously stated arguments for more investigative reporting by television and for a more comprehensive overview by show producers and news directors. If the commission's conclusion is correct, and we have no evidence that it is not, television news failed the American people dismally in one of the primary functions of a responsible news medium, which is to search out and report concealed trends and conditions which, however few people they may affect immediately, are the ultimate concern of all in the community. Television was so surprised by the riots that it failed to interpret them accurately, and to that extent the public remained unaware of the nature of the crisis even after it was upon us. Thus bad art led directly to more violence.

The commission report also substantiates the view that this concern relates more directly to television than to any other medium: "Television is the formal news source most relied upon in the ghetto. According to one report, more than 75 per cent of the sample turned to television for national and international news, and a larger percentage of the sample (86 per cent) regularly watched television from 5 to 7 P.M., the dinner hours when the evening news programs are broadcast."[15] Regarding newspaper reading, the commission reported: "When ghetto residents do turn to newspapers, most read tabloids, if available, far more frequently than standard size newspapers and rely on the tabloids primarily for light features, racing charts, comic strips, fashion news, and display advertising."[16]

---

[11] *Report of the National Advisory Commission on Civil Disorders* (New York: Bantam Books, Inc., 1968), p. 363.

[12] *Ibid.*, p. 363.

[13] *Ibid.*, p. 369.

[14] *Ibid.*, p. 373.

[15] *Ibid.*, p. 376.

[16] *Ibid.*, p. 377.

In McLuhanesque terms, the urban ghetto is already an oral, tribal subculture, reachable most easily by television and therefore more susceptible to the influence of television than to that of any other medium. By definition, then, television's responsibility toward the ghetto is the greatest.

To fulfill this responsibility, television must be more searching and more sensitive in both its reporting of ghetto affairs and its examination of the problems which arise from the ghetto and affect all of society. Demands for law and order, for an end to divisiveness in the nation, will fall on deaf ears both in the ghetto and outside it until the underlying causes of disrespect and divisiveness are exposed, explained, understood, and uprooted. In the last several hundred years, we have had successive revolutions in favor of the mercantile class, the manufacturing class, and the working class. Today's revolution, of which urban violence is only a symptom, is the revolution of the poor demanding a fair share of the fruits of the affluent society. It is, perhaps, the last revolution, the final process leading to as classless a society as man can devise. When the nation comprehends that every man must have a chance to participate in the workings of society and derive its benefits, that the American system cannot endure only part free and part equal, then the nation will either act to remedy the problem or it will fail to act and cease to endure. The heaviest responsibility for creating such understanding lies upon television.

Conclusion

Looking far beyond the problem of urban violence, the television newsman needs to consider the nature of the species which by its self-bestowed generic title of *Homo sapiens* arrogates to itself the right to think. If the opinions of the more recent and relevant students of man can be relied upon, the arrogation was somewhat inaccurate. Man is more prone to violence than to thought.

Zoologist Niko Tinbergen of the Oxford University Animal Behavior Research Group goes so far as to call man an "unhinged killer" whose unthinking attitudes have "truly lethal potentialities" for the species.[17] Tinbergen finds man the only animal which engages in the mass murder of its own kind, a creature combining "cultural excesses" in the form of technology with a type of self-brainwashing which deprives him of the social tools (such as displays of meekness and distress) by which other species avoid extinction.

---

[17] Niko Tinbergen, speech at San Francisco State College, reported by the *Los Angeles Times* (May 12, 1968), Section A, p. B. Copyright, 1968, by the Los Angeles Times. Reprinted by permission.

Man's killer instinct has been variously ascribed to blind tribal loyalties, the instinct to defend territory, and improper instincts acquired during his evolution as a misfit member of the ape family. Whatever its cause, man's tendency to substitute emotion for reason and to rationalize his killer instinct has recently become the object of widespread concern. And this sudden concern is, comfortingly, the result of his ability to think. Having invented the hydrogen bomb, he cannot uninvent it, and so it hangs over his head, suspended by a thin thread of reason. At least he knows it is there.

The critical question is whether he can learn enough about himself, and learn it quickly enough, to keep himself from cutting the thread and eliminating himself from the planet. Or, like the dinosaur, has he become so successfully specialized that his very success is an evolutionary trap from which he cannot escape? Will he die of the technology which has given him such admirable control over his environment? Can he control himself as well?

The fascinating experiment that began millions of years ago, when the first technological ape picked up the first crude club or hurled the first rock missile, is not yet over. As long as it continues, and man recognizes the nature of the experiment, there is hope. If he can grow in wisdom as he has grown in knowledge, he may survive.

And the very instrument which so well portrays man's violence may be the means of his survival. If television can disillusion man with war and enable him to use his emotional capacities for discernment, he may still have a chance. By the very nature of the course he has taken, he has no other chance. That is why he must place his faith in television, and why he must learn to understand how it really works and then make it work to his benefit. The medium of emotion is the medium through which he may ultimately conquer emotion and become a truly thinking animal. The most fascinating part of the experiment lies just ahead.

Television's greatest challenge may thus be said to arise from the communications equivalent of the Heisenberg uncertainty principle of physics, according to which the very act of attempting to measure the velocity and position of an electron alters its velocity and position. Neither can ever be known for certain. Equally, television, by its very existence, alters war, politics, social relations—all of man's affairs—in uncertain ways.

But the electronic age is not going to disappear unless we all disappear with it. We shall not return to Bryan and his breathless audience. We must learn to live with this instrument and make it serve us well. We must learn because the tiger still stalks outside the cave; and if we let ourselves be mesmerized into inattention, we shall surely feed the tiger. We are both tiger and victim.

The effects of electronic communication must be transmuted into evolutionary changes in the social and political structures of which it is irrevocably a part, and most importantly into a revolutionary new concept of man himself. And the first and greatest understanding of this must come from the electronic journalist. He is the proxy for all mankind, and his medium is the new town hall of the world. His is not merely the greatest challenge of our time; his is the greatest opportunity of all time. He alone can make television the instrument through which man not merely endures, but prevails.

Summary

If television news conveys its message more by emotion than by reason, its effects on society should be analyzed in that light.

By mirroring the animal instincts which make possible the rationale of war, and by revealing clearly the futility of war, television may have made war obsolete.

The Democratic National Convention in Chicago in 1968 extended the "credibility gap" to include television news. This public reaction, by which both television and the public may be the ultimate losers, demonstrates the absolute necessity for irreproachable coverage of controversial events.

Future political conventions almost certainly will be altered to fit the needs of television coverage, because the democratizing force of television has made the traditional convention format obsolete.

The psychological x-ray eye of television penetrates most efforts at personal image-making, and thus may help make a pluralistic, continental democracy viable.

Television appears to be responsible in some degree for contributing to the American climate of violence, by offering an entertainment art which life has imitated. The newsman has contributed by the imperfection of his art, by his failure to grasp the inner meaning of events. His responsibility is greater than any other newsman's, and by corollary his opportunity to quiet the impulse to violence is also greater.

If man's actions are dictated more by his emotion than by his reason, television, with its capacity to generate emotion, may be the greatest—perhaps the only—means of man's survival.

Suggested Assignments

1. State your own ambitions in television and your reasons for wishing to enter the medium.

2. Give your own opinion of the effect of television on war, supporting your argument by specific examples.

3. Discuss the relationship of television news and "image" candidates with respect to a local election.

4. Compare the effect on yourself of television coverage of a political campaign event and newspaper coverage of the same event.

5. Cite examples of television political coverage which generated emotional effects which were (a) harmful and (b) beneficial.

6. Compare the relative influence of (a) image and (b) issues in a specific political campaign.

7. From your own experience cite one or more examples of the phenomenon of inattention.

8. Define the responsibility of the television newsman in reporting filmed incidents of violence of a nature likely to inflame public opinion.

9. Assuming it is true that television is the most influential news medium in the urban ghetto, explain why this might be so.

10. State your own view of television's responsibility to society, and discuss measures which might be taken to make the medium more responsible.

Appendix A

Actual Job Openings (1968)

Note: The following job offers were culled by the author from placement lists of the Radio Television News Directors Association, and the words used in the right-hand column are those of the prospective employers. Salaries quoted up to $392 are weekly, from $550 to $675 monthly, and from $8,000 up yearly. In addition, the code, in the left-hand column, indicates the skills expected. The symbol # indicates a network job; all others are at local stations; it might be noted that few network or major-market station positions need advertising.

A–Air work	R–Reporter
C–Cameraman	W–Writer
E–Film editor	X–News executive
P–Producer	

Skills	Location	Station's Job Description
A	Atlanta, Ga.	Anchorman, mature, experienced. $15,000.
C	do	Cameraman, $125.
AW	Cedar Rapids, Ia.	TV airman for 2 half-hour shows a day. Write shows too. $10,000–$12,000.
ERW	Cincinnati, O.	Writer-reporter, also handle film equipment. Up to $200 maximum to start.
RW	Columbus, O.	Reporter, leg man, writer, do interviews. Experienced. $6,000–$7,000.
AR	do	Investigative reporter-newscaster with good radio or TV record. $200.
RWX	do	Night news director. Assignments, writing, some reporting. Plan show. $8,000–$10,000.

AX	Columbia, S.C.	Asst. news director. Anchor major newscasts, other duties. Prefer journ. degree and 3–5 yrs. TV news experience. To $10,000.
ACRW	Evansville, Ind.	Reporter-writer-photographer. Some on-camera work. $125 range.
ACR	Fort Wayne, Ind.	Trained reporter. Also to handle camera. Will teach. Prefer journ. degree or experience. Sports, weather, and air capability all helpful. $500–$550 range.
RW	Grand Rapids, Mich.	Reporter-writer. $130–$170.
PW	Green Bay, Wis.	Producer-writer for late half-hour news block. $130 or more to right man.
APRW	High Point, N.C.	Night TV editor. Reporting, writing skills. Film knowledge. Air work. $130–$145.
ARW	Idaho Falls, Id.	Writer-reporter-TV air man. Degree preferred. Political knowledge necessary. Sports background helpful. $550–$675 range.
PW	Miami, Fla.	Writer-producer. Experienced. $135–$150 range.
PRW	Minneapolis, Minn.	News editor familiar with expanded format. Good writer. BA, experience. Some outside work. Send writing samples, salary needs, standup film piece with application. $8,000–$10,000.
AEW	Montgomery, Ala.	Newsman. On-air reporting. Young, enthusiastic. Writing, editing, newsfilm. $130–$140.
ACR	Nashville, Tenn.	Reporter. Self-starter. Helpful if can handle camera and do air work. $150 range.
CRW	Peoria, Ill.	Radio-TV newsman-reporter-cameraman. Start $125–$135.
AERWX	Phoenix, Ariz.	Assignment editor. Writing, reporting, some standups. Film know-how. About $9,000.
AER	Portland, Me.	Radio-TV reporter, handle film, air work. Prefer journ. grad. $130–$144 plus talent.
AR	Saginaw, Mich.	Morning man for radio and TV. Young college graduate to handle on-air radio and TV, do some city, county reporting. $125 to start.
ACW	St. Joseph, Mo.	Asst. farm director. Knowledge of Midwest farming. Prefer experience with broadcasting and 16 mm. photography. $130.
AW	Scranton, Pa.	11 P.M. anchorman. Also write. $175–$200.

ACR	San Diego, Cal.	Field reporter. Air work. Must be able to handle silent camera. $195.
APRW	San Francisco, Cal.	Sportscaster, for inserts on 6 and 11 P.M. shows. Write, produce own material. $392 per week.
ACRW	Steubenville, O.	Writer-reporter, some air work, handle 16 mm. camera. About $8,000.
ACERW	Tampa, Fla.	Newsman to report, handle cameras, edit, script, some air work. Prefer man with college journ. $6,500–$8,000.
AR	Washington, D.C.	TV reporter. Also handle air work regular 10 P.M. cast. Experienced newsman with good air appearance. $18,000.
X	do	Editor for TV assignment desk. Handle crews. $200–$250 range. #
X	Zanesville, O.	News director for radio-TV. Experienced. Up to $9,000.

Appendix B

Television Code

Section V of the Television Code of the National Association of Broadcasters, thirteenth edition, August, 1968, states the following to be acceptable practice in the treatment of news and public events:

1. A television station's news schedule should be adequate and well balanced.

2. News reporting should be factual, fair and without bias.

3. A television broadcaster should exercise particular discrimination in the acceptance, placement and presentation of advertising in news programs so that such advertising should be clearly distinguishable from the news content.

4. At all times, pictorial and verbal material for both news and comment should conform to other sections of these standards, wherever such sections are reasonably applicable.

5. Good taste should prevail in the selection and handling of news: Morbid, sensational or alarming details not essential to the factual report, especially in connection with stories of crime or sex, should be avoided. News should be telecast in such a manner as to avoid panic and unnecessary alarm.

6. Commentary and analysis should be clearly identified as such.

7. Pictorial material should be chosen with care and not presented in a misleading manner.

8. All news interview programs should be governed by accepted standards of ethical journalism, under which the interviewer selects the questions to be asked. Where there is advance agreement materially restricting an important or newsworthy area of questioning, the interviewer will state on the program that such limitation has been agreed upon. Such disclosure should be made if the person being interviewed requires that questions be

submitted in advance or if he participates in editing a recording of the interview prior to its use on the air.

9. A television broadcaster should exercise due care in his supervision of content, format, and presentation of newscasts originated by his station and in his selection of newscasters, commentators, and analysts.

The following portions of the NAB Television Code are also of relevance in news programming:

I, 7. It is in the interest of television as a vital medium to encourage and promote the broadcast of programs presenting genuine artistic or literary material, valid moral and social issues, significant controversial and challenging concepts and other subject matter involving adult themes. Accordingly, none of the provisions of this Code, including those relating to the responsibility toward children, should be construed to prevent or impede their broadcast. All such programs, however, should be broadcast with due regard to the composition of the audience. The highest degree of care should be exercised to preserve the integrity of such programs and to ensure that the selection of themes, their treatment and presentation are made in good faith upon the basis of true instructional and entertainment values, and not for the purposes of sensationalism, to shock or exploit the audience or to appeal to prurient interests or morbid curiosity.

II, 1. The education of children involves giving them a sense of the world at large. It is not enough that only those programs which are intended for viewing by children shall be suitable to the young and immature. In addition, those programs which might reasonably be expected to hold the attention of children and which are broadcast during times of the day when children may be normally expected to constitute a substantial part of the audience should be presented with due regard for their effect on children.

III, 1. A television broadcaster and his staff occupy a position of responsibility in the community and should conscientiously endeavor to be acquainted fully with its needs and characteristics in order better to serve the welfare of its citizens.

IV, 1. Program materials should enlarge the horizons of the viewer, provide him with wholesome entertainment, afford helpful stimulation, and remind him of the responsibilities which the citizen has toward his society. The intimacy and confidence placed in television demand of the broadcaster, the network and other program sources that they be vigilant in protecting the audience from deceptive program practices.

IV, 2. Profanity, obscenity, smut and vulgarity are forbidden, even when likely to be understood only by part of the audience. From time to time, words which have been acceptable acquire undesirable meanings, and telecasters should be alert to eliminate such words.

IV, 3. Words (especially slang) derisive of any race, color, creed, nationality or national derivation, except wherein such usage would be for the specific purpose of effective dramatization such as combating prejudice, are forbidden, even when likely to be understood only by part of the audience. From time to time, words which have been acceptable acquire undesirable meanings, and telecasters should be alert to eliminate such words.

IV, 4. Racial or nationality types shall not be shown on television in such a manner as to ridicule the race or nationality.

IV, 5. Attacks on religion and religious faiths are not allowed. Reverence is to mark any mention of the name of God, His attributes and powers. When religious rites are included in other than religious programs the rites shall be accurately presented. The office of minister, priest or rabbi shall not be presented in such a manner as to ridicule or impair its dignity.

IV, 6. Respect is maintained for the sanctity of marriage and the value of the home. Divorce is not treated casually as a solution for marital problems.

IV, 7. In reference to physical or mental afflictions and deformities, special precautions must be taken to avoid ridiculing sufferers from similar ailments and offending them or members of their families.

IV, 9. Law enforcement shall be upheld and, except where essential to the program plot, officers of the law portrayed with respect and dignity.

IV, 10. Legal, medical and other professional advice, diagnosis and treatment will be permitted only in conformity with law and recognized ethical and professional standards.

IV, 13. Criminality shall be presented as undesirable and unsympathetic. The condoning of crime and the treatment of the commission of crime in a frivolous, cynical or callous manner is unacceptable.

The presentation of techniques of crime in such detail as to invite imitation shall be avoided.

IV, 16. Illicit sex relations are not treated as commendable. Sex crimes and abnormalities are generally unacceptable as program material. The use of locations closely associated with sexual life or with sexual sin must be governed by good taste and delicacy.

IV, 17. Drunkenness should never be presented as desirable or prevalent . . .

IV, 18. Narcotic addiction shall not be presented except as a vicious habit. The administration of illegal drugs will not be displayed. The use of hallucinogenic drugs shall not be shown or encouraged as desirable or socially acceptable.

IV, 19. The use of gambling devices or scenes necessary to the development of plot or as appropriate background is acceptable only when presented with discretion and in moderation, and in a manner which would not excite interest in, or foster, betting nor be instructional in nature.

IV, 20. Telecasts of actual sports programs at which on-the-scene betting is permitted by law should be presented in a manner in keeping with Federal, state and local laws, and should concentrate on the subject as a public sporting event.

IV, 23. No program shall be presented in a manner which through artifice or simulation would mislead the audience as to any material fact. Each broadcaster must exercise reasonable judgment to determine whether a particular method of presentation would constitute a material deception, or would be accepted by the audience as normal theatrical illusion.

IV, 24. The appearances or dramatization of persons featured in actual crime news will be permitted only in such light as to aid law enforcement or to report the news event.

IV, 25. The use of horror for its own sake will be eliminated; the use of visual or aural effects which would shock or alarm the viewer, and the detailed presentation of brutality or physical agony by sight or by sound are not permissible.

IV, 29. Camera angles shall avoid such views of performers as to emphasize anatomical details indecently.

IV, 30. The use of the television medium to transmit information of any kind by the use of the process called "subliminal perception," or by the use of any similar technique whereby an attempt is made to convey information to the viewer by transmitting messages below the threshold of normal awareness, is not permitted.

IV, 31. The broadcaster shall be constantly alert to prevent activities that may lead to such practices as the use of scenic properties, the choice and identification of prizes, the selection of music and other creative program elements and inclusion of any identification of commercial products or services, their trade names or advertising slogans, within a program dictated by factors other than the requirements of the program itself. The acceptance of cash payments or other considerations in return for including any of the above within the program is prohibited except in accordance with Section 317 and 508 of the Communications Act.

IV, 32. A television broadcaster should not present fictional events or other non-news material as authentic news telecasts or announcements, nor should he permit dramatizations in any program which would give the false impression that the dramatized material constitutes news. . . .

IV, 33. Program content should be confined to those elements which entertain or inform the viewer and to the extent that titles, teasers and credits do not meet these criteria, they should be restricted or eliminated.

VI, 1. Television provides a valuable forum for the expression of responsible views on public issues of a controversial nature. The television broadcaster should seek out and develop with accountable individuals, groups and organizations, programs relating to controversial public issues of import to his fellow citizens; and to give fair representation to opposing sides of issues which materially affect the life or welfare of a substantial segment of the public.

VI, 4. Broadcasts in which stations express their own opinions about issues of general public interest should be clearly identified as editorials. They should be unmistakably identified as statements of station opinion and should be appropriately distinguished from news and other program material.

Appendix C

Canon 35

Canon 35 of the American Bar Association's Canons of Judicial Ethics is purely a recommendation of the ABA, which is nothing more than an organization of lawyers and not an arm of the courts. Nevertheless, Canon 35 has come to have the effect and force of law in almost every court the land. Its result has been a ban on still photography, filming, or video recording of almost all court proceedings. In some cases the courts have also construed Canon 35 or similar judicial council recommendations to ban photography in empty courtrooms and the immediate environs of courtrooms, such as nearby corridors. Canon 35 reads as follows:

Proceedings in court should be conducted with fitting dignity and decorum. The taking of photographs in the courtroom during sessions of court or recesses between sessions, and the broadcasting or televising of court proceedings detract from the essential dignity of the proceedings, distract participants and witnesses in giving testimony, and create misconceptions with respect thereto in the mind of the public and should not be permitted.

In connection with Canon 35, it is worth rereading the First and Sixth Articles of the Bill of Rights of the Constitution of the United States:

Article I. Congress shall make no law respecting an establishment of religion, or prohibiting the free exercise thereof; or abridging the freedom of speech, or of the press; or the right of the people peaceably to assemble, and to petition the Government for a redress of grievances.

Article VI. In all criminal prosecutions, the accused shall enjoy the right to a speedy and public trial, by an impartial jury of the State and district wherein the crime shall have been committed, which district shall have been previously ascertained by law, and to be informed of the nature and cause of the accusation; to be confronted with the witnesses against him; to have compulsory process for obtaining witnesses in his favor, and to have the Assistance of Counsel for his defence.

It is a long reach from these two Articles of the Bill of Rights to the prohibition of photography in the courtroom. And while that prohibition might have been unquestionable before the advent of television, or even before the development of video equipment so unobtrusive that it became possible to televise trials without anyone in the courtroom being aware of it, it is no longer so.

Unquestionably the lawyers conceived the ban on photography out of concern for the rights of the accused and the process of justice. However, even leaving aside the fact that most of the past abuses were aided and abetted by the laxity of the presiding judge, Canon 35 skirts the questions raised by the guarantee of a "public" trial. It is highly questionable whether a trial of national significance and wide public interest can any longer truly be called "public" in the sense intended by the framers of the Constitution. Few members of the public are admitted to such trials because of lack of space in the courtroom; the public at large is represented only by the newsmen present, including television newsmen. The means by which that public can see and hear such a trial is now available; it is television. There are many arguments against televising trials, some valid and some irrelevant, but still untested is the question whether the ban on televising trials violates the Constitutional rights of the accused, the press, and the public.

Suggested
Additional
Reading

The following list is not intended to be comprehensive. However, it includes works by which, with a minimum of study, the reader can rapidly broaden his knowledge of television news. Most of the suggestions relating to film theory are drawn from the literature of the theatrical film, because little has been written in exploration of news film as an art form. While the works are listed by topics, most contain material of broader interest than the topical listings indicate; this is particularly true of the works listed under "Concept and Technique."

Concept and Technique

Atkins, Jim, Jr., and Leo Willette, *Filming TV News and Documentaries*. Philadelphia: Chilton Company; and New York: American Photographic Book Publishing Co., Inc., 1965. An excellent book on practical aspects of television reporting, with emphasis on film coverage; loaded with helpful hints.

Bluem, A. William, *Documentary in American Television*. New York: Hastings House, 1965. The definitive work on television documentaries, with innumerable conceptual applications for the television journalist; of particular value for the producer of news specials.

CBS News, *Television News Reporting*. New York, Toronto, London: McGraw-Hill Book Company, Inc., 1958. Written by a "committee," but worth rapid skimming for general information about television news.

Downs, Hugh, and Mike Wallace, "The Craft of Interviewing," *Television Quarterly*, Vol. IV, No. 3 (Summer 1965), pp. 9–19. Pertinent, practical comment by two expert practitioners of the craft of interviewing.

Fang, Irving E., *Television News*. New York: Hastings House, 1968. Basic discussion of television news writing, filming, editing, and production.

Wood, William A., *Electronic Journalism.* New York and London: Columbia University Press, 1967. A thoughtful study of the conceptual aspects of broadcast journalism.

Zettl, Herbert, *Television Production Handbook, Second Edition.* Belmont, California: Wadsworth Publishing Company, Inc., 1968. Perhaps the best available work covering every possible technical aspect of television production.

Film Theory

Arnheim, Rudolf, *Film as Art,* pp. 8–160. Berkeley and Los Angeles: University of California Press, 1966. An examination, somewhat disorganized but often stimulating, of conceptual principles and mechanisms by which film creates its effects.

Eisenstein, Sergei, *Film Form* and *The Film Sense.* New York: Meridian Books, 1957. These essays by the great seminal filmmaker and theorist are required reading for every serious student of film. While Eisenstein places perhaps excessive emphasis on picture composition and geometrical relationships, his perceptions of film technique as art have had profound influence on all films made in the last half century.

Lawson, John Howard, *Film: The Creative Process.* New York: Hill and Wang, 1964. Theory of film drama by one of its foremost theorists; pp. 221–359 especially contain many ideas directly applicable to television news.

Lindgren, Ernest, *The Art of the Film.* New York: The Macmillan Company, 1963. Presents valuable and fundamental concepts of film editing (pp. 55–96), the use of sound (pp. 97–113), and camera work in terms of composition and the directorial function (pp. 114–133).

Spottiswoode, Raymond, *A Grammar of the Film.* Berkeley and Los Angeles: University of California Press, 1950. Although sometimes overly insistent on the verity of subjective factors, the author explains in considerable detail the psychological effects created by various shots, angles, transitions, and montages; valuable reading for both the film reporter and the film editor, especially pp. 113–274.

Social Effects

Friendly, Fred W., *Due to Circumstances beyond Our Control.* New York: Random House, Inc., 1967. An astringent look at the inside workings of the American system of commercial network television and its decision-making processes, by the former president of CBS News.

Herman W. Land Associates, Inc., *Television and the Wired City.* Washington, D.C.: National Association of Broadcasters, 1968. A study of television's relationship to the national community, favoring continuation of the broadcast mode of distribution; the section on news (pp. 175–196) documents the "news explosion" of the 1960s.

Loevinger, Lee, "The Ambiguous Mirror: The Reflective-Projective Theory of Broadcasting and Mass Communications," *Journal of Broadcasting,* Vol. 12,

No. 2 (Spring 1968), pp. 97–115. An FCC commissioner's view of the nature and function of broadcasting.

McLuhan, Marshall, *Understanding Media: The Extensions of Man*. New York: The New American Library, Inc., 1964. A provocative if sometimes repetitive or undecipherable view of the influence of electronic mass media on society; the section on television (pp. 268–294) is especially applicable.

Report of the National Advisory Commission on Civil Disorders, pp. 362–389. New York: Bantam Books, Inc., 1968. The commission's conclusions on the relationship of the news media to civil disorder.

Rubin, Bernard, *Political Television*. Belmont, California: Wadsworth Publishing Company, Inc., 1967. Detailed examples of the interaction of television and politics, with particular emphasis on the presidential campaign debates of 1960 and the presidential campaigns and conventions of 1964. The book unhappily leaves the reader wishing for more in the way of conclusions.

Schramm, Wilbur, ed., *The Process and Effects of Mass Communication*. Urbana, Illinois: University of Illinois Press, 1961. Many detailed examples; especially pertinent are the sections on comparative effects of media (pp. 87–105), meaning and perception (pp. 109–137), and source credibility and effectiveness (pp. 274–320).

Schramm, Wilbur, ed., *The Science of Human Communication*. New York and London: Basic Books, Inc., Publishers, 1963. A compendium of various theories on mass media and their effects.

Schramm, Wilbur, Jack Lyle, and Edwin B. Parker, *Television in the Lives of Our Children*. Stanford, California: Stanford University Press, 1961. A thoroughly researched study of the effects of television on children, demolishing a number of myths and raising some questions which remain unanswered.

Summers, Robert E., and Harrison B. Summers, *Broadcasting and the Public*. Belmont, California: Wadsworth Publishing Company, Inc., 1966. Detailed factual information on the history of broadcasting, its current practices, and its effects; of particular interest to the journalist are the discussions of news and information programs (pp. 297–332) and of the public interest (pp. 359–380).

Writing

Bywater, Ingram, and W. Rhys Roberts, trans., *The Rhetoric and the Poetics of Aristotle*, pp. 233–237. New York: The Modern Library, 1954. Despite recent tendencies toward the episodic, this remains the classic treatment of effective story structure, as applicable to television news as to the drama.

Fergusson, Francis, *The Idea of a Theater*. Garden City, N.Y.: Doubleday and Company, Inc., 1953. A study of the changing concepts of form and purpose in the theater, from Sophocles to T. S. Eliot.

Fairlie, Henry, "Can You Believe Your Eyes?", *Horizon* (Spring 1967), pp. 24–27. An excellent brief discussion of the manner in which the news motion picture deceives, and of the need for counterpoint in writing.

Lawson, John Howard, *Theory and Technique of Playwriting and Screenwriting*, pp. 367–439. New York: G. P. Putnam's Sons, 1949. Perhaps the best philosophical exploration of the structure of the dramatic motion picture, with innumerable applications to television news. The reader must salt his understanding of this work with due consideration for Lawson's admitted bias for socialism.

Hilliard, Robert L., *Writing for Television and Radio, Second Edition*. New York: Hastings House, Publishers, 1967. Highly practical instruction, especially for the writer of news and sports (pp. 91–118), special events, features, and documentaries (pp. 119–163); and talk programs (pp. 164–195).

(Note: The works of Fang and Wood, listed under "Concept and Technique" above, also contain information on television writing.)

Glossary

AB Announce booth.

Academy leader A type of film leader, with time markings on each frame, used to time the roll cue.

Adjacency A broadcast or program immediately preceding or following another; of importance because of the audience advantage a highly-rated show confers on the show immediately following.

Aerial shot A shot taken from mid-air, as from a plane.

Air man Anyone who performs for the video camera.

Anchorman An air man who anchors a show; the featured performer who narrates the news and leads in to reports delivered by subsidiary performers.

A-reel (B-reel, etc.) Designation of edited film reels in a multiple-chain story.

Audio Sound.

Audio mixer A control room technician who assembles ("mixes") sound from different sources.

Backdrop A cloth used as the visual background for a studio scene.

Backtime To plan the closing of a show by timing the final section for use intact; cuts or additions are made earlier in the show.

Backup lead-in A silent lead-in to sound film or VTR in which the original recording preceding the sound is uncut; the lead-in sound may be blooped, or it may be faded out by the audio mixer.

Beeper A telephone interview or narration containing sound beeps at regular intervals.

Beep-tape A magnetic tape which reproduces a continuous beep.

Billboard A brief announcement identifying the sponsor of a show or portion of a show.

Bloop To erase a sound track, if magnetic, by degaussing; if optical, by covering the track with an opaque material.

Boom A pole or arm, sometimes carried on a dolly, used to suspend a microphone in space.

Breakup Video picture distortion caused by interference with or improper transmission of the video signal.

331

B&W Black and white.

Cam Camera (used only in writing).

Camera left (right) Left (or right) as viewed by the camera.

Camera negative An original negative film as shot by the camera.

Chroma-key An electronic process for matting one picture into another; also called "shooting the blue."

Close shot A shot of an object in which the object fills the frame, viz., a shot of a face in which virtually none of the surroundings are visible.

Closeup A close shot.

Composite A sound track containing a mix of all the desired sounds.

Continuity The flow, in a show, of script from one story or segment to another.

Control room Location where the show is assembled electronically by the director, technical director, and audio mixer.

Convention (film or VTR) A method of achieving an effect, usually in transitions from one shot to another; the effect is not necessarily inherent in the medium, but may be the result of usage and custom.

Crane shot A shot taken from a mobile crane in which the camera rides.

Cross-cut Intercut.

Cue Any direction—written, spoken, or visual—for a change in sound or picture or for the performance of any action.

Cue card A card displaying a cue.

Cut An instantaneous transition from one film or video picture to another; used as noun or verb.

Cutaway shot A shot which takes the action away from the master shot, usually to avoid a jump-cut.

Director Person in charge of assembling a program electronically.

Dissolve A transition device in which one picture fades in while another fades out.

Dolly A wheeled vehicle used to move cameras or microphones.

Dolly shot A shot during which the camera is moved on a dolly; the reference is usually to movement closer to or farther from the subject.

Double-chain Refers to a film story using two film chains simultaneously.

Double spot Two commercials run back to back.

Double-system Film in which picture and sound are recorded on separate film tracks.

Dropout Loss of sound volume.

Dub To transfer sound from one track to another.

Dupe neg Duplicate negative.

Duplicate negative A negative film which is an exact duplicate of another film, usually of a master positive.

Electrical transcription A phonograph record made by individual inscribing rather than multiple pressing; by extension, any phonograph record, however made.

Establishing shot A shot which establishes the scene of action; most often a wide shot.

ET Electrical transcription.

Extreme closeup An extremely close shot of an object, as in showing only the eyes and lips of a person.

Fade A transition device in which the picture fades in from black, or fades out to black.

False reverse A reverse shot taken from an angle other than that of a true reverse but giving the same impression.

Fax Facilities, usually in reference to video facilities.

Feed An electronic signal; used as noun or verb.

Fill copy Pad copy.

Film chain A combination of motion picture film projector, slide projector, and television camera, used to convert film pictures and sound, or still pictures mounted on slides, into electronic signals.

Film counter A device used to measure film length during editing.

Film lineup List of films in order of airing.

Film rundown List of cues for a film story.

Filter A device for distorting sound; the resulting sound is said to be filtered.

Flat A vertical surface used to simulate a wall in studio; rigid in structure.

Following shot A shot in which the camera follows behind a subject.

FP Front projection.

Frame A single still picture in a series constituting a motion picture; also, the outer boundary of a picture.

Front projection A picture projected on a screen from the front and viewed from the front.

Frozen frame A single frame of film used in the manner of a still picture; while it is so used the film reel must be stopped.

Gain Sound volume.

Gel Gelatin, a transparent sheet of colored plastic used to alter the color of a still or graphic.

Generation Any one in a series of identical copies of film, VTR, or audio tape, each in the series being made from the preceding one in the series. The original is the first gen-

eration, a duplicate made from the original is the second generation, etc. Quality diminishes somewhat with each generation.

Gopher A hanger-on who may be ordered to "go for" things someone else wants.

Graphics All visual displays, such as art work, maps, and charts, designed to be photographed by the video camera; the term often includes still pictures, especially when they are combined with art work.

Hard (sound) Used in reference to the sound in a room with hard, bare surfaces which cause an echo.

Hard news Spot news, or news of immediacy, the value of which declines rapidly with the passage of time.

HFR Hold for release.

High-angle shot A shot taken from a high point looking downward.

ID Identification; used in reference to the station break or program interruption during which the station identifies itself.

Idiot card A card or sheet bearing, in large letters, parts of a script or cue words; it is displayed off camera, and read by the performer to refresh his memory.

Insert (film) A shot, usually close, inserted in the master shot to explain a detail.

Insert (show) A section of a show which is inserted, either live or VTR; the news insert is often an update, and may originate from a location other than that from which the rest of the show originates.

Intercut (film or VTR) To cut back and forth between two or more lines of action.

Investigative reporting A redundant term applied to reporting which involves more investigation than the average.

Jump-cut A cut in which objects in the picture change position abruptly in a way which is impossible in reality.

Lap dissolve A dissolve, usually of longer than normal duration.

Lavalier mike A microphone suspended around the neck.

Leader A section of blank film stock, used between film stories and also within stories at portions where the film is not to be seen; see also Academy leader.

Lead-in A section of film, VTR, or standup copy preceding and leading into another section, the latter usually being film or VTR accompanied by sound.

Lip-flap Movement of the lips without sound, encountered most frequently at the beginning of a single-system film shot.

Lip sync Lip movements synchronized with sound track.

Live Descriptive of any picture or sound broadcast at the instant it occurs.

Long shot A shot encompassing a wide area, or an object and its surroundings; virtually indistinguishable from a wide shot.

Loop A section of film spliced to itself to form an endless loop; also (in sound) to dub.

Low-angle shot A shot taken from a low point looking upward.

Magazine A film container which can be attached to the camera; unexposed film is fed from the magazine into the camera, and after exposure it is returned to the magazine for storage.

Magazine format A show format in which the various elements are not prefixed as to time or relative position; the converse of segmented.

Master control Location where all of a station's program inputs and outputs are controlled.

Master positive A positive film made from the edited camera negative and the composite sound track, and including optical effects.

Master shot A shot of an entire action, usually but not always from a single point of view; a shot to which all other shots in a sequence are related editorially.

Medium close shot A shot halfway between medium and close, as in showing a person from the waist up.

Medium shot A shot showing an object in the middle distance, or a person in full and nearly filling the frame.

Mix To blend two or more sound tracks.

Monitor A television receiver used to watch or monitor programs, usually on closed circuit.

Montage A nonchronological film or VTR sequence designed to create a specific artistic effect; in common usage synonymous with sequence, but used as above in this book.

MOS Sound film on which no sound is recorded; literally, "mitout sound."

Movieola A device used for viewing film during editing.

Moving shot A shot in which the camera follows a moving object.

Natural sound The sound of whatever is natural for the location, without narration.

Neg (film) Negative.

Network option time Broadcast hours preempted by a network on its owned and affiliated stations.

News wheel A news show in which the content is repeated, sometimes with updated material.

Nostril shot A ridiculously extreme closeup.

O&O Owned and operated, used in reference to network-owned stations.

One (two, etc.) shot A shot showing a specified number of persons.

Optical effects Transition devices or other effects achieved in film by laboratory processing, in video by electronics.

Outs Discarded portions of a film story.

Over Term used to describe the relationship of simultaneous, unsynchronized sound to picture, or vice versa; also, to indicate a sound intended to dominate (be louder than) another sound. In the first sense "over" and "under" are used synonymously, strange as this may seem; in the second sense they are antonymous.

Overlap A single-system film splice in which lip-flap at the beginning of the second shot is covered by sound at the end of the first shot.

Pad copy Scripted copy designed primarily to fill time, but not necessarily planned for use otherwise; fill copy.

Pan To move a camera's field of view across a subject or from one subject to another while the camera remains in one location, thus obtaining a panoramic view; usually the movement is horizontal.

Pan shot A shot obtained by panning.

Patch An electronic connection; used as noun or verb.

Playback A repeat of a recorded film or tape.

Plug Free advertising.

Pot Device by which sound volume is controlled.

POV Point of view.

POV shot A shot taken from a point of view previously established.

Presence (sound) The quality of sound in a given location; used especially in reference to the "sound" of silence.

Presentational Refers to a type of performance in which the camera is treated as the audience and addressed directly; antonym: representational.

Presidential patch A portable sound system with outlets for several amplifier connections.

Print A positive film.

Producer Person in charge of a show.

Promo A promotional statement, film, VTR, slide, or combination of the same; used as noun or verb.

Prop Property; stage furnishings such as sets or chairs.

Pull A graphic display to which movement is imparted by pulling one sheet or card beneath a perforated sheet or card.

Raw stock Unexposed film.

Reaction shot A shot showing reaction.

Rear projection A picture projected on a screen from the rear and viewed from the front.

Release print The film print made from the duplicate negative and distributed, as to theaters, for public viewing.

Remote A broadcast, live or VTR, from a location outside the studio; also, the unit which originates such a broadcast.

Representational Refers to a type of performance in which the performer ignores the camera; antonym: presentational.

Reversal print A positive film recorded in the camera, not derived from a negative.

Reverse shot A shot taken from an angle which is the reverse of the angle of the master shot.

Rewind Device used to hold and rotate a film reel during editing.

Ride the pot To control sound gain or volume.

Roll cue Cue on which film or VTR is rolled.

Rollover Undesirable vertical movement of the video picture resulting in apparent "roll" from one frame to the next.

Rollthru A section of film or VTR which continues to roll unseen.

RP Rear projection.

Rule of 180 degrees The rule governing the shooting of reverses: master shot and reverse cameras must both shoot from the same side of an imaginary line between the two (or more) persons in the frame.

Running shot A shot in which the camera is moved past a subject or series of subjects; a trucking shot.

Run-through shot A shot in which an object passes through the frame.

Segment Any portion of a show; sometimes, more specifically, a regularly scheduled and separately sponsored portion of a show.

Segue (pronounced *seg*-way) An uninterrupted transition from one musical section or composition to another; a sound dissolve; used as noun or verb.

Sequence A series of film or video shots, usually, but not always, chronological; in common usage synonymous with montage, but used as above in this book.

Setup Positioning of camera, lights, and subject for shooting; each move of the camera requires another setup.

Shader A device, operated automatically or manually, which alters the shading of the video picture.

Shooting the blue Chroma-key.

Shot The series of film frames recorded from the instant a camera starts until it stops; or, similarly, the electronic picture taken by a single video camera without interruption; also, in either film or VTR, that portion of the recorded shot which is used after editing.

Shotgun mike A highly directional microphone used to pick up sound at a distance.

Signal area Geographic area within which a broadcast video signal can be received.

Single-chain Refers to a film story using only one film chain.

Single-system Film in which picture and sound are recorded on the same film track.

Slide A still picture transparency recorded on a 35-millimeter or 2- by 2-inch slide.

Snow Spots on a video picture caused by interference or weakness of the signal. In B&W the spots are white; in color they are multi-colored like confetti.

SOF Sound on film.

Soft news Features and news of current events which lose value comparatively slowly with loss of immediacy.

SOF transposer A device used to transpose the magnetic sound track on single-system film, either to eliminate or to re-establish the 28-frame separation between sound and corresponding picture.

Sound track A sound recording (film or tape).

Special A broadcast or program deviating from the regular program schedule.

Speed The rolling speed at which film or VTR reproduces a usable picture and sound.

Splice The physical connection by which one film or VTR shot is affixed to another; used as noun or verb.

Splicer Device for making a film or VTR splice.

Split screen An arrested wipe, showing parts of 2 or more pictures simultaneously.

Stage manager Worker in command of studio activity; one of his principal duties is to cue the performer.

Standup copy Script written to be delivered presentationally without visuals over; despite the name, standup copy may be delivered while sitting.

Station manager Chief executive of a television station.

Still A still photograph shot by a video camera; in the broader sense, any graphic shot by the video camera.

Strip show Any show broadcast on a regular basis several times a week.

Strobe To appear to move in the discontinuous manner of action observed under a rapidly flashing stroboscopic light.

Studio Location from which a show originates.

Super Superimposition; used as noun or verb.

Superimposition Two pictures simultaneously occupying the full screen.

Superslide A slide superimposed on another picture.

Swishpan A pan shot in which the camera movement is so rapid that the picture blurs; also, a stock transition device which creates an effect resembling a swishpan shot.

Sync Synchronization.

Sync pulse An electric pulse generated for the purpose of running devices in synchronization, as, a camera and an audio tape recorder; or to indicate points of synchronization on two separate tracks, as on a film picture track and a film sound track.

Tag The final section of a story, used especially with reference to a standup section following film or VTR.

Take A shot; also, to take a shot.

Take cue Cue on which film or VTR appears on the air.

Talent Anyone who performs on the air, regardless of ability.

Tally light A light, usually red, on a video camera, used to indicate when the picture transmitted by the camera is being used.

TD Technical director.

Tease A statement or hint concerning an upcoming story or stories, designed to "tease" the viewer into watching; used as noun or verb.

Technical director Control room technician who performs the picture-switching operations and creates video optical effects.

Telecine Location of film chains and sometimes VTR machines.

Tilt shot A vertical pan shot.

Time compression Effect obtained by editing film or VTR to portray an event in less time than its occurrence required.

Title slide A slide displaying the title or name of the show.

Track A recording of either sound or picture.

Transition device Any device used to effect a transition from one shot to another.

Trucking shot A shot in which the camera is moved past a subject or series of subjects; a running shot.

Tubby (sound) Refers to the echoing quality of sound in a hard room.

Under Term used to describe the relationship of simultaneous, unsynchronized sound to picture, or vice versa; also, to indicate a sound to be dominated by (not as loud as) another sound. In the first sense "under" and "over" are oddly synonymous; in the second sense they are antonymous.

Upcut To overlap sound-picture with other sound unintentionally, most commonly to overlap lead-in narration with film or VTR sound.

Update To alter a broadcast, in whole or in part, in order to bring it up to date by including new events or late developments.

UHF Ultra high frequency; used in reference to television stations broadcasting on the higher frequencies of channels above 13.

Video Refers to the electronic picture.

Visuals Any and all visual elements in a television show.

VHF Very high frequency; used in reference to television stations broadcasting on the lower frequencies of Channels 2 through 13.

VO Voice over.

VTR Video tape recording.

Walking shot A shot taken by a cameraman while walking; also, a shot of someone walking.

Wide shot A shot encompassing a wide area, usually showing a subject with its surroundings; virtually indistinguishable from a long shot.

Wild track A sound track not synchronized with picture.

Wipe A transition device in which one film or video picture appears to wipe another off the screen.

Work print A film print used to determine the original editing of the picture.

WOW Variation or distortion in the pitch of sound, caused by variation in the speed of film or tape.

Yak Narration.

Zoom lens A lens of variable focal length.

Zoom shot A shot during which the focal length of the lens is varied to give the impression of moving closer to or farther away from the subject.

Index